CONFESSIONS

of a

LONELY LOVER

An Exploration of Online Dating Scams

A TRUE STORY

Joe Eweka, PMP.
(a.k.a. African Joe)

THIS PAGE WAS INTENTIONALLY LEFT BLANK

CONFESSIONS OF A LONELY LOVER

An Exploration of Online Dating Scams

By:

PRINCE JOE EWEKA, PMP.®
(a.k.a. AFRICAN JOE)

THIS IS A TRUE STORY.

Front and Back Covers Designed By: Prince Joe Eweka, PMP.®

CONFESSIONS OF A LONELY LOVER

An Exploration of Online Dating Scams

By:

PRINCE JOE EWEKA, PMP.®
(a.k.a. AFRICAN JOE in the Music Industry.)

Joe Eweka Group, LLC.

Publisher: Joe Eweka Group, LLC.
2009 - 2021

Books By Prince Joe Eweka, PMP.®

1. Confessions Of A Lonely Lover: *An Exploration Of Online Dating Scams.*

2. This Star Is An African: *Oberservations From the Land of Alkebulan.* (*A Collection of Poems, Songs, and Plays Based on Real-Life Experiences and Observations.*)

Upcoming Books By Prince Joe Eweka, PMP.®

3. Readings – Volume One: *An Interdisciplinary Collection of Essays, Articles, Research Studies, Discussions, and White Papers.*

4. Readings – Volume Two: *A Scholarly Collection of Essays, Articles, Research Studies, Discussions, and White Papers.*

5. Pleadings: *Hearings, Transcripts, Pleadings, and Legal Brief*s.

6. Taking A Walk In My Shoes – Volume One: *A Victim of Circumstance.* (Autobiography)

7. Taking A Walk In My Shoes – Volume Two: *Pursuit of "The American Dream."* (Autobiography)

8. Taking A Walk In My Shoes – Volume Three: *The Tyranny of the American Justice System – More Than A Decade of Misery!* (Autobiography)

9. Taking A Walk In My Shoes – Volume Four: *Another Half-a-Decade of Misery – Just Because They Can!* (Autobiography)

10. How America Betrayed Its Citizens.

11. Disasters: *Act of God or Man-Made?*

Reggae Music CD Albums By African Joe

1. Africanism
2. Beauty In Diversity
3. Child Abuse
4. Mighty Babylon
5. My Hoopty Has Got AC
6. Unforgiving Society
7. War In No Man's Land

Websites
https://www.Joe-Eweka.com
https://www.African-Joe.com
https://www.Joe-Eweka.org

Printed: 2021
ISBN: 978-1-944429-01-0   (Hardcover Version)
ISBN: 978-1-944429-90-4   (Paperback Version)
ISBN: 978-1-944429-00-3   (eBook Kindle Edition)
ISBN: 978-1-944429-02-7   (eBook)

Publisher: Joe Eweka Group, LLC.
13395 Coppermine Road, Unit 206
Herndon, Virginia, 20171.

Website: https://www.Joe-Eweka.com
https://www.Joe-Eweka.org
https://www.African-Joe.com

Telephone: 703-957-5466
Email: Books@Joe-Eweka.com
Info@Joe-Eweka.com
Publisher@Joe-Eweka.com
Info@African-Joe.com

Bulk Ordering Information:

Special discounts may be available on quantity purchases by U.S. trade bookstores, wholesalers, associations, corporations, educators, and other groups, etc. Please contact the publisher for details at the addresses listed above.

Library of Congress Control Number: 2021910856

DEDICATION

It is often said by people that "a friend in need is a friend indeed." Therefore, this book is dedicated to my very good friend, Natasha Ashley, for her help, tender care, and concerns during my disability. You are a good friend that is like a sister to me. Special thanks to you, Natasha!

THIS PAGE WAS INTENTIONALLY LEFT BLANK

TABLE OF CONTENTS

PREFACE

This book, *Confessions of a Lonely Lover* is a true account of real "chat" conversations between Dave Washington and other individuals. (*Some names have been changed.*) Dave's brother in Italy had sent an email to Dave to join Flixster, an online social networking site. Dave was not interested in chatting with anybody online due to the anonymity involved, but he decided to join anyway because of his younger brother's invitation. Some Flixster friends of Dave's brother invited him to become their friends too. Hence Dave accepted their invitations with no ulterior motive whatsoever than to connect with people. However, the sad thing is, after Dave joined Flixster, his brother in Italy did not communicate with him on Flixster. Instead, they continued with their usual methods of communication; or lack thereof.

This book came into existence by accident. It was not planned, as the author did not intend to write the book. Rather, after his personal experiences with the online scammers he encountered on the Internet, he decided to compile their conversations into what now turned out to be this book. The critical points when the author decided to write this book occurred in Chapters 17 and 18, where jealousy on the part of Gracy caused a strain on her relationship with Dave, as well as the ensuing two weeks period when Dave ignored Gracy and her attempts to contact him.

The purpose of this book is to warn innocent and honest hearted people (male or female) of the dangers of social media and online dating. The conversations between Dave and other individuals in this book are real. The statements of all the participants are reproduced in this book, with all the grammatical and typographical errors, without editing them. The author has included commentaries where necessary for clarification purposes. The events described in this book happened in 2009.

The publication of this book is an appetizer just to test the waters in book publishing. The real "meats" or "main courses" of bookish buffets will follow soon. Please stay tuned.

THIS PAGE WAS INTENTIONALLY LEFT BLANK

CHAPTER 1
INTRODUCTION: HOW IT ALL STARTED

Dave's younger brother in Italy invited him to join the social networking site called Flixster. Once Dave joined Flixster, he began to receive Friend Requests from some Flixster members. Initially, he ignored them all. Later, however, he accepted some of the invitations for friendship. Dave also began to view the profiles of some members. One day, he received a friend request from someone who called herself Rose. Rose claimed to be a Manager at an Omni Hotel in Toronto, Canada, and that she was hiring for the vacancies she had open. She invited members to contact her privately for instructions on how to apply for the jobs. Dave knew right away as an experienced investigator that this was a fraud because, even though Rose claimed that she was living and working in Canada, she listed a United Kingdom telephone number. Dave immediately blocked Rose from posting any further messages on his profile and then reported her to the Flixster Administration.

Upon further exploration, Dave noticed that Rose had become viral on the Flixster network, as she[1] had posted hundreds of fraudulent messages on the profiles of Flixster members and they were falling for it. Rose had also used several other names on Flixster to defraud people. Dave then posted warnings on some of the members' profiles to alert them that Rose was a fraud and a scammer. Some members heeded Dave's warnings and responded by posting expressions of gratitude on Dave's profile. One of the people who thanked Dave for his warning, and who could have been defrauded by Rose, was Ibrahim Issifu (usernames: Musahissfu and Morro.Issifu). Ironically, this same Ibrahim Issifu, whom Dave saved from being defrauded, later tried without success to defraud Dave too. The others, especially Rasheed Zakari[2] (username: Rasheed-Zakari), tried to use "love" to gain Dave's trust and then defraud him. Below are brief descriptions of the individuals involved, and the true accounts of their actual conversations in the chat rooms are presented chronologically in the following chapters.

---

[1]   Although the real gender of the person posing as "Rose" is unknown, the pronoun "she" will be used in this book because the person claimed to be a female.

[2]   Rasheed Zakari is another fraudster who is not what she claimed to be online.

1

* * * * * * *

Username: **Friends4Dave**
Web address: **http://www.flixster.com/user/Friends4Dave.**[3]

This is Dave Washington, the *"Lonely Lover."* He is honest and sincere in his dealings with people. He usually speaks what is on his mind and expects people to do the same. His greatest faults are that he is too honest, too kind, and initially trusts others too much. However, he has learned the hard way on several occasions that he cannot depend on anyone for anything except the Almighty God. He had posted detailed information about himself on his profile; but he deleted it later when he discovered that most (if not all) the people that contacted him on Flixster.com were scammers. Just a few of such scammers are discussed in this book, and the scammers are identified under the brief introductions below in this chapter.

* * * * * * *

Username: **RasheedZakari**
Web address: **http://www.flixster.com/user/rasheedzakar**i.

Rasheed Zakari is a female. She claimed that she was 30 years old during her communications with Dave in May 2009. She also stated that she lives in "Adams, Ma" (wherever that is). Dave initially thought that she lives somewhere in Massachusetts (MA), but it turned out that she lives in Ghana, in West Africa. However, she does not have a Ghanaian accent; she sounds more like an American or a Canadian.[4] During his Skype video conversations with her, Dave established that Rasheed was really a female; but he also discovered that she looked White – a long-dark-haired young lady with some Middle Eastern ancestry. Even though she may have some Middle Eastern background, but she is probably an American or Canadian because of her accent.

Before their telephone and Skype conversations, Dave thought that Rasheed was a Ghanaian. Although this sounded strange at first, it was no longer

---

[3] Dave's web address has been changed.
[4] Rasheed's accent was confirmed during Dave's telephone and Skype conversations with her. She had a Ghanaian telephone number.

---

surprising later on; because after further investigation into the activities of many scammers who claimed to be Nigerians or Ghanaians, Dave discovered that these scammers are not Nigerians or Ghanaians at all. Many of them are actually Chinese, Lebanese, Indians, Russians, and other nationals in Europe claiming to be Nigerians online. Some even have Nigerian local cellular telephone numbers which they then call-forwarded to their real numbers abroad. Nevertheless, many of these Chinese actually now live in Nigeria and Ghana, which makes it easier for them to impersonate real Nigerians and Ghanaians.

Rasheed stated that she was an accounting student. Her profile message declared that she was 29 years old at the time (which Dave thought was probably a typographical error, since she also said that she was 30 years old in her message to Dave). Rasheed is an intelligent person. She is greedy and very pushy. She goes for the kill fast, and she will rob you blind before you even know what is happening, if you are not careful. Dave seriously doubts if *Rasheed Zakari* is her real name.

Rasheed likes to use *IMvironments* to woo men emotionally; but that did not work for her in her attempts to enamor Dave. For example, she often used the *"Falling Hearts"* and *"Falling Leaves"* IMvironments whenever she sensed that Dave was upset with her. She had an accomplice working with her in her fraudulent schemes. Her collaborator's name is Hanson Opare (probably a male), whom she claimed to be her mother. However, Dave now thinks that this Hanson Opare is possibly her boyfriend, because Rasheed tells her victims to send her money through Western Union under the name "Hanson Opare."

Rasheed Zakari's Profile Comment: "My name is Rasheed 29 years of age single with no kids and a student studying accounting who is now searching for the right man to spend the rest of my life with."

Invitation Message posted on Dave's Profile by **RasheedZakari** (**Rasheed Zakari**):

"My name is Rasheed 30 years of age single with no kids and a student studying accounting who is now searching for the right man to spend the rest of her life with and i will like to know more about u and so if u have access to yahoo instant messenger then u can add me there as rasheed_zakari@yahoo.com so that we can chat there and know more about each other."

* * * * * * *

Username: **Lovemandycare**
Web address: **http://www.flixster.com/user/lovemandycare**.

On one of her online profiles[5] on flixster.com, Abigail Osei listed her name as "*Mandy KImmy Anderson*" with a photograph of a very attractive Black lady. She claimed to be a female[6], 28 years old, and living in Accra, Ghana. Abigail Osei was also found on the websites www.Friendster.com and www.Minekey.com with totally different photographs; but it was the same person, as the results of Dave's investigation into "Abigail Osei" profiles indicated.

Although Abigail Osei claimed to be a Ghanaian, Dave now has valid reasons to believe that Abigail is not a Ghanaian at all, and may not even be a female. For one thing, Abigail declined[7] any telephone or Skype contacts, and may be one of those Chinese or other nationals who impersonate Nigerians and Ghanaians online (and via emails) in their fraudulent schemes. Although Abigail claimed that she was looking for her "Mr. Right", her real intention is to defraud innocent people of their money – and lots of it.

Abigail Osei's Profile Comment: "I am Mandy and i very caring, honest, lovely, faithful and loyal. I am very Attractive looking woman that is searching for her Mr. Right and hope to find him here."

Invitation Messages posted on Dave's Profile by **Lovemandycare** **(Abigail Osei):**

---

[5] Abigail Osei had many different profiles on Flixter.com and a few other social media sites, all intended to defraud people, as Dave's investigation revealed.
[6] The true gender of Abigail Osei could not be ascertained during the investigation; but it is doubtful if the person is even a female.
[7] Although she promised to talk on the phone or do video conferencing with Dave, she never did it whenever Dave asked for a telephone or video conversation.

"Hello Dear,

How are you today? and how is things moving with you? hope
fine and you are in good health. My name is Abigail Osei, I am
looking for a very nice person of love, caring, sincere, easy
going, matured, and understanding, then after going through
your profile now on this site (flixter.com) i pick interest in you,
so i will like you to write me via my email address which is as
follow (loveangle200@yahoo.com) so that i will give you my
picture for further discussion, because i am really looking
forward for a serious friendship with you,

Yours New Friend Abigail."

Dave found the lady in the picture on Abigail's profile to be very attractive.
So, he responded with interest online to her invitation for friendship.
Abigail immediately writes Dave back with the following:

Lovemandycare:

"Hello Dave, I am happy to hear from you and you have a
nice profile and a lot of friends too. I will like us to know
each other if you don't mind. I will like to send you a mail
and tell you more about me and if you don't mind given me
your email address. Take care and hope to hear from you
soon ... Abigail."

* * * * * * *

Username: **Talk2bryan2001**
Web address: **http://www.flixster.com/user/Talk2bryan2001**.

This girl called herself "Gracy Isy." The picture on her profile was not hers.
Although the photograph on her online profile indicated that she was
probably from India or Pakistan area, it turned out that she is from Nigeria.
Dave found it somewhat disheartening later on when he discovered that she

was a scammer too; because this gives further ammunition to some people who erroneously think that most "Nigerians are scammers and fraudsters." Even though she sent Dave another picture she claimed to be her, Dave has good reasons to doubt whether that second photograph was really her true picture. *Gracy Isy* is not her true name either. She also appeared to be undecided between defrauding Dave and falling in love with him.

Dave initially thought that Gracy was different from the other people, whom he soon discovered were scammers; and he initially trusted her. She posted little to no information about herself on her flixster.com online profile at the time of their encounter in 2009. Dave's telephone conversations with Gracy revealed that she was reserved and reluctant to answer questions. But she was also very sweet and sensitive. Dave later fell in love with her … until towards the end of the book, when everything went awry.

***Invitation Message posted on Dave's Profile by* Talk2bryan2001 (Gracy Isy):**

> "U welcome. Here is my email id **Talk2bryan2001**. Just add me. Ok. I am always on line on my yahoo messenger."

* * * * * * *

Username: **Musahissifu**
Web address: **http://www.flixster.com/user/musahissifu**.

This guy[8] is an ungrateful and determined criminal. He is a real scoundrel. The photograph on his online profile may or may not be his real picture. He claimed that his name was Musah Issifu. But on *Yahoo! Messenger*, he used the name "Moro Issifu." But he did not post any personal information on his profile on flixster.com. He was the scammer who, although Dave saved him from being scammed by "Rose", later tried to defraud Dave himself. When Dave insisted on knowing his real name before sending him the money he asked Dave to send to him, Musah/Moro then admitted that

---

[8] For the purpose of this book, this person is assumed to be a male because that is what he claimed to be; although the person's real identity is uncertain.

his real name is Ibrahim Issifu.

Musah/Moro/Ibrahim, or whatever his name really is, declined any telephone or Skype conversation, which would have provided Dave with clues as to this scoundrel's real identity. Dave was not even sure whether the Ibrahim Issifu is a male or female, even though the person claimed to be a male. Ibrahim's refusal to talk on the telephone or Skype was perhaps indicative of his impersonation of someone else. He may be one of those instances where other nationals impersonate Nigerians and Ghanaians when perpetuating their online and email fraudulent schemes.

* * * * * * *

CHAPTER 2
FIRST SIGNS OF FRAUD ON FLIXSTER'S WEBSITE

Soon after Dave began to explore the contents of Flixster.com, he discovered the first signs of fraud on the website. He noticed one particular member, who called herself "Rose Grand". Rose had posted what appeared to be obvious fraudulent messages on the profiles of many members of Flixster.com. Surprisingly, some of the members were falling for Rose's scams. Dave considered Rose's practices to be very unsettling. Rose also posted the same fraudulent message on Dave's profile. Dave wrote a reply message for Rose, warning her not to post any more fraudulent messages on his profile, and Dave immediately deleted her message. When Dave viewed some other member's profiles, he noticed that "Rose Grand" has posted similar messages on their profiles too.

For example, below was one of the messages that Rose Grand posted on Musah Issifu's profile on Flixster.com (as well as on hundreds of other members' profiles, including Dave's profile). Rose used about 40 different profiles accounts with different pictures on Flixster.com to defraud people. Dave did not believe that any of the pictures used actually belonged to this scammer, nor did he believe that "Rose Grand" was the scammer's real name. Here is one example:

> "Hotel Omni Mont-Royal
> 1050 Sherbrooke Street West
> Montreal, H3A 2R6 CA.
>
> Welcome To Omni Mont-Royal Hotel Canadian Employment Offer
>
> Good day,
>
> I am Rose from Canada, the manager of Omni canadian hotel, pls i want to inform you about the vacancies in our hotel, The management needs men and women, married and not married, who will work and live in canada .The hotel will pay for his flight ticket and assist him to process

his visa in his country, if you are interested contact us via
E-mail: omni.montroyalhotels@yahoo.ca. And the Hotel
informations will be sent to you immediately.

Thanks.

From the Hotel manager.
TEL...   001-606-259-4052   OR   +44-703-187-1148.
Fax: (440)348-7275.
E-MAIL: omni.montroyalhotels@yahoo.ca
HOTEL WEBSITE. www.omnimontroyalhotels.com

Do you notice anything that was obviously wrong with Rose Grand's
message above? The point here was not necessarily about how grandiose
her assumed name (Rose Grand) was, although that might also be a clue.
Rather, it was something else. Do you see the obvious clues of fraud?
When Dave read the above message for the first time, he knew right away
that this was a scam. For example, listing a United Kingdom telephone
number, a Kentucky (USA) telephone number, and an Ohio (USA) fax
number, while at the same time claiming to live in Canada and without any
Canadian telephone number at all, simply did not make any sense to Dave;
except, of course, that this was a fraud.

Besides, Rose Grand's writing skills were definitely deplorable for a
manager; and she did not write as a real manager of a reputable hotel in
Canada should. To make matters worse, she listed a *Yahoo!* email address
as her business email. No reputable hotel in North America used a *Yahoo!*
email address as its official email. Furthermore, the website address she
gave was not the real hotel's website URL. Rose Grand, or whatever her/his
real name was, intentionally set up this fake hotel website for the sole
purpose of defrauding innocent victims. She even had a copied-and-pasted
picture of the real hotel on her fake hotel website, as Dave's investigation
revealed.[9] Dave had reasons to believe that Rose Grand was perhaps a
Russian or Chinese, and possibly a male.

---

[9] More on the results of Dave investigation on Rose Grand will be presented in Chapter 25
of this book.

Below is another one of Rose Grand's many different profiles and advertisements that Dave found on **Flixster.com**. "**Vinayaamatya**" was the name for her assumed profile on this particular posting at http://www.flixster.com/user/ vinayaamatya:

> "hotelcanadians …
>
> i am rose from canada, i am the manager of canada hotels, pls hotel need man and woman who can work and live in canadian hotel Canada, hotel will pay for his ticket and his visa in his country, if you are interested contact me back o.k email hotelcanadians@yahoo.com."

When Dave queried "Rose Grand" on Flixster.com, he discovered from the search results that Rose still had about forty active profiles/accounts on the website, as of 2009.

Based on this information and the obvious fraud that "Rose Grand" perpetuated online, Dave posted warnings on as many members' profiles as possible. Some of the members responded with messages of gratitude; including Ibrahim Issifu (a.k.a. "Musa Issifu" and "Moro Issifu") who, in turn, later tried to defraud Dave too. Below was Dave's warning message on Ibrahim's profile:

> **Friends4Dave:**
>
> "WARNING: I just wanted to post a response to the message by this lady who calls herself "Rose". She claims to be the Manager of a major hotel in Canada and that she is hiring. Well, there is no major hotel in existence in the United States and Canada that uses a *Yahoo!* email address. Besides, one of her telephone numbers is a United Kingdom phone number, not Canadian. The second phone number and the fax number are both in the United States. Before you fall for such an obvious fraud, you may want to ask her to post publicly online here the name and address of the hotel, as well as her supervisor's name. Then "Google" (search for) the hotel at www.google.com or go to www.whitepages.com

and try to locate the hotel's information. If you are able locate it, then call the number listed in the results on google.com or whitepages.com to see if a person by the name of "Rose Grand" really works there as a manager. Please do not call the phone numbers she listed in her profile. Just be careful ... all of you reading her profile. You don't even know if this person is truly a female as claimed to be."

Shortly thereafter, Ibrahim Issifu responded to Dave's warning (already deleted from Dave's profile), and he informed Dave that he (Ibrahim) had already contacted Rose Grand, and that she wanted him to send her four hundred US dollars ($400.00) to start processing his "paperwork". Consequently, Dave posted another warning for Ibrahim below:

Friends4Dave:

"Please do not give her any money. It is fraud! If you give her any money, you will never hear from her again. And there is nothing you can do to get your money back."

Subsequently, Ibrahim responded to Dave's further warning by posting another message for Dave on his profile. He also invited Dave to be his online friend:

Invitation Message posted on Dave's Profile by Musahissifu:

"Ok I understand you. Thank u very much. Please can you give me your yahoo or msn id so that we can chat? Ok?"

Dave did as Ibrahim requested. Although Dave did not have any *Yahoo!* account at the time of the request, he decided to sign up for one, and he gave Ibrahim his new *Yahoo!* ID (which Dave intended to cancel in due time).

CHAPTER 3
DAVE OPENS A *YAHOO!* ACCOUNT

𝔇ave opened a *Yahoo!* account for the first time. Since Dave now had a Yahoo account, through which he could chat with people, he accepted invitations from some other Flixster members to add them to his list of contacts on *Yahoo!*. About a week or more later, on May 22nd, Musah responded with a different name. Dave noticed that his name had changed from Musah Issifu to Moro Issifu.

Moro.Issifu (May 22 - 3:46:13 PM):   Hello dear how are you doing today. (*Dave felt rather uncomfortable that a man was calling him "dear", but he decided to give Musah the benefit of the doubt, as such endearment from a complete stranger may be due to cultural differences.*)

Dave was not online at the time that Musah/Moro left the message above. Therefore, he was not able to respond in real time. So, on May 23rd, Moro tried to contact Dave again.

Moro.Issifu (May 23 - 7:23:40 AM):   Hello.

Dave was also not online this time either. His online unavailability caused Musah to miss a chance to chat with him. Nevertheless, Dave wondered why this person was trying to contact him online live, as if he was right there. Could this guy not ascertain Dave's online status ("Unavailable") before he tried to communicate with him as though he was right there by saying: "Hello"?

* * * * * * *

Now, let us switch gears to someone else for a moment. A couple of weeks ago, Rasheed Zakari had also invited Dave to be her friend; and she had since been trying to get in contact with Dave (without success) after he had added her to his *Yahoo!* contacts, per Rasheed's Flixster Friend request below:

Rasheedzakari: My name is Rasheed 30 years of age single with no kids and a student studying accounting who is now searching for the right man to spend the rest of her life with and i will like to know more about u and so if u have access to yahoo instant messenger then u can add me there as rasheed_zakari@yahoo.com so that we can chat there and know more about each other.

* * * * * * *

Rasheed tried again many times to contact Dave, but he still was not available online each time. After a few futile attempts to synchronize their meeting times online, due to the difference in time zones, Dave decided to respond on May 23rd, and he left the following message for Rasheed:

Friends4Dave (May 23 - 12:35:58 AM): I apologize, Rasheed, for not been online when you were here. I accidentally deleted your messages before I could copy down your mobile phone number. It appears that you are on a different time zone than I am. I live in the United States. Where do you live? (*Rasheed was not online at the time.*)

* * * * * * *

Later that day, on May 23rd, Rasheed left the following messages for Dave:

Rasheed Zakari (May 23 - 12:02:11 PM): Hi and how are you doing today?

Rasheed Zakari (May 23 - 1:25:34 PM): My phone number is +233241913379

Rasheed Zakari (May 23 - 1:25:59 PM): Call me or send me a text message.

Dave tried to call the telephone number that Rasheed had left for him. It was an invalid phone number. He tried to send text messages to the number, he continued to get "Invalid number" error messages. Dave thought that either the number was a typographical error, or it was obviously a bogus telephone number that Rasheed intentionally gave to him.

* * * * * * *

Two days later, on May 25th, Dave responded with the following message:

Friends4Dave (May 25 - 4:30:16 PM):　　　Hi Rasheed. I tried many times to send you a text message, but it would not go through. I also called the phone number to speak with you, but no one answered. Hope to talk to you soon....

Rasheed was not online.

* * * * * * *

Let's return to Musah/Moro/Ibrahim. That same day, on May 25th, 2009, Ibrahim left the following message for Dave, and Dave responded when he read the message later in the day.

Moro.Issifu (May 25 - 7:29:39 AM):　　　Hi.

Friends4Dave (May 25 - 5:51:18 PM):　　　Hi Moro ... Sorry I missed your text again. I guess our time zones are different. I live in the United States. Where do you live?

CHAPTER 4
DAVE CHATS FOR THE FIRST TIME!

On May 25th, Gracy Isy had left a message for Dave in the wee hours of the morning. Hence, Dave decided to chat with her online for the first time. So, later that day, when Dave was online, he began to chat with Gracy. Weeks earlier, Gracy had invited Dave to become her friend on Flixster, and Dave accepted. But for a few weeks, Dave did not hear from her. So, he sent a message to her to find out how she was doing. She responded and gave Dave her *Yahoo!* ID, which was Talk2bryan2001 .

Talk2bryan2001 (May 25 - 1:52:26 AM):   Hi, Mr. Dave[10]. Well... just thought I should say hellooow.... Stay blessed.

Friends4Dave (May 25 - 12:29:20 PM):   Hi Gracy! How are you?

Talk2bryan2001 (May 25 - 12:29:43 PM):   Am fine and you?

Friends4Dave (May 25 - 12:30:00 PM):   I'm Blessed. Thanks.

Talk2bryan2001 (May 25 - 12:30:41 PM):   Where are you from?

Friends4Dave (May 25 - 12:31:10 PM):   I kind of missed talking to you on Flixster. I am a Nigerian-American living in the United States.

Friends4Dave (May 25 - 12:31:36 PM):   Where are you from?

Talk2bryan2001 (May 25 - 12:31:55 PM):   How old are you? (*Gracy did not answer Dave's question.*)

Friends4Dave (May 25 - 12:32:13 PM):   47. And you?

---

10   As previously indicated, this name has been changed.

Talk2bryan2001(May 25 - 12:32:30 PM):   Is that really your picture?
(Again, she avoided answering his question.)

Friends4Dave (May 25 - 12:33:08 PM):   Yes. I am everything I say I
am. No tricks. No games.

Talk2bryan2001 (May 25 - 12:33:58 PM):   Then I guess I am safe.

Friends4Dave (May 25 - 12:35:06 PM):   Yes, you are. *(Sensing her
sigh of relief, Dave somewhat began to think
that Gracy perhaps could be trusted.)* Tell me
about yourself. I hope that is your picture I saw
on Flixster. If you have a webcam, you can see
me live.

Talk2bryan2001 (May 25 - 12:36:40 PM):   And what if I say that's not
my picture?

Talk2bryan2001 (May 25 - 12:37:26 PM):   Do you discriminate?

Friends4Dave (May 25 - 12:38:38 PM):   It really does not matter, as
long as you are really what you say you are. I
just want to know whom I am talking to...
that's all. I really do not want anything from
you. And no, I do not discriminate. In fact, I
hate discrimination of any kind.

Talk2bryan2001 (May 25 - 12:38:43 PM):   What part of Nigeria are you
from my dear friend? *(She continued on her
line of questioning without really answering
Dave's questions.)*

Friends4Dave (May 25 - 12:39:09 PM):   *(Dave decided to give her the
benefit of doubt in order to ease her fears and
suspicions.)* I am from Benin City.

Talk2bryan2001 (May 25 - 12:39:51 PM):   Ok.

Talk2bryan2001 (May 25 - 12:40:00 PM):   Ok good.

Talk2bryan2001 (May 25 - 12:40:19 PM):   *(She continued with her questioning.)* Are you married?

Friends4Dave (May 25 - 12:40:22 PM):   *(Dave ignored her last question and insisted that she answer his questions for a change.)*   Now, what is your real name and where are you from? And how old are you?

Friends4Dave (May 25 - 12:40:42 PM):   *(As an afterthought, Dave decided to answer her last question anyway.)* I am divorced. Since 2008.

Talk2bryan2001 (May 25 - 12:44:11 PM):   Hope I will still be your friend when I tell you about myself. Would anything change? Please tell me.

Friends4Dave (May 25 - 12:44:43 PM):   No. As I said, I don't want anything from you.

Friends4Dave (May 25 - 12:45:19 PM):   You will still be my friend, as long as you are law-abiding.

Talk2bryan2001 (May 25 - 12:45:56 PM):   Ok dear, I promise. Ok? *(She hesitated and didn't want to answer Dave's questions. This is because the very attractive picture of a young lady on her profile indicated that she was probably from India, or someone living elsewhere but of Indian descent.)*

Friends4Dave (May 25 - 12:47:04 PM):   If you don't want to tell me who you are, you don't have to. But it would be nice for me to know who really I am talking to.

Talk2bryan2001 (May 25 - 12:47:26 PM):   *(She decided to confess her true origin, but she still left Dave wondering as to whether she was a Nigerian or an American.)* Well, I am Gracy from the same country and I am 22 years old.

Friends4Dave (May 25 - 12:48:11 PM):   That's good. What part of Nigeria or the United States are you from?

Talk2bryan2001 (May 25 - 12:48:30 PM):   *(Again, she ignored Dave's question.)* When was the last time you visited your country?

Friends4Dave (May 25 - 12:49:29 PM):   *(Dave was displeased with her failure to answer his questions fully, but he decided to give her a little more time.)* I have two countries. I live in one (United States), and the last time I visited the other one (Nigeria) was in 2001.

Talk2bryan2001 (May 25 - 12:49:58 PM):   Ok.

Friends4Dave (May 25 - 12:50:12 PM):   *(Sensing that Gracy might not be an American, Dave asked her a pointed question.)* What part of Nigeria are you from?

Talk2bryan2001(May 25 - 12:50:52 PM):   Delta State.

Talk2bryan2001 (May 25 - 12:51:19 PM):   But stay in Lagos.

Friends4Dave (May 25 - 12:51:21 PM):   That's good. Are you from Warri?

Friends4Dave (May 25 - 12:52:36 PM):   And I have family in Lagos.

Friends4Dave (May 25 - 12:53:25 PM):   *(Since it was now obvious that the picture on her profile was not hers, Dave decided to determine what the gender of the person really was.)* Are you a male or a female?

Talk2bryan2001 (May 25 - 12:53:38 PM):   Nope. Not from Warri.

Talk2bryan2001 (May 25 - 12:54:58 PM):   Female.

Talk2bryan2001 (May 25 - 12:55:22 PM):   Male right?

Friends4Dave (May 25 - 12:56:59 PM):   Yes, I am a male. Like I said before, I am everything I say I am. I do not like lying to people and do not like to be lied to either. Now, don't be afraid to use your true picture on Flixster. If people don't like what they see in you, that is their problem.

Talk2bryan2001 (May 25 - 12:58:08 PM):   Thanks dear.

Talk2bryan2001 (May 25 - 12:58:21 PM):   I like that.

Friends4Dave (May 25 - 12:58:28 PM):   Be proud of what you are.... That's what God made you to be. There is a reason God made you like that.... So be proud of what you are.

Talk2bryan2001 (May 25 - 12:59:07 PM):   I like you.

Friends4Dave (May 25 - 12:59:48 PM):   Thank you. What you see in me is what I truly am. I am nothing more and nothing less.

Friends4Dave (May 25 - 1:01:49 PM):   What do you currently do?

Talk2bryan2001 (May 25 - 1:03:14 PM):   What I like most about you is that you are a GOD fearing man. I like that a lot. Good to have you as a friend.

Friends4Dave (May 25 - 1:04:38 PM):   No problem. It's good to have you as my friend, too. I was raised as a Jehovah's Witness, even though I am no longer a Jehovah's Witness.

Friends4Dave (May 25 - 1:06:38 PM):   What time is it in Nigeria now?

Friends4Dave (May 25 - 1:10:06 PM):   *(Gracy did not respond.)* Are you still there?

Friends4Dave (May 25 - 1:12:30 PM):   Okay, then... I will talk to you some other time. I need to go now and call my family in Nigeria. Goodbye and be blessed. *(Dave remained logged on to Yahoo! Messenger while, at the same time, he called a family member in Nigeria.)*

Talk2bryan2001 (May 25 - 1:19:38 PM):   *(After about 13 minutes of silence, Gracy resumed her chat with Dave.)* Hi dear ... you still there?

Friends4Dave (May 25 - 1:20:22 PM):   Yes, I am. I am trying to call my sister in Nigeria.

Talk2bryan2001 (May 25 - 1:20:39 PM):   Ok.

Talk2bryan2001(May 25 - 1:21:22 PM):   You've got children?

Friends4Dave (May 25 - 1:21:45 PM):   One. And you?

Talk2bryan2001 (May 25 - 1:21:48 PM):   If yes, how many?

Talk2bryan2001 (May 25 - 1:22:22 PM):   None.

Friends4Dave (May 25 - 1:22:43 PM):   Ok. What time is it in Nigeria now?

Talk2bryan2001 (May 25 - 1:23:48 PM):   (*She ignored Dave's question.*) How old is your child and where is your child now?

Friends4Dave (May 25 - 1:24:09 PM):   Hold on a minute, please. I'm talking to my sister's husband in Lagos now....

Talk2bryan2001 (May 25 - 1:24:52 PM):   6:25 p.m.

Talk2bryan2001 (May 25 - 1:25:29 PM):   I am waiting...

Friends4Dave (May 25 - 1:26:19 PM):   Ok. I'm back. My daughter is 17.

Talk2bryan2001 (May 25 - 1:26:50 PM):   Where is she?

Friends4Dave (May 25 - 1:27:03 PM):   She lives here in the United States. She is an American.

Talk2bryan2001 (May 25 - 1:27:21 PM):   With you? What time is it?

Friends4Dave (May 25 - 1:27:55 PM):   She sometimes lives with me, and she lives with her mother most of the time.

Friends4Dave (May 25 - 1:28:38 PM):   That's the way the system is here in America.

Friends4Dave (May 25 - 1:30:20 PM):   It's 13:30 hrs (1:30 p.m.) here.

Friends4Dave (May 25 - 1:31:03 PM):   Do you live with your parents?

Talk2bryan2001 (May 25 - 1:32:34 PM):   Yeah. But now in school.

Friends4Dave (May 25 - 1:32:56 PM):   What school do you attend?

Talk2bryan2001 (May 25 - 1:33:39 PM):   DELSU.

Friends4Dave (May 25 - 1:34:00 PM):   That's good. What is your
                             major?

Talk2bryan2001 May 25 - 1:34:14 PM):   Delta State University.

Talk2bryan2001 (May 25 - 1:35:52 PM):   I study political science... 300
                             levels.

Friends4Dave (May 25 - 1:36:32 PM):   That's good. So you have only
one tear to go after this. What do you plan to
do after that?

Friends4Dave (May 25 - 1:37:10 PM):   Only one year to go, not
                             "tear"... sorry.

Talk2bryan2001 (May 25 - 1:37:48 PM):   Maybe Masters or work.

Friends4Dave (May 25 - 1:38:20 PM):   You have wonderful plans!

Talk2bryan2001 (May 25 - 1:38:41 PM):   Thanks.

Friends4Dave (May 25 - 1:38:43 PM):   What part of Delta State are
                             you from?

Talk2bryan2001 (May 25 - 1:39:05 PM):   So what do you do?

Friends4Dave (May 25 - 1:39:50 PM):   *(Dave quickly thought for a
few seconds. He decided not to tell her that he
was currently disabled and unable to work at*

the moment... at least he should not tell her the truth yet because he did not want to scare her away because of the stigma of being disabled.) I am a Realtor, Consultant, and Project Manager.

Talk2bryan2001 (May 25 - 1:40:26 PM):   Would you like us to call each other on our cell phone?

Talk2bryan2001 (May 25 - 1:40:37 PM):   Ok good.

Talk2bryan2001 (May 25 - 1:40:58 PM):   Good for you my friend.

Friends4Dave (May 25 - 1:42:01 PM):   But I also studied Criminal Justice, Law, and Information Systems ... up to Ph.D level.

Talk2bryan2001 (May 25 - 1:42:55 PM):   Good for you my friend.

Friends4Dave (May 25 - 1:43:25 PM):   If you want to call me, my home number is 757-271-6756. Please do not give my number to anybody else.

Talk2bryan2001 (May 25 - 1:43:47 PM):   Ok.

Talk2bryan2001 (May 25 - 1:45:21 PM):   Do you need mine? Would you love to talk to me on phone?

Friends4Dave (May 25 - 1:45:44 PM):   Yes, please. (*Dave sensed that Gracy was having second thoughts about giving him her phone number because of the delay in sending him her number.*)

Talk2bryan2001 (May 25 - 1:48:08 PM):   Here: +2347062042902.

Friends4Dave (May 25 - 1:48:28 PM):   Thanks.

Talk2bryan2001 (May 25 - 1:49:03 PM):   You are welcome my friend.

Friends4Dave (May 25 - 1:49:03 PM):   If you like, you may check out my website. (*Dave gave her his real website URL.*) https://www.dave-washington.com.[11] You can also check me out on http://www.YouTube.com Just type my name in the search box. (*Dave sent Gracy two of his pictures through the file-sharing feature.*) I just sent you two of my pictures.

Friends4Dave (May 25 - 1:52:38 PM):   (*Dave called Gracy on the phone. A female picked up and said "hello"; but as soon as Dave spoke, she hung up the phone.*) That was me that just called you, Gracy.

Talk2bryan2001 (May 25 - 1:54:27 PM):   Sorry I did not get your call here. Please check the number and just call. Ok.?

Friends4Dave (May 25 - 1:55:41 PM):   I am going to try again...

Talk2bryan2001 (May 25 - 1:56:24 PM):   +234-70-6204-2902. (*Dave called Gracy again. The phone rang but got disconnected.*)

Talk2bryan2001 (May 25 - 1:58:17 PM):   I can't here you.

Friends4Dave (May 25 - 1:58:37 PM):   It rang but the call was disconnected. Don't worry... I will try it some other time. Sometimes, calls to Nigeria do not go through easily.

---

[11] The website URL has been changed.

Talk2bryan2001 (May 25 - 1:58:41 PM):   I can't hear you.

Talk2bryan2001 (May 25 - 1:59:41 PM):   I want to hear your voice. Ok.

Friends4Dave (May 25 - 1:59:56 PM):   I am calling you now...

Talk2bryan2001 (May 25 - 2:00:05 PM):   Please call me... ok.

Friends4Dave (May 25 - 2:00:08 PM):   It is ringing on my end.

Talk2bryan2001 (May 25 - 2:00:54 PM):   But it's not ringing here.

Talk2bryan2001 (May 25 - 2:01:44 PM):   *(She changed the subject.)* Do you keep friends?

Friends4Dave (May 25 - 2:03:14 PM):   Yes. I do keep worthy friends. I was using the *Yahoo! Voice* to call you. Let me call you directly from my home phone number please.

Talk2bryan2001 (May 25 - 2:23:47 PM):   You could have lots of friends, but I want to be different.

Talk2bryan2001 (May 25 - 2:25:03 PM):   Are you there?

Friends4Dave (May 25 - 2:26:09 PM):   I can't log off yet because you will not be able to receive the pictures I sent you if I log off now. I will wait until you accept the pictures before I turn off my computer.

Friends4Dave (May 25 - 2:26:48 PM):   But I am leaving here to do other things.

Talk2bryan2001 (May 25 - 2:28:21 PM):   Oh sorry dear, I'm using my phone to chat now... ok? So, I can't get the pictures now.

Talk2bryan2001 (May 25 - 2:29:41 PM):   My picture needs to be fixed
but I don't have enough money to fix it now.

Talk2bryan2001 (May 25 - 2:31:27 PM):   Still there? (*Dave was already
gone.*)

Talk2bryan2001 (May 25 - 3:41:45 PM):   Are you there? (*She logged
off before Dave returned.*)

CHAPTER 5
DAVE FINALLY CATCHES UP WITH MORRO ISSIFU

On May 26[12], Ibrahim Issifu[12] left a one-word message for Dave again:

Moro.Issifu (May 26 - 5:55:13 PM):   Hello.

Dave was not online.

* * * * * * *

On May 27th, Moro Issifu left another one-word message for Dave again:

Moro.Issifu (May 27 - 9:57:30 AM):   Hello.

Dave was not online.

* * * * * * *

That same day, on May 27th, 2009, Dave sent the following message to Rasheed Zakari:

Friends4Dave (May 27 - 1:10:57 PM):   Hi Rasheed. I just tried again to call you two times, but nobody picked up. Please let me know the best time to call you. By the way, where do you live?

But Rasheed was not online.

* * * * * * *

Since Gracy was already online on *Yahoo!* at the time Dave went online, Dave and Gracy chatted with each other on May 27th, as indicated below:

---

[12]   Moro Issifu or Musah Issifu.

Friends4Dave (May 27 - 12:04:57 PM):   Hi Gracy, how are you? (*But Gracy did not respond for a while.*)

Friends4Dave (May 27 - 12:08:17 PM):   I guess you are currently indisposed. Goodbye.

Talk2bryan2001(May 27 - 12:08:27 PM):   No! (*She finally responded.*)

Talk2bryan2001 (May 27 - 12:09:05 PM):   I am fine, and you?

Friends4Dave (May 27 - 12:09:09 PM):   Do you have time to chat for about five minutes?

Friends4Dave (May 27 - 12:09:30 PM):   I'm blessed, thank you.

Friends4Dave (May 27 - 12:11:04 PM):   Did you receive my pictures?

Talk2bryan2001 (May 27 - 12:11:45 PM):   I have not checked my box.

Talk2bryan2001 (May 27 - 12:11:59 PM):   I missed you.

Friends4Dave (May 27 - 12:12:22 PM):   Thanks. So did I.

Friends4Dave (May 27 - 12:12:50 PM):   I emailed you the pictures.

Friends4Dave (May 27 - 12:13:48 PM):   How is the weather now where you are?

Talk2bryan2001 (May 27 - 12:14:07 PM):   (*Probably misunderstood Dave's question.*) Home.

Friends4Dave (May 27 - 12:14:28 PM):   (*Dave asked the question again.*) How is the weather there?

Friends4Dave (May 27 - 12:17:11 PM):   (*Gracy did not respond for about three minutes. So, Dave decided to end the conversation.*) I have to go now. I took a little break just to chat with you... Goodbye.

---

* * * * * * *

On May 30th, Dave left another message for Rasheed. Evidently, she had not been online since the last time Dave sent her the previous message.

Friends4Dave (May 30 - 3:28:43 PM):   Hi Rasheed. I just tried to call you again and the system said that your number "is switched off." You can call me if you like at my home number at 757-271-6756. Hope to hear from you soon. Be blessed .... Dave.

* * * * * * *

Earlier on May 30th, Moro Issifu had left a message for Dave. Later on in the day, Dave and Moro were able to get in touch with each other and chat online:

Moro.Issifu (May 30 - 5:43:52 AM):   Hello.

Friends4Dave (May 30 - 3:05:12 PM):   Hi Moro. How are you?

Moro.Issifu (May 30 - 3:05:30 PM):   I am fine.

Moro.Issifu (May 30 - 3:05:32 PM):   And you?

Friends4Dave (May 30 - 3:05:53 PM):   I am fine, thank you. I saw that you are online now.

Friends4Dave (May 30 - 3:06:24 PM):   We have been missing each other online. Thanks for your messages.

Moro.Issifu (May 30 - 3:06:27 PM):   Ohh yes.

Moro.Issifu (May 30 - 3:06:35 PM):   Ohh yes.

Friends4Dave (May 30 - 3:06:39 PM):   Where are you from?

Moro.Issifu (May 30 - 3:06:40 PM): Do I know you please? (*Dave was thinking, "Something must be wrong with this guy's memory; but he is polite though. This is the same guy who has been leaving me messages online and now he is asking if he knows me?"*)

Moro.Issifu (May 30 - 3:06:52 PM): I am from Ghana.

Moro.Issifu (May 30 - 3:06:53 PM): And you?

Friends4Dave (May 30 - 3:08:06 PM): I am Dave. We met on Flixster. I was the one that posted warning messages on your Flixster profile about "Rose Grand" who claimed to be the manager of the hotel in Canada. And I am from Nigeria, but I live in the United States.

Moro.Issifu (May 30 - 3:08:34 PM): Are you there?

Friends4Dave (May 30 - 3:08:44 PM): I am here.

Friends4Dave (May 30 - 3:09:15 PM): Do you remember me now?

Moro.Issifu (May 30 - 3:09:16 PM): Ohh I see.

Moro.Issifu (May 30 - 3:09:23 PM): So how is your day now?

Moro.Issifu (May 30 - 3:09:34 PM): Wait for me... ok?

Friends4Dave (May 30 - 3:09:46 PM): I am blessed... thanks. (*Dave waited for about eight minutes or so, during which time Ibrahim kept logging in and out without chatting with Dave.*)

Friends4Dave (May 30 - 3:17:56 PM): Alright, Moro.... I waited for you but you came in and out without chatting and then disappeared. Goodbye. (*Dave logged out.*)

Moro.Issifu (May 30 - 3:27:29 PM):   (*Ibrahim returned about ten minutes after Dave logged out. Dave was now offline.*) Ohh no!

CHAPTER 6
DAVE AND ABIGAIL OSEI
COMMUNICATE BY EMAIL

Dave and Abigail Osei Communicated by email. Upon request, Dave had sent "Mandy Klmmy Anderson"[13] his email Address, and she wrote him with the name "Abigail Osei," which is different from the name she used on Flixster's website. Dave also sent her a reply email that same day. Abigail's email is reproduced below exactly as written, without editing:[14]

"Hello dear,

I am very glad to hear from you and at the same time thanks for the mail you sent to me. I even don't know where to start from? I am Abigail Osei as you know and i am 25 years single without a child. I am from Ghana that is Madina and I am Single (five years ago), Black, dark black hair, brown eyes, 5' 9", 141 lbs., long Hair and a healthy Lady. I am self-sufficient, Beautiful, happy, secure, self-confident, psychologically aware, emotionally and not financially secure and I stay with my sister, I lost my Mom Years back and that is a long story. I come from a caring and honest family that i like it a lot. Well I am a woman who needs the best for myself and will like to meet the right man who is very handsome, caring, faithful, respectful, God fearing, loyal and will be there for me when i need him. My desire is to meet a Handsome, sensitive, sensuous, warm, assertive single man who wants a serious relationship.

My interpretation of a man I am looking for is one to whom you can pour out all the contents of your heart, chaff and grain together, knowing that the gentleness of hands

---

[13] Also known as Abigail Osei.
[14] In hindsight, Dave now believes that Abigail Osei sends the same email to all her male targets.

will take it all, sift it, keep that which is worth keeping and, with a breath of kindness, blow the rest away and I am looking for a special, loving relationship with a unique Man who is affectionate, Handsome, with a shapely figure, sincere, easygoing, with interests and characteristics similar to mine...someone who wants a meaningful, serious, long-term relationship...not just a few dates. I am looking for someone who has a great sense of humor and big heart, is curious about new things that would like to share new experiences or old habits and I am looking for someone who believes that a true intimate partner looks out for the other and vice versa. While navigating life together, we are caring and concerned for each other's well-being because we make each other so happy and we love each other very much. Looking for a serious long term relationship with someone who possesses strong character and is goal-oriented. He must love the Lord with all of his heart, then I know he will love me with all his heart and he should enjoy good humor, love to laugh, and be a hopeless romantic. So that would make him a God-loving romantic guy......and God will approve.lol. My ideal partner must love to take long walks...holding hands.....when I am not giving him a "walk for his money"....His yes must be yes, and his no, no. I am more concerning on the distance but when i saw your mail in which u said distance is not a problem with you i was glad and i think one day you will find a time to pay me a visit here.

I think one day we should have a chat and see each other on cam what do you think about that and i think through that we can see each other as real..Take care and hope to hear from you soon… Abigail."

* * * * * * *

One particular statement that Abigail made in her email struck Dave as odd. This is when Abigail stated in her email, "I am more concerning on the distance but when i saw your mail in which u said distance is not a problem with you i was glad and i think one day you will find a time to pay me a visit here." The fact is, Dave never told her that "distance is not a problem." That issue had never been discussed in the very scant conversation between Dave and Abigail until Dave received her email. Dave thought that she was probably mistaking him for someone else with whom she had discussed distance-dating relationship. However, giving Abigail the benefit of doubt, Dave sent a reply email to her, a copy of which is reprinted below:

"Hi Abigail:

Hope this letter meets you well. I am very pleased to receive your email, which I believe is very insightful.[15] It shows you are intelligent and know exactly what you want in a man. The characteristics you desire in a man are not superficial but they are truly godly qualities, which I cherish in my life. I could sense the genuineness of your heart as I read your email.

Before I continue, please allow me to express my condolences to you for the loss of your Mom. I know how painful that can be because I lost my Mom in July 2008. May God give you and the rest of your family the strength to deal with the loss and the courage to move on with life, knowing that you will see her again in the future (John 5:28, 29; Revelation 21:3-5; and John 11:21-27).

Again, my name is Dave Washington. I am a Nigerian-American. I live in Virginia in the United States. I'm 47 years old, 5'9" tall, 196 lbs, brown eyes, black hair with a few specks of gray (I had my first gray hair when I was about 20 years old). I shave my hair every two days; so most people think I'm bald. I am muscular and naturally very strong. I was once married for 18 years to a beautiful woman, but we ended the marriage in 2005 due to irreconcilable differences and adultery (we had gotten married within three months of meeting each other for the first time in Brooklyn, New York). We were divorced

---

[15] Although Dave was not impressed by Abigail's diction and writing style, he felt that she was beautiful and appeared to have some other qualities which he was looking for.

shortly thereafter 2008. I tried to make it work because I really don't believe in divorce; but the marriage could not work and it ended on the grounds of adultery. My ex-wife and I are still good friends until today and we still help each other out; but our romance ended in 2005 when we separated. I have a daughter who lives with my ex-wife, and my daughter visits me periodically whenever she is able to do so.

I have not had any girlfriend (lover) for years now, and I did not want any woman. Recently, however, I have been praying to God to give me the right woman. And even though I prayed to God to give me the right woman, I was not actively looking for a woman. I joined Flixster because one of my brothers (Morgan One) in Italy asked me to join so that we could communicate there. So, I joined but did not frequent Flixster and did not give details about my profile either. I was only interested in communicating privately with my brother ... that's it. I happened to come across your profile on Flixster by chance, while I was responding to people postings on my profile. When I saw your profile, something came over me (which I cannot explain); so I sent you a friend request. And you accepted almost immediately. Then I logged back in and updated my profile and sent you another message informing you that I had just updated my profile if you want to review it. And you did and sent me another message complimenting me on my profile; and thanks again. So that's how you and I met.

Back to my not wanting a girlfriend until I met you: I just don't want to get any woman. I can get most women I want, anytime I want, including some married women who keep telling me that they want to be with me; but I do not want them because I do not want to sin against my God. I only want a woman I can love deeply, honor, cherish, and marry. Yes, I want a woman I can make my queen and the essence of my life. I have no time for games (too many sexually transmitted diseases are floating around, I don't want them to come near me).

I have been living alone in a three-bedroom apartment
since my ex-wife and I separated and later got divorced on
the grounds of adultery. My daughter visits me here
sometimes (so, she has her own bedroom here). I left the
house we owned together to my ex-wife when we decided
to separate in 2005. I believe she deserves to have the
house because my daughter lives in the house with her.
Nevertheless, I hope and plan to buy another house within
the next two years, by the grace of God.

To more effectively describe myself to you, it is best that I
use some of the expressions which people, who know me
very well, have used to describe me to others. According to
them, and I agree, I am well-educated; self-confident, yet
humble; independent, yet cooperative; kind, yet disciplined
and a disciplinarian; loyal; faithful; honest and sincere;
psychologically stable and competent; emotionally secure;
warm; sensitive; respectful; assertive, yet considerate of
other's opinions and feelings; compassionate when
justified; intelligent; scholarly; goal-oriented; romantic;
caring; loving and lovely; Man of God; generous; have a
good sense of humor; funny; affectionate; have a strong
character; decisive; and very patient. Moreover, many
people say that I am also good-looking. As for the good-
looking part, that will be for you to judge. While I am not
the most handsome person in the world, I also believe that
I am not the ugliest person either. ☺ Factually, though, I
am muscular and naturally strong, even though I had a
back injury years ago.

Currently, I am not as financially secure as I used to be; but
that will change for the better again in the near future.
Compared to what I used to be as a millionaire, I am
currently a very poor man (but I can take care of myself,
though). However, all that will change for the best once I
complete the few projects I am currently planning and/or
executing. And with God's help, I will be much better off

than I have ever been in my life. I just hope that you will be there with me if, according to God's Will, you are the right woman for me and I am the right man for you.

I said "I hope you will be there with me" because, from the description of yourself in the email, you seem to have the qualities I need in a woman. Furthermore, as for the qualities, which you expressed in your email that you desire in the right man for you, God has already put those qualities in me. You see, I was raised a Jehovah's Witness. I learned and cultivated those qualities in me from my childhood onward, just as I have tried to cultivate similar qualities in my daughter. Although I was disfellowshipped from Jehovah Witnesses' organization a few years ago, I have recently resumed attending the meetings again at a local Kingdom Hall of Jehovah's Witnesses; although I have not been reinstated yet. My association with the organization during a major part of my life enabled me to develop all the good qualities that I have, which people who know me very well use to describe me as I indicated earlier above. Moreover, these are the same qualities that you have delineated in your email that you desire in a man; and which you will definitely and pleasantly discover in me if our relationship proceeds further. The more you get to know me, the happier you will become.

Therefore, please pray about me, and I will about you, for God's guidance; and if it is God's Will, you and I will be together and for each other for the rest of our lives. Yes, I like taking long walks along scenic places, holding hands affectionately and giving kisses of endearment to each other both in private and in public. When you need sustenance, I will be there to sustain you. When you need moral support, I will be there to give you that moral support without hesitation. When you need someone special to lean on, I will be there to give you my shoulders, arms, chest, and any other part of me you need to lean on. In addition, when need someone just to listen to you talk, I will be there to listen too.

Until then, may your beauty continue to glow with excellence amongst the peoples of the world; may the sparkle of your effervescent brown eyes shine like the stars of the heavens; and may your angelic smile (yes, I saw your smile on Flixster) find favor among men and women and, most of all, find favor in the eyes of God.

Finally, I agree that we should chat and see each other through the webcam. That really would be very nice. Please let me know when you want us to meet online Remember that I am about five or six hours behind your time. When it is 12 noon in Ghana, it is about 5 a.m. or 6 a.m. here in the part of the United States where I live. Until I hear from you again, I wish you pleasant thoughts to accompany you during the days and sweet dreams during the nights.

Be blessed,

Dave."

CHAPTER 7
RASHEED IS ELUSIVE.
GRACY AND ABIGAIL CHAT WITH DAVE.

Rasheed was elusive for about 11 days. Gracy and Abigail chatted with Dave on the same day. Finally, on May 31st, Rasheed Zakari left the following message for Dave on *Yahoo! Messenger* to call her on a phone number that did not work. Dave wondered why Rasheed kept asking him to call her on an invalid phone number.

Rasheed Zakari (May 31 - 1:12:54 PM):   I am sorry.

Rasheed Zakari (May 31 - 1:16:51 PM):   Try calling me again when you come online and you are going to get me to talk to you.

Rasheed Zakari (May 31 - 1:16:59 PM):   I really want to chat with you too.

* * * * * *

Gracy Isy (Grace Nwaokoro)[16] was online when Dave logged in. Gracy initiated a conversation with Dave and Dave began to chat with her. Few minutes later, however, Abigail Osei came online too, and she initiated a conversation with Dave. Therefore, Dave began to chat with both ladies simultaneously, even though he did not like to do so. The conversation between Gracy and Dave is presented first below. Immediately after that, Dave's conversation with Abigail is presented next.

Talk2bryan2001 (May 31 - 5:20:38 PM):   I miss you.

Friends4Dave (May 31 - 5:20:57 PM):   I missed you too. How are you?

---

[16] Dave discovered that Gracy Isy's name is Grace Nwaokoro; but later on in this book, Dave began to doubt whether Grace Nwaokoro is even her real name.

Talk2bryan2001 (May 31 - 5:21:04 PM):   Did you get my offline
                                            message?

Talk2bryan2001 (May 31 - 5:21:26 PM):   I'm blessed.

Talk2bryan2001 (May 31 - 5:21:30 PM):   And you?

Friends4Dave (May 31 - 5:21:43 PM):   No. I did not. What was the
                                         message?

Friends4Dave (May 31 - 5:21:58 PM):   I'm blessed, too. Thanks.
                                        (Dave checked to see if there was any message
                                        from Gracy for him, but there was none.
                                        Therefore, he wondered if Gracy was
                                        confusing him with someone else.)

Talk2bryan2001 (May 31 - 5:23:17 PM):   That I long to hear from you.

Talk2bryan2001 (May 31 - 5:24:05 PM):   And that you should please
                                            call me if you can.

Friends4Dave (May 31 - 5:24:15 PM):   I was just checking my online
                                         messages to see if I had any from you. I do not
                                         see any. But thanks for your longing.

Friends4Dave (May 31 - 5:24:44 PM):   I would have called you if I
                                         got the message.

Friends4Dave (May 31 - 5:25:13 PM):   How is everything in Nigeria?

Talk2bryan2001 (May 31 - 5:26:25 PM):   We bless GOD. I am just
                                            doing great.

Talk2bryan2001 (May 31 - 5:26:34 PM):   How is work?

Friends4Dave (May 31 - 5:27:04 PM):   That's great! Work is fine.
(Dave did not want to tell her that he was currently disabled .... It was not time to tell her yet.)

Friends4Dave (May 31 - 5:27:21 PM):   How is your schooling?

Talk2bryan2001 (May 31 - 5:27:51 PM):   Looks like you've been busy. You hardly come online.

Talk2bryan2001 (May 31 - 5:28:21 PM):   My exams are starting next week.

Friends4Dave (May 31 - 5:28:45 PM):   That is true. I do not come online that frequently. I only came online once on Monday, and also today just to chat with you. But I ended up chatting with someone else too.[17]

Friends4Dave (May 31 - 5:29:09 PM):   I wish you the best on your exams!

Talk2bryan2001 (May 31 - 5:31:03 PM):   I will send you my pictures .... Ok? When I go to the Internet Café because I don't have a PC anymore. At least that would be faster.

Friends4Dave (May 31 - 5:31:30 PM):   No problems. Please send them to me at your convenience.

Talk2bryan2001 (May 31 - 5:31:50 PM):   Ok.

Talk2bryan2001 (May 31 - 5:32:13 PM):   I really like you... you know.

Friends4Dave (May 31 - 5:32:56 PM):   Thanks. I like you, too. Did

---

[17] Abigail Osei.

you get my pictures?

Talk2bryan2001 (May 31 - 5:33:10 PM):   Well, I really don't know why; but I just like you.

Talk2bryan2001 (May 31 - 5:34:28 PM):   No, I checked. Maybe I will still check my mail box again.

Friends4Dave (May 31 - 5:34:46 PM):   Thanks again. Let me know when you get my pictures. I emailed them to you. You may want to check your email *Inbox* and *Spam* folders.

Talk2bryan2001 (May 31 - 5:35:29 PM):   Ok, I will, but how?

Talk2bryan2001 (May 31 - 5:36:07 PM):   I tried your number but it was not going through. Why?

Friends4Dave (May 31 - 5:36:51 PM):   Please go to yahoo.com website. Once you log into your email account, click on check messages or the envelope icon.

Talk2bryan2001 (May 31 - 5:37:45 PM):   I am using my phone to chat now.

Talk2bryan2001 (May 31 - 5:38:15 PM):   So, that's not possible.

Friends4Dave (May 31 - 5:39:31 PM):   Sorry you could not reach me on the phone. To call me, please dial 1-757-271-6756.

Friends4Dave (May 31 - 5:39:44 PM):   Call me later then. Any time.

Talk2bryan2001 (May 31 - 5:40:30 PM):   But this was not the number you gave me. Right?

Friends4Dave (May 31 - 5:40:56 PM):   It is the same number. My home number.

Talk2bryan2001 (May 31 - 5:41:31 PM):   Ok, yeah… that's it.

Talk2bryan2001 (May 31 - 5:42:03 PM):   It's not going through.

Friends4Dave (May 31 - 5:42:54 PM):   Perhaps the network is down. Try calling me later. Is that ok?

Talk2bryan2001 (May 31 - 5:43:44 PM):   I want two hear from you almost all the time. That's how much I miss you. Ok? (*These statements indicated that Gracy appeared to be falling in love with Dave.*)

Friends4Dave (May 31 - 5:44:45 PM):   Ok. I will wait for some time. If don't hear from you, I will call you. Is that alright?

Talk2bryan2001 (May 31 - 5:45:56 PM):   Fair enough.

Friends4Dave (May 31 - 5:48:16 PM):   I am really looking forward to speaking to you, tomorrow. Like I said, I will first wait for you to call me, so that you know that I gave you my real home number. But, if I do not hear from you, I will call you tomorrow.

Friends4Dave (May 31 - 5:50:14 PM):   Are you still there Gracy?

Talk2bryan2001 (May 31 - 5:50:59 PM):   Well, for now I am not having much on me.

Friends4Dave (May 31 - 5:51:28 PM):   What do you mean?

Talk2bryan2001 (May 31 - 5:53:04 PM):   Now that I am in school and my exam is soon, I hardly buy airtime to make calls. That's what I mean dear.

Talk2bryan2001 (May 31 - 5:53:42 PM):   I do not have enough money.

Friends4Dave (May 31 - 5:54:05 PM):   Ok. I can call you tomorrow if you don't mind, instead of you calling me. Is that ok?

Talk2bryan2001 (May 31 - 5:54:28 PM):   Maybe you do the calling for now… ok.

Friends4Dave (May 31 - 5:55:17 PM):   That is fine with me.

Friends4Dave (May 31 - 5:55:41 PM):   I need to go now. I will call you tomorrow.

Talk2bryan2001 (May 31 - 5:55:49 PM):   Thanks.

Talk2bryan2001 (May 31 - 5:55:58 PM):   Ok.

Friends4Dave (May 31 - 5:56:01 PM):   You are welcome. (*Dave ended the conversation and Gracy logged out.*)

* * * * * * *

Earlier that same day, May 31st, Dave and Abigail Osei ("Mandy Klmmy Anderson" on Flixster.com) chatted on Flixster for a short while, but Dave lost connection. Later, however, Dave and Abigail met again on *Yahoo! Messenger*, while Dave was about nine minutes into his conversation with Gracy. Dave and Abigail resumed chatting from where they had left off on their Flixster chats; and while Dave was simultaneously chatting with Gracy above on *Yahoo! Messenger*.

Abigail Osei (May 31 - 5:29:32 PM):   Hello.

Chapter 7: Rasheed Is Elusive. Gracy And Abigail Chat With Dave.

Friends4Dave (May 31 - 5:29:47 PM):   Hi Abigail.

Abigail Osei (May 31 - 5:30:13 PM):   Hello.

Abigail Osei (May 31 - 5:30:20 PM):   Dave, how are you doing?

Friends4Dave (May 31 - 5:30:42 PM):   I'm blessed! And you? Did you get my email?

Abigail Osei (May 31 - 5:31:05 PM):   No, I didn't. I check it but there was no email.

Abigail Osei (May 31 - 5:31:12 PM):   I want you to send it to me again.

Friends4Dave (May 31 - 5:31:57 PM):   I sent it again today.

Abigail Osei (May 31 - 5:32:18 PM):   Ok wait and let me check.

Abigail Osei (May 31 - 5:34:42 PM):   Let's chat while it's loading.

Abigail Osei (May 31 - 5:34:47 PM):   So how was your day??

Abigail Osei (May 31 - 5:35:14 PM):   When was it last you've been to Nigeria??

Friends4Dave (May 31 - 5:35:45 PM):   My day was beautiful. I went to the Kingdom Hall in the morning. I have been busy working on some reports before and after I first chatted with you on Flixster.

Abigail Osei (May 31 - 5:36:30 PM):   Ok and you went without saying bye.

Abigail Osei (May 31 - 5:37:09 PM):   I have received your email.

Abigail Osei (May 31 - 5:37:43 PM):   Wow you told me more about yourself.

Friends4Dave (May 31 - 5:37:55 PM):   No, I didn't leave without saying goodbye. I was logged off by Flixster. Flixster is unreliable. By the time I logged on again, you were already gone. But I am truly sorry.

Abigail Osei (May 31 - 5:38:22 PM):   So where is your daughter??

Friends4Dave (May 31 - 5:39:21 PM):   She is with her mother now. She may be visiting me sometime in the Summer. Thanks for asking about her.

Abigail Osei (May 31 - 5:39:54 PM):   Ok where are they now?? Nigeria or where??

Friends4Dave (May 31 - 5:40:22 PM):   Here in the United States. She and her mother are Americans.

Abigail Osei (May 31 - 5:41:16 PM):   Oh ok.

Abigail Osei (May 31 - 5:41:45 PM):   Are you there??

Friends4Dave (May 31 - 5:42:00 PM):   Yes, dear. I am here.

Abigail Osei (May 31 - 5:42:13 PM):   Ok.

Abigail Osei (May 31 - 5:42:20 PM):   So what is the time there now??

Friends4Dave (May 31 - 5:43:47 PM):   It is 17:43 hrs. (5:43 p.m.). Where exactly is Medina?

Abigail Osei (May 31 - 5:44:04 PM):   Ghana.

Friends4Dave (May 31 - 5:45:13 PM):   I know it is Ghana. But is it near Accra or near Kumasi?

Abigail Osei (May 31 - 5:45:39 PM):   Accra.

Abigail Osei (May 31 - 5:45:43 PM):   Have you been to Ghana before??

Friends4Dave (May 31 - 5:46:48 PM):   I would like to visit you in Ghana sometime in the future. I have only been to Accra in transit (from Nigeria to Germany) on my way back home in the United States.

Friends4Dave (May 31 - 5:48:35 PM):   *(After about three minutes of no response from Abigail.)* Are you there, Abigail?

Abigail Osei (May 31 - 5:48:55 PM):   Yes I am here.

Abigail Osei (May 31 - 5:49:02 PM):   I was reading what you wrote to me.

Abigail Osei (May 31 - 5:49:20 PM):   So are you trying to tell me that you are still single??

Friends4Dave (May 31 - 5:49:24 PM):   Please, take your time. Just let me know when you are done.

Abigail Osei (May 31 - 5:49:40 PM):   I am done.

Friends4Dave (May 31 - 5:49:50 PM):   Yes, I am single by choice.

Abigail Osei (May 31 - 5:50:30 PM):   Ok.

Abigail Osei (May 31 - 5:51:33 PM):   I have to go. It is late here.

Abigail Osei (May 31 - 5:51:43 PM):   I will send you a mail.

Friends4Dave (May 31 - 5:51:50 PM):   Ok. What time is it there?

Abigail Osei (May 31 - 5:52:09 PM):   9:50 p.m.

Friends4Dave (May 31 - 5:52:35 PM):   Good bye. And it was a
pleasure chatting with you today. Yes, it is
really late. Good night then.

Abigail Osei (May 31 - 5:53:06 PM):   Ok.

Abigail Osei (May 31 - 5:53:08 PM):   I will send you a mail.

Friends4Dave (May 31 - 5:53:47 PM):   Ok.

Abigail Osei (May 31 - 5:54:16 PM):   I am sorry about that.

Friends4Dave (May 31 - 5:54:37 PM):   No apologies necessary. I
understand.

Abigail Osei (May 31 - 5:54:41 PM):   So what are your plans in life
now??

Friends4Dave (May 31 - 5:54:44 PM):   *(Dave thought to himself, "I
thought you said that you have to go? Why are
you now asking me about my plans in life?"
He wanted to discuss the issue another time.)*
Good night.

Abigail Osei (May 31 - 5:55:11 PM):   Night.

Dave's conversations with Gracy Isy and Abigail Osei ended almost at the same time.

CHAPTER 8
DAVE FINALLY CATCHES UP WITH RASHEED

𝔇ave finally caught up with Rasheed. Dave was able to interact live with Rasheed on *Yahoo! Messenger* about five hours after she had left her last message for Dave earlier in the day. Rasheed came online shortly after Dave's conversations with Gracy Isy (Grace Nwaokoro) and Abigail Osei (Mandy Klimmy Anderson) ended.

Friends4Dave (May 31 - 5:11:54 PM):   (*In response to Rasheed's message about four hours ago, Dave left this message for her when he came online.*) I tried again many times today to call you, but the system said it "cannot detect any voice signals from Rasheed Zakari." You may want to try calling me instead. Or let me know when you are normally online and the country you live in so that I can arrange to be online at the same time; in order that we can chat. Thanks. Be blessed .... Dave.

* * * * * *

Rasheed Zakari (May 31 - 6:06:43 PM):   (*Approximately one hour after Dave left the above message for Rasheed, she came online and left this message for him. Dave was not online at the time.*)   Oh ok. I will let you know when you are going to call.

Friends4Dave (May 31 - 6:10:06 PM):   (*However, a few minutes later, Dave came back online and noticed that he had just missed Rasheed. But, as he was leaving this message for her, she came back online and they began to chat.*) Hi Rasheed. I just missed you again. Just by a few minutes.

Rasheed Zakari (May 31 - 6:10:25 PM): OOh yes, how are you doing? (*Glad to be able to reconnect with Dave.*)

Friends4Dave (May 31 - 6:10:43 PM): I'm blessed, and you?

Rasheed Zakari (May 31 - 6:10:54 PM): I am also good, thanks.

Rasheed Zakari (May 31 - 6:11:06 PM): How was your day?

Friends4Dave (May 31 - 6:11:54 PM): My day was great! I first went to the Kingdom Hall in the morning, and now I am just having fun and relaxing.

Friends4Dave (May 31 - 6:12:18 PM): How was your day?

Rasheed Zakari (May 31 - 6:12:39 PM): Oh yes me too, went to the church as well and came to Mom and helped her with some home work.

Friends4Dave (May 31 - 6:13:10 PM): (*Dave thought to himself, "She must be a very good girl since she helps her mother with household chores.*) That's great. Good values with helping your Mom.

Friends4Dave (May 31 - 6:13:34 PM): Which country do you live in Rasheed?

Rasheed Zakari (May 31 - 6:14:10 PM): Oh I live in Ghana.

Rasheed Zakari (May 31 - 6:14:28 PM): Have you talked with someone from there before?

Friends4Dave (May 31 - 6:14:34 PM): (*Dave ignored Rasheed's question because he did not want to lie about talking to someone else in Ghana.*) Ok. That's very good. Where in Ghana?

Rasheed Zakari (May 31 - 6:15:09 PM):   I live in Greater Accra.

Friends4Dave (May 31 - 6:15:38 PM):   Ok. I live in Virginia in the United States.

Rasheed Zakari (May 31 - 6:16:06 PM):   Oh great.

Friends4Dave (May 31 - 6:16:46 PM):   Do you have access to a webcam so that you can see me and I can see you?

Rasheed Zakari (May 31 - 6:17:07 PM):   (*She did not answer Dave's question.*) Do you have one?

Friends4Dave (May 31 - 6:17:17 PM):   Yes, I do.

Rasheed Zakari (May 31 - 6:17:32 PM):   Ok can I see you??

Friends4Dave (May 31 - 6:17:53 PM):   Yes, you can.

Rasheed Zakari (May 31 - 6:18:01 PM):   Ok invite me then.

Friends4Dave (May 31 - 6:18:57 PM):   (*Dave invited Rasheed to view him on her the webcam.*) Do you see me?

Rasheed Zakari (May 31 - 6:19:04 PM):   Oh you are looking great and handsome.

Rasheed Zakari (May 31 - 6:19:08 PM):   Have you talked with someone from there before?

Friends4Dave (May 31 - 6:19:53 PM):   Thanks. Yes, I have talked to someone there.

Friends4Dave (May 31 - 6:20:22 PM):   Do you have a web cam?

Rasheed Zakari (May 31 - 6:20:47 PM):   Oh ok that is cool. Are you married with kids?? Yes I have a webcam but not sure how to fix it … (*She lied about not knowing how to use the web cam, though.*)[18]

Rasheed Zakari (May 31 - 6:20:56 PM):   I have to Install the CD.

Friends4Dave (May 31 - 6:21:27 PM):   Ok. No, I'm not married, but I have a daughter.

Friends4Dave (May 31 - 6:22:10 PM):   Are you married?

Rasheed Zakari (May 31 - 6:22:11 PM):   Oh great, I am single, never been married with no kids. Tell me … what are you looking for and have you found it yet?

Friends4Dave (May 31 - 6:23:30 PM):   (*Dave was stunned at her boldness and directness.*)   I am really not actively looking for anybody right now, but if the right woman comes along, I am also ready. My wife and I separated in 2005; and we were divorced shortly thereafter.

Rasheed Zakari (May 31 - 6:24:01 PM):   Oh ok, so tell me what happened in your relationship?

Friends4Dave (May 31 - 6:24:21 PM):   However, the right woman must be honest, clean, and God-fearing.

Friends4Dave (May 31 - 6:25:01 PM):   We ended the marriage due to irreconcilable differences and adultery. (*Dave*

---

[18] She lied about not being able to use her webcam because she later proved to be very proficient in using the webcam and in her ability to manipulate the images that you see on your end. Since she was not expecting Dave to ask her about connecting through video conferencing, she was just buying time to doctor up the images that she wanted Dave to see; as would be discussed later in this book.

did not want to go into details; as he did not want to tell other people how terrible, his ex-wife really is. As far as he is concerned, it is none of their business.)

Rasheed Zakari (May 31 - 6:26:22 PM):   I am a serious Christian woman and I am Guided by my relationship with Jesus Christ. I say that up front because my faith is very important to me. I will touch on that more later. So I want a man of faith who has principles and values. We have all made mistakes in life but need to be guided by something...

Friends4Dave (May 31 - 6:26:23 PM):   Are you there?

Rasheed Zakari (May 31 - 6:28:14 PM):   I am looking for the real man of my life whom is a sincere, honest, dedicated, responsible, romantic, and passionate young gentleman with a good sense of humor and strong values in search of a best friend, life-long partner, and a true love. Love is like trust, when you find your special someone it is as if you're trusting them with your heart.

Friends4Dave (May 31 - 6:30:26 PM):   (*Dave was impressed by her statement and reasoning. Since Dave wanted an intelligent woman in his life, he began to think that Rasheed might have the potential to be just the person he was looking for.*) And I agree. I am only interested in true love also.

Friends4Dave (May 31 - 6:30:39 PM):   How old are you?

Rasheed Zakari (May 31 - 6:30:54 PM):   I am 30 years of age and what about you??

Rasheed Zakari (May 31 - 6:31:07 PM):   I value friendship, honesty, loyalty, romance, passion, spirituality, family, and a good laugh. I have had many experiences in my life that make me an intelligent, well-rounded, understanding, and compassionate person.

Friends4Dave (May 31 - 6:31:55 PM):   *(Dave noticed some inconsistencies in her statements about how old she claimed she was. For example, she wrote 29 years, 30 years, and 32 years on her Flixster profiles.[19] At the same time, Dave felt such inconsistencies were minor.)* I am 47. I am everything that I said I am in my Flixster profile. My yes means yes, and my no means no.

Rasheed Zakari (May 31 - 6:32:54 PM):   Oh ok I understand.

Rasheed Zakari (May 31 - 6:33:41 PM):   Well, I want you to know that I am not here to play games or to play with some one's feelings and I don't want mine to be played as well. I hope you are trying to understand me. *(Dave liked what he was reading so far.)*

Friends4Dave (May 31 - 6:34:07 PM):   *(Dave confessed.)* I am resisting an urge to admit that you have described the kind of woman that I want.

Rasheed Zakari (May 31 - 6:34:56 PM):   What do you do for a living?

Friends4Dave (May 31 - 6:37:22 PM):   *(Dave could not respond in time to her question above because he was writing this comment at the time.)* I understand you very well. I am hesitant in opening up my

---

[19] Dave discovered later that Rasheed had multiple accounts profiles on Flixster.

heart to you because I really do not know whom I am talking to yet. However, whatever I say under any given circumstance is factual. I do not deceive people and do not want to be deceived. Moreover, the qualities you have just enumerated are quite virtuous and admirable; certainly, those are some of the characteristics, which I possess; and they are the characteristics that I desire in a woman.

Friends4Dave (May 31 - 6:38:23 PM):   (*Dave now responded to Rasheed's last question.*) I am a Realtor, Consultant, and Project Manager by profession. I also studied Criminal Justice, Law, Human Services, as wells as Information Systems in college and graduate schools. Please visit the website I listed on my Flixster profile to find out more about me.

Rasheed Zakari (May 31 - 6:39:01 PM):   Oh ok cool.

Friends4Dave (May 31 - 6:40:04 PM):   (*Dave thought to himself, "Ok, cool? That sounds like she is an American, not a Ghanaian."*) What do you do for a living?

Rasheed Zakari (May 31 - 6:40:28 PM):   I help my mom to sell in a super market.

Friends4Dave (May 31 - 6:41:10 PM):   (*Another yellow flag for Dave: "Super Market? That's also an American terminology."*) That's good. Do you live by yourself or with your Mom at present?

Rasheed Zakari (May 31 - 6:41:35 PM):   I live with my Mom.

Rasheed Zakari (May 31 - 6:41:43 PM):   And do you live alone?

Friends4Dave (May 31 - 6:43:14 PM):   There is nothing wrong with living with your Mom. Yes, I live alone. When my ex-wife and I separated in 2005, I left our house and everything for her. I have been living in a three-bedroom apartment since then. But, I hope to buy another house in the next two years.

Rasheed Zakari (May 31 - 6:43:48 PM):   That is great. So what do you do for fun?

Friends4Dave (May 31 - 6:47:19 PM):   Quite frankly, I have not been having much fun for a few years now. On the other hand, when I do, I go to the movies with my daughter, dine out in restaurants, go the Busch Gardens, and bowling. I also enjoy reading a lot (everyday), and watching some wholesome TV programs. When I find the right woman, I would like to resume visiting the parks, taking long walks, holding hands (privately and publicly); and, of course, doing what she really loves to do, whatever that may be, as long as it is legal.

Rasheed Zakari (May 31 - 6:49:21 PM):   I weight 136 lbs and 5'6" ft tall. I helped my mom to sell in a super market. I did gradated school at the University of Ghana Legon. I study Journalism and want to be a journalist one day in the future. I enjoy cooking, watching movie, and my favourite movies are Adventure, cartoons, Comedy, etc. I do play Video games with my Friends such as XBox 360. I love to play that much, but I always lose… lol. I like to listen to RNB music, Jazz, Hip life and Gospel. Like I said, I am looking for a soul mate to spend my life with a man who can make me happy for the rest of my life and also a man who is genuine and also a good Christian as well.

Friends4Dave (May 31 - 6:53:58 PM):   *(Dave was impressed by her acclaimed academic achievements. Dave noticed also that she wrote in British English, as opposed to the American English. For example, she used the British word "favourite", instead of the American word "favorite". Was she British?.... Or perhaps an Australian?)* Congratulations on your Journalism degree. Well, I like jazz, R&B, reggae, and some country music. I don't know how to play the games on Xbox either, so you are not alone .... Besides, when I do play games, I enjoy just the fun of playing the games, whether I win or lose. If you enjoyed playing the games with your friends, it doesn't really matter if you lost. The only thing that matters is that you had a great time and that's good for your soul.

Rasheed Zakari (May 31 - 6:54:47 PM):   Yes, I agree.

Friends4Dave (May 31 - 6:55:35 PM):   There is no doubt in my mind that my next wife is going to be very happy. However, I am taking my time in finding that right woman, because I don't ever want to divorce again. I hate divorce!

Rasheed Zakari (May 31 - 6:56:14 PM):   Hmm, I hope that will never happen in my relationship... ever.

Rasheed Zakari (May 31 - 6:56:27 PM):   So, do you have a cell phone?

Friends4Dave (May 31 - 6:57:55 PM):   Yes, I do. But, I do not receive signals at home.[20] I am home now. My cell

---

[20] Dave's telephone carrier, T-Mobile, recently cancelled its roaming contract with AT&T

phone number is 757-358-4757.[21] My home number is 757-271-6756.[22] You can call me at home if you would like to.

Rasheed Zakari (May 31 - 6:58:52 PM): *(Rasheed was very smooth and very slick. She began to manipulate Dave without him realizing what was happening at first.)* Oh well, I do have a cell phone as well, but I don't have a calling card to call you. Can you call outside your country?

Friends4Dave (May 31 - 6:59:09 PM): I will show you my cell phone so you can see that I don't receive signals here. *(Dave brought out his Blackberry 8800 cell phone and showed it to Rasheed on the web cam.)*

Rasheed Zakari (May 31 - 6:59:41 PM): Ok I see it.

Friends4Dave (May 31 - 7:01:26 PM): Please, just a minute.... I will be right back. I need to turn off what I am heating up (food) on the stove in the kitchen. *(Dave went to the kitchen to turn off the stove.)*

Rasheed Zakari (May 31 - 7:01:45 PM): Oh ok. I am here with you.

Friends4Dave (May 31 - 7:03:09 PM): *(Dave returned.)* Sorry about that.

Rasheed Zakari (May 31 - 7:03:16 PM): Oh it's ok.

Friends4Dave (May 31 - 7:03:54 PM): *(Dave was curious to see whom he was chatting with; now that she has*

---

and, as such, Dave could no longer receive cellular telephone call whenever he was at home because there was no cellular signal in his neighborhood.

[21] Dave no longer owns this phone number.

[22] Dave no longer owns this phone number.

---

seen him on the webcam.) What do you look like? Not that it matters much, but I like to know whom I am speaking to.

Rasheed Zakari (May 31 - 7:04:22 PM):   Oh ok. Well, I will show you my picture and fix my webcam in 2 minutes. (*Rasheed invited Dave to view her on the web cam.*)

Rasheed Zakari (May 31 - 7:06:52 PM):   Can you see me?

Friends4Dave (May 31 - 7:06:54 PM):   (*Dave saw a very beautiful young lady on his computer screen, approximately 23-28 years old, with long dark hair. She appeared to be of Middle Eastern lineage, or perhaps an Australian.*) You are beautiful.

Rasheed Zakari (May 31 - 7:07:00 PM):   Thank you so much. (*But the video image soon began to wobble badly and then turned off. Rasheed invited Dave again to view the web cam. Dave accepted again.*)

Rasheed Zakari (May 31 - 7:07:46 PM):   Can you see me now?

Friends4Dave (May 31 - 7:08:42 PM):   I see you. Like I said, you are very beautiful. (*But the video image soon began to wobble badly and then turned off again.*)

Rasheed Zakari (May 31 - 7:08:49 PM):   Thank you so much.

Rasheed Zakari (May 31 - 7:08:55 PM):   I think my cam went off...

Rasheed Zakari (May 31 - 7:08:57 PM):   Accept.

Friends4Dave (May 31 - 7:09:43 PM):   (*Dave's level of trust for*

Rasheed was elevated.) Now that I know whom I am speaking to, I can give you a tour of my apartment, if you like.

Rasheed Zakari (May 31 - 7:09:53 PM):   Ok.

Rasheed Zakari (May 31 - 7:09:58 PM):   Thanks. Let me see it then.

Friends4Dave (May 31 - 7:11:08 PM):   Wait a minute please. First, I have to disconnect the power and put it on battery. Then, I will switch from IEEE to wireless connection. Please bear with me. (*Dave did exactly what he said he would do.*)

Rasheed Zakari (May 31 - 7:11:26 PM):   Oh ok. I am here with you. Don't worry at all.

Friends4Dave (May 31 - 7:13:11 PM):   (*Done. Dave reconnected.*) Are you still there?

Rasheed Zakari (May 31 - 7:13:31 PM):   Yes, I am here with ya.

Rasheed Zakari (May 31 - 7:14:21 PM):   (*Dave began to pan around with the web cam and show Rasheed some of his surroundings.*) Wow you have a great House and very good building. I can see outside USA.

Rasheed Zakari (May 31 - 7:15:25 PM):   Great living Room.

Rasheed Zakari (May 31 - 7:16:40 PM):   Wow! Do you live in this Big house ?????????????

Rasheed Zakari (May 31 - 7:16:45 PM):   Wow! Wonderful.

Friends4Dave (May 31 - 7:21:49 PM):   (*The webcam he was using got *disconnected at some point, but Dave did not know it until a few minutes later.*) Sorry, we got disconnected.

Rasheed Zakari (May 31 - 7:22:14 PM): Oh yes, I guess so.

Friends4Dave (May 31 - 7:22:17 PM): The apartment is big for one person.

Rasheed Zakari (May 31 - 7:22:22 PM): You went off and I don't know what happened.

Rasheed Zakari (May 31 - 7:22:34 PM): Yes. Can I come join you? ... lol.

Friends4Dave (May 31 - 7:22:45 PM): Where did it get disconnected... in the living room?

Rasheed Zakari (May 31 - 7:22:57 PM): No, in the kitchen I guess.

Friends4Dave (May 31 - 7:23:42 PM): That's great. I'll love to have you. This is not really big for my standard. The house I am going to buy will be big.

Friends4Dave (May 31 - 7:24:05 PM): I will show you again. You really didn't see it all.

Rasheed Zakari (May 31 - 7:24:32 PM): Ok thanks.

Friends4Dave (May 31 - 7:24:34 PM): Please wait a minute. (*Dave began again to give Rasheed a tour of some parts of his apartment. He rushed through the remainder of the apartment that Rasheed had not previously seen. But he did not show Rasheed his daughter's room. He did not want to show that to anyone because he wanted to maintain his daughter's privacy.*)

Rasheed Zakari (May 31 - 7:26:53 PM):   Wow.

Rasheed Zakari (May 31 - 7:28:54 PM):   Are you in conference room or what?

Rasheed Zakari (May 31 - 7:36:59 PM):   (*Dave completed the virtual tour of his apartment and returned to his study.*) I guess you are very tired.

Friends4Dave (May 31 - 7:37:26 PM):   LOL. Not really. Did you see everything?

Rasheed Zakari (May 31 - 7:37:54 PM):   Yes I saw everything. Is this the President's house or what?

Rasheed Zakari (May 31 - 7:37:55 PM):   Lol.

Friends4Dave (May 31 - 7:38:18 PM):   (*Even though Dave knew that his apartment was really nice and looked expensive, he didn't want to fall for nor accept Rasheed's obvious flattery saying that Dave's apartment looked like the President's house.*) Nope. Just a poor man's apartment.

Friends4Dave (May 31 - 7:38:44 PM):   Do you still see me on the cam?

Rasheed Zakari (May 31 - 7:38:51 PM):   Hey, I know you are not poor. Don't pretend.

Rasheed Zakari (May 31 - 7:39:00 PM):   Yes I can still see ya on webcam.

Friends4Dave (May 31 - 7:40:26 PM):   (*Dave honestly reiterated his true current financial status.*) Really. I am poor now. However, I used to be a millionaire. And I believe that I will become a become millionaire again within the next few years, I hope, by the grace of God.

Rasheed Zakari (May 31 - 7:40:45 PM):   Wow that is very great.

Rasheed Zakari (May 31 - 7:40:55 PM):   (*This was the opportunity that Rasheed had been steering Dave towards, so that she could extort some money out of him without him realizing it. How unusually stupid he was!*) Well can you get me the calling card so I can call you??

Friends4Dave (May 31 - 7:41:24 PM):   (*Since Dave really did not see Rasheed clearly before her web cam kept turning off, he now wanted to see her again on the web cam.*) Would you please let me see you again on the webcam?

Rasheed Zakari (May 31 - 7:41:35 PM):   Oh ok let me turn it on. Ok? (*She turned the web cam on again.*)

Rasheed Zakari (May 31 - 7:43:32 PM):   Can you see me now?

Friends4Dave (May 31 - 7:43:49 PM):   Are you at home?

Rasheed Zakari (May 31 - 7:43:56 PM):   Yes, in my bedroom.

Friends4Dave (May 31 - 7:44:02 PM):   Yes, I can see you. Thanks.

Rasheed Zakari (May 31 - 7:44:10 PM):   You are welcome. (*Rasheed's webcam flickered and went off again; and Dave began to suspect that maybe Rasheed was manipulating the webcam and turning it off on purpose.*)

Friends4Dave (May 31 - 7:44:28 PM):   Do you see me, though?

Friends4Dave (May 31 - 7:45:29 PM):   Are you still there?

Friends4Dave (May 31 - 7:49:14 PM):   Did we get disconnected?

Rasheed Zakari (May 31 - 7:52:02 PM):   Hello. Sorry I got disconnected for some minutes.

Rasheed Zakari (May 31 - 7:52:03 PM):   Sorry.

Friends4Dave (May 31 - 7:52:20 PM):   I thought so. You have beautiful lambent eyes, and your effervescent smile is captivating. (*Dave was not trying to flatter her. The young lady Dave saw on the web cam was really very beautiful and had a captivating smile.*)

Rasheed Zakari (May 31 - 7:53:02 PM):   Really??

Friends4Dave (May 31 - 7:53:33 PM):   Yes... really. You are beautiful and do not let anyone tell you differently.

Rasheed Zakari (May 31 - 7:54:05 PM):   Oh ok. Thank you so much and you are handsome as well.

Friends4Dave (May 31 - 7:54:20 PM):   Thanks.

Friends4Dave (May 31 - 7:54:33 PM):   Have you ever been to the United States?

Rasheed Zakari (May 31 - 7:54:51 PM):   No, I have never been to the United States.

Rasheed Zakari (May 31 - 7:55:08 PM):   But one day, I love to travel all over the country.

Friends4Dave (May 31 - 7:55:33 PM):   So do I. Do you want to live
in the United States?

Rasheed Zakari (May 31 - 7:55:51 PM):   Yes, sometimes… when I
meet my man.

Friends4Dave (May 31 - 7:56:26 PM):   Great then. That can be
arranged when the time comes.

Rasheed Zakari (May 31 - 7:56:45 PM):   (*Rasheed tried to redirect
Dave to her main objective, which was to
extort money from him.*) Yes… so can you get
me the calling card?

Friends4Dave (May 31 - 7:57:04 PM):   (*Dave fell for her scam.*) What
type of calling card?

Rasheed Zakari (May 31 - 7:57:20 PM):   Well… Akasanoma calling
card.

Rasheed Zakari (May 31 - 7:57:41 PM):   I wanna call you.

Friends4Dave (May 31 - 7:57:48 PM):   Can I get it on the Internet?

Rasheed Zakari (May 31 - 7:58:14 PM):   (*Rasheed was ready for Dave,
and she provided him the information almost
immediately.*) Well yes, but my network is
MTN ... www.ghanaairtime.com.

Rasheed Zakari (May 31 - 7:58:28 PM):   **WWW.GHANAAIRTIME.COM**

Friends4Dave (May 31 - 7:59:09 PM):   Ok. I will check into it. How
do I reach you once I get it?

Rasheed Zakari (May 31 - 7:59:29 PM):   Oh well, I am here. If you have any problem, let me know.

Friends4Dave (May 31 - 8:00:17 PM):   Ok. Wait a minute. Let me go to the website and check it out.

Rasheed Zakari (May 31 - 8:00:52 PM):   Ok. I am here.

Rasheed Zakari (May 31 - 8:13:01 PM):   *(Dave was having a lot of problems trying to pay for the calling card through his PayPal account. The website would not accept it. Rasheed was also obviously concerned because it was taking Dave too long to buy her the calling card.)* Am here…. Are you there with me?

Friends4Dave (May 31 - 8:13:50 PM):   Yes, Sorry. PayPal was giving me a hard time. I will be back when I am done buying the card.

Rasheed Zakari (May 31 - 8:14:18 PM):   Oh ok. Do you need my number then?

Rasheed Zakari (May 31 - 8:14:22 PM):   Ok cool.

Friends4Dave (May 31 - 8:14:43 PM):   Yes. Please give me your number.

Rasheed Zakari (May 31 - 8:14:55 PM):   Okay I will do that. Ok.

Rasheed Zakari (May 31 - 8:15:28 PM):   +233 541533719.

Friends4Dave (May 31 - 8:16:00 PM):   *(Dave noticed that this number is different from the phone numbers she had previously given to Dave and which Dave was not able to call many times for the past couple of weeks.)* Great. I will be back.

Rasheed Zakari (May 31 - 8:16:08 PM):   Ok.

Rasheed Zakari (May 31 - 8:16:09 PM):   Am here.

Friends4Dave (May 31 - 8:24:57 PM):   *(Dave was still having a problem with the website because it would not accept payment through his PayPal account even though there is a PayPal payment option.)* There is a problem. PayPal is not accepting the phone number. It says that it is not a valid phone number. I think it is because I am in the USA. Let me keep on trying to see if there is another way. I typed in +233-54153-3719. Is that correct?

Rasheed Zakari (May 31 - 8:25:31 PM):   Yes.

Rasheed Zakari (May 31 - 8:27:36 PM):   That is my correct number.

Rasheed Zakari (May 31 - 8:28:29 PM):   If you try and not accepting, well I would like you to send me some funds so I can get it here.

Friends4Dave (May 31 - 8:28:52 PM):   *(Dave thought to himself, "Men, this girl is really bold and pushy. This is the first time she is really chatting with him and she is already demanding that I send her some funds." But, at the same time, Dave liked the fact that she knew exactly what she wanted and how to get it when she wanted.)* OK. I am trying to figure out if I can pay with a credit card directly without going through PayPal.

Rasheed Zakari (May 31 - 8:29:03 PM):   Oh ok.

Friends4Dave (May 31 - 8:32:47 PM):   *(Dave finally got the calling*

*card and then returns to the chatting room.
Because he was having so much problem with
trying to pay with PayPal, Dave decided to try
a smaller amount of just $25 first ... an amount
much smaller than he initially wanted to send
to her. That way, it would not be a big deal if
he lost the money.)* Done. It says that someone
will call me to verify the order.

Friends4Dave (May 31 - 8:32:55 PM):   I bought $25.00 worth of
calling card for you.

Rasheed Zakari (May 31 - 8:33:03 PM):   Ok.

Rasheed Zakari (May 31 - 8:33:06 PM):   Thanks.

Friends4Dave (May 31 - 8:33:37 PM):   No problem. Sorry for the
delay. Now I know how...

Rasheed Zakari (May 31 - 8:33:54 PM):   Oh ok. That is alright. Thanks.

Rasheed Zakari (May 31 - 8:34:10 PM):   Well if it is done I will get a
text message from them.

Friends4Dave (May 31 - 8:34:36 PM):   How long does it usually take
for them to call to confirm?

Rasheed Zakari (May 31 - 8:34:50 PM):   Oh well don't think so.

Rasheed Zakari (May 31 - 8:35:25 PM):   Well, you have to wait till they
call to confirm. Ok?

Friends4Dave (May 31 - 8:36:10 PM):   No problem.

Rasheed Zakari (May 31 - 8:36:33 PM):   So what are you doing now?

Friends4Dave (May 31 - 8:39:00 PM): *(Dave's phone rang. It was the calling card company calling Dave to confirm the $25.00 purchase he just did online.)* He just called me. I was speaking with him. He said he would send the airtime to your phone number.

Rasheed Zakari (May 31 - 8:39:19 PM): Oh ok, thanks.

Rasheed Zakari (May 31 - 8:39:30 PM): Thank you so much for the air time then.

Friends4Dave (May 31 - 8:39:46 PM): And he also said he would send a copy of the airtime receipt to my email.

Rasheed Zakari (May 31 - 8:40:05 PM): Oh ok, that is alright and good as well. Thanks.

Friends4Dave (May 31 - 8:40:14 PM): That is not a problem. I like you; so I don't mind doing it.

Rasheed Zakari (May 31 - 8:40:42 PM): Oh ok ...

Rasheed Zakari (May 31 - 8:40:45 PM): Alright.

Friends4Dave (May 31 - 8:40:46 PM): Please let me know when you get it.

Rasheed Zakari (May 31 - 8:41:04 PM): Oh ok. I will be waiting for it as we chat. Ok?

Friends4Dave (May 31 - 8:41:16 PM): Ok.

Friends4Dave (May 31 - 8:41:44 PM): When did you graduate from the University?

Rasheed Zakari (May 31 - 8:41:55 PM): Ok I just received the airtime.

Rasheed Zakari (May 31 - 8:42:05 PM): Last year. And you?

Friends4Dave (May 31 - 8:42:22 PM): Great!

Rasheed Zakari (May 31 - 8:42:49 PM): Thank you so much. Which school did you attend?

Friends4Dave (May 31 - 8:45:10 PM): I attended John Jay College of Criminal Justice, City University of New York, for my Bachelors and first Master's degrees in Criminal Justice and Law. Then I attended Walden University for my Ph.D. program in Human Services. Thereafter, I attended Strayer University for my second Masters degree program in Information Systems. I also have some diplomas from other schools of higher learning.

Friends4Dave (May 31 - 8:45:47 PM): You are welcome. Please don't mention it again. That's a small change.

Rasheed Zakari (May 31 - 8:46:39 PM): Oh okay.

Rasheed Zakari (May 31 - 8:47:07 PM): Well that is ok…. Well, but I was not able to continue my education after all this…

Rasheed Zakari (May 31 - 8:48:09 PM): And I still wanna continue my education.

Friends4Dave (May 31 - 8:49:11 PM): It is never too late to go school, if you really want to. If you like me and our relationship progresses beyond just chatting online, as I would hope it will be, then you can go to school as high a degree as you want, if that is what you want to do. (*At the same time, Dave noticed some inconsistencies in her statements about graduating from college with a degree in journalism; and, now, that she was not able to continue her education. However, he was not sure whether she meant she was not able to continue to graduate school or whether she could not finish college. He decided to leave the matter alone.*)

Rasheed Zakari (May 31 - 8:50:16 PM):   Yes and I want to be a journalist in the future. Because I was not able to continue,[23] I did not get that job doing what I want ... and now, I am helping my Mom in the super market... and soon I wanna get my own super market to start working.

Friends4Dave (May 31 - 8:51:17 PM):   (*Dave thought to himself, "Why does she keep using American slangs? Is she perhaps an American or Canadian?" Nevertheless, he continued to chat with her.*) I will support you in whatever wholesome endeavors you want to embark on in life.

Rasheed Zakari (May 31 - 8:51:34 PM):   Thank you so much ...

Rasheed Zakari (May 31 - 8:51:44 PM):   (*Now that she was ahead of the game, she decided to go further in her fraudulent scheme, but she would not be that fortunate this time because Dave was now catching on to her schemes.*) Well when is your birthday?

---

[23] Dave noticed an inconsistency and wondered (as he read her statements that she was not able to continue): Did she not say earlier that she graduated from the "University of Ghana Legon" with a "Journalism" degree? Did she not also just say that she graduated "last year"?

Rasheed Zakari (May 31 - 8:52:48 PM):   Mine is on the 6th of this month and I just finished sending my friends email telling them about my b-day.

Friends4Dave (May 31 - 8:52:54 PM):   (*Responding now to her expression of gratitude.*) You are welcome. I am glad we finally chatted. I apologize I was hesitant at first. That's because I did not know whom I was talking with.

Friends4Dave (May 31 - 8:53:11 PM):   My birthday is in February. (*Dave gave a fake birth date.*)[24]

Friends4Dave (May 31 - 8:53:22 PM):   February 1st.

Rasheed Zakari (May 31 - 8:53:22 PM):   Me too. I was very happy to correspond with you, and so excited now.

Rasheed Zakari (May 31 - 8:53:48 PM):   Oh ok, February. Just soon and mine is in a few days …

Rasheed Zakari (May 31 - 8:53:59 PM):   Well what will you like for your birthday?

Friends4Dave (May 31 - 8:54:21 PM):   Nothing, but just your friendship. I don't celebrate birthdays.

Rasheed Zakari (May 31 - 8:54:52 PM):   Wow, thank you so much and I promise to be a good friend to you, and I will never do something to hurt your feelings or to make you upset with me.

Friends4Dave (May 31 - 8:56:27 PM):   (*Dave was thinking to himself, "Why is she saying that she would not hurt my*

---

[24] He did not want to reveal his real birthday for several reasons, including security reasons and the fact that he does not celebrate birthdays.

feelings? Is she planning to something to hurt me?" Dave was glad that he did not give Rasheed his real birth date. Anyway, Dave continued to be polite.) I appreciate that.... And I promise you the same. What I promise and what people promise me are very important to me. My yes means yes, and my no means no.

Rasheed Zakari (May 31 - 8:56:56 PM):   That is very good. I understand your feelings.... (*Then she redirected Dave to her main objective: to defraud him.*) So what do you have for my birthday then?

Rasheed Zakari (May 31 - 8:56:57 PM):   ??   (*She queried again.*)

Friends4Dave (May 31 - 8:57:12 PM):   (*For religious* [25] *and other reasons, Dave does not believe in any birthday celebrations or in birthday gifts. But out of curiosity, since he was beginning to have some suspicions about her motives, he decided to play along for the moment in order to see where this was leading.*) What do you want?

Rasheed Zakari (May 31 - 8:57:25 PM):   Something from your heart.

Friends4Dave (May 31 - 8:57:40 PM):   Ok.

Friends4Dave (May 31 - 8:57:59 PM):   What do you like, though?

Rasheed Zakari (May 31 - 8:58:22 PM):   Oh ok. Well I would like you to get me some Cake, pastries, and dress as well.

---

[25] Dave was raised as a Jehovah's Witness; but at the time of the events described in this book, he was no longer a Jehovah's Witness because he had been disfellowshipped. Yet, he still adhered to many of the Bible's principles.

Friends4Dave (May 31 - 8:58:59 PM):   What would that cost?

Rasheed Zakari (May 31 - 8:59:06 PM): $400.00. *(This was in US Dollars.)*[26]

Rasheed Zakari (May 31 - 8:59:14 PM):   I think.

Friends4Dave (May 31 - 9:00:05 PM):   *(Dave was stunned that Rasheed asked him for $400.00 on their first chat, and he then became suspicious. He thought to himself, "So, I see… that's what all this is about." He then decided to play along further in her game.)* I will not have $400.00 dollars to give to you by your birthday. Remember I said I am a poor man now. I meant that. I do not lie. Besides, like I said before, I do not celebrate birthdays. So, if I send you money, it would not be for your birthday.

Rasheed Zakari (May 31 - 9:00:29 PM):   Oh ok. How much can you get then my dear?

Rasheed Zakari (May 31 - 9:01:00 PM):   Even if you get $150 for me, it is alright with me. *(Dave was silent for a few seconds.)*

Rasheed Zakari (May 31 - 9:01:15 PM):   Anything you can afford to give me.

Friends4Dave (May 31 - 9:01:27 PM):   *(Still trying to figure her*

---

[26] What! Four hundred US Dollars? Dave began to realize that this lady may be a scammer, or she was just being foolhardily greedy. Why in the world would he give a $400 birthday gift to someone he had never met – assuming he was the type that celebrated birthdays? Still, Dave decided to play along for now, in order to determine if she was a scammer or just an extremely greedy person.)

out...) I will try to send you about $100.00.

Rasheed Zakari (May 31 - 9:01:58 PM):   Ok, thank you so much. Why can't you do it like you did for the airtime?

Friends4Dave (May 31 - 9:03:35 PM):   (*Dave was thinking, and he wanted her to notice his hesitation. Besides, he was not comfortable with sending money online to someone he really did not know; and he definitely would not send any birthday gifts to anyone. Period. So, he decided to stall for a while until he had time to dig into Rasheed's background.*) No. I do not have the ability to send money like that. I will have to go into a place where they send money, like MoneyGram, and send it in person.

Rasheed Zakari (May 31 - 9:04:16 PM):   Oh ok. But we don't have MoneyGram near. But Westernunion.com is the nearest.

Friends4Dave (May 31 - 9:05:01 PM):   (*Dave did not want to go to Western Union's website to send her money, so he pretended that he did not know anything about Western Union.*) I will check to see if they have Western Union around here.

Rasheed Zakari (May 31 - 9:05:19 PM):   Oh ok. Right now?

Friends4Dave (May 31 - 9:05:47 PM):   What time is it now where you are? (*Trying to figure out her real location from her time zone.*)

Rasheed Zakari (May 31 - 9:06:00 PM):   It is 12 a.m. now here. (*That ruled out the possibility that she was physically in the United States. Nevertheless, there was a possibility that she was somewhere in eastern*

Canada – Nova Scotia perhaps, or somewhere in Europe, or in Ghana as she claims, etc. But Dave could not really tell at that moment.)

Rasheed Zakari (May 31 - 9:06:04 PM): What is the time there now?

Friends4Dave (May 31 - 9:06:31 PM): It's 21:06 hrs.

Rasheed Zakari (May 31 - 9:06:59 PM): Oh ok. Well, it means I'm 4 hours ahead…

Rasheed Zakari (May 31 - 9:07:27 PM): It's 1st June.

Friends4Dave (May 31 - 9:07:43 PM): So, yours is 01:00 hrs. then?

Rasheed Zakari (May 31 - 9:07:53 PM): Yes.

Friends4Dave (May 31 - 9:08:03 PM): I see. *(Dave thought: "Then she must be somewhere in Europe or West Africa ... perhaps even from Ghana as she claims.")*

Rasheed Zakari (May 31 - 9:08:11 PM): Oh ok cool.

Rasheed Zakari (May 31 - 9:08:31 PM): What did you have for dinner?

Friends4Dave (May 31 - 9:08:55 PM): Jolloff rice.

Rasheed Zakari (May 31 - 9:09:02 PM): Wowwwwwwwwwwwww.

Friends4Dave (May 31 - 9:09:02 PM): And you?

Rasheed Zakari (May 31 - 9:09:23 PM): I took potatoes and stew. *(Again, that did not sound like a typical West African dish for dinner. Besides, most West Africans do not call evening meal "dinner", they call it "supper".)*

Friends4Dave (May 31 - 9:09:37 PM):   Humnn…. That's good.

Friends4Dave (May 31 - 9:10:10 PM):   *(Dave's suspicion of Rasheed was growing.)* Are you on a computer or are you using a mobile device to chat with me?

Rasheed Zakari (May 31 - 9:10:28 PM):   I am using a computer.

Rasheed Zakari (May 31 - 9:10:34 PM):   What's wrong ?

Friends4Dave (May 31 - 9:11:29 PM):   Ok. You know you can also call me on the computer right now for free? You don't have to use your credits to call me.

Rasheed Zakari (May 31 - 9:11:58 PM):   Oh well I can, but I don't have speakers… I have given it to my younger sister to use.

Rasheed Zakari (May 31 - 9:12:31 PM):   I don't have a microphone either. So, I have to call you with the credit. Ok?

Friends4Dave (May 31 - 9:12:32 PM):   Ok.

Friends4Dave (May 31 - 9:12:59 PM):   Hmnnn … *(Dave started to think more like Dave now, as an analytical person and investigator, and no longer blinded by the emotions of someone who was love-struck. He thought to himself, "This girl is good. She claims to be a Ghanaian, but he is completely White." He knew that even though there are White Ghanaians and White Nigerians, such occurrences are very rare. "Besides, why is she in such a hurry to get the money now? What else is she planning to do?*

Is it possible that she lives here in the United States or somewhere in Europe or Canada, but has an accomplice in Ghana. Could the person Dave is chatting with now actually be a male posing as a female? How long has she been soliciting money from people? And how many people has she gotten money from this way?" So, he decided to query Rasheed further about her heritage.) I know you told me that you live in Ghana now. But where are you originally from?

Rasheed Zakari (May 31 - 9:13:25 PM):   I was Born and raised in Ghana. What is wrong with that?

Rasheed Zakari (May 31 - 9:13:36 PM):   But my Mom is from Australia.

Friends4Dave (May 31 - 9:14:00 PM):   There is absolutely nothing wrong with that.

Rasheed Zakari (May 31 - 9:14:09 PM):   Good.

Rasheed Zakari (May 31 - 9:14:18 PM):   I really wanna chat with you all the time. (*Trying to change the subject.*)

Rasheed Zakari (May 31 - 9:14:39 PM):   Can I have your Number again? ... I will text you a message.

Friends4Dave (May 31 - 9:14:40 PM):   There is nothing wrong with you being from Ghana. For example, I was born in Nigeria, as I told you before, but I now live in the United States.

Rasheed Zakari (May 31 - 9:14:53 PM):   Yes, you told me before.

Rasheed Zakari (May 31 - 9:15:05 PM):   But I was born and raised in

Ghana.

Rasheed Zakari (May 31 - 9:15:12 PM):   Never travelled outside my country.

Friends4Dave (May 31 - 9:15:48 PM):   (*Dave was now really suspicious that Rasheed may be lying to him, but he continued to play along.*) Ok. My number (cell) is 757-358-4757.[27]

Rasheed Zakari (May 31 - 9:15:54 PM):   Ok.

Friends4Dave (May 31 - 9:16:42 PM):   I may not get the text message, unless I am about a mile or more away from home. I no longer get signals here.

Rasheed Zakari (May 31 - 9:17:26 PM):   Oh ok. I understand. That is cool. Well I will try and call you then.

Friends4Dave (May 31 - 9:18:07 PM):   That's fine. You may call me at home. Do you still see me on the webcam?

Rasheed Zakari (May 31 - 9:18:19 PM):   Oh no, I can't see you on webcam dear.

Rasheed Zakari (May 31 - 9:18:23 PM):   It is gone.

Friends4Dave (May 31 - 9:18:38 PM):   I lost you a long time ago, too.

Rasheed Zakari (May 31 - 9:18:53 PM):   Oh really? Ok, I will turn it on. Ok? (*Dave and Rasheed turned on their webcams.*)

Rasheed Zakari (May 31 - 9:19:40 PM):   Wow, you are looking good. (*Dave saw this comment as pure flattery.*)

---

[27] Dave's mobile number has changed and this is no longer valid.

Rasheed Zakari (May 31 - 9:20:01 PM):   It's getting late there.

Friends4Dave (May 31 - 9:20:44 PM):   Thank you very much. And you look spectacular. (*Dave lost Rasheed's web cam image again.*) But I lost you again.

Rasheed Zakari (May 31 - 9:20:52 PM):   Oh, okay accept.

Rasheed Zakari (May 31 - 9:21:09 PM):   Yes, I have a problem on my webcam. Don't know what is wrong with it. (*Dave tried hard to believe her, but he suspected that she might be the one manipulating the images. He continued to think critically.*)

Rasheed Zakari (May 31 - 9:22:44 PM):   My puppy is here.

Rasheed Zakari (May 31 - 9:24:17 PM):   Why are you so quiet?

Friends4Dave (May 31 - 9:25:00 PM):   I was thinking and trying to see if I could see you on the webcam.

Rasheed Zakari (May 31 - 9:25:06 PM):   My puppy is here now... he is disturbing me.

Friends4Dave (May 31 - 9:25:29 PM):   I would like to see him!

Rasheed Zakari (May 31 - 9:25:39 PM):   Oh ok. You will see him now… (*Rasheed turned on her webcam again and, for the first time, the image was clearly focused on a small dog. Cute dog. Pretty thing. Dave does not like tiny little dogs, and he especially dislikes Chihuahuas, but this particular one was cute. Nevertheless, even the webcam image of the dog did not stay on long either, even though it was clearer and more focused than Rasheed's rather blurry and unsteady webcam images. Dave was now positive that Rasheed had been manipulating the images. Nonetheless, he continued to play along.)*

Rasheed Zakari (May 31 - 9:26:04 PM):   Did you see him?

Friends4Dave (May 31 - 9:26:14 PM):   He is cute.

Rasheed Zakari (May 31 - 9:26:18 PM):   Thank you.

Friends4Dave (May 31 - 9:26:32 PM):   Is he a Chihuahua?

Rasheed Zakari (May 31 - 9:26:42 PM):   Yes, Chihuahua.

Rasheed Zakari (May 31 - 9:26:49 PM):   You are right... he is called Leo.

Friends4Dave (May 31 - 9:27:14 PM):   Hi Leo!

Rasheed Zakari (May 31 - 9:27:25 PM):   Haha... lol.

Rasheed Zakari (May 31 - 9:27:28 PM):   You make me smile.

Friends4Dave (May 31 - 9:27:46 PM):   That is a good thing... right?

Rasheed Zakari (May 31 - 9:28:07 PM):   Yes, very good. You make me happy and excited.

Rasheed Zakari (May 31 - 9:28:40 PM):   *(Rasheed was sidetracked for a little while, but she was really good at her scams. She soon redirected Dave to her main objective again – to swindle money from him before he even knew what was happening.)*
So, why don't you try and send me the money

online?... My uncle used to do it for me before he died.

Friends4Dave (May 31 - 9:28:49 PM):   (*Dave ignored that her latest attempt and instead responded to her saying that he made her "happy and excited.*) That's wonderful, then. That's what I intend to make the right woman for me be ... happy and excited.

Rasheed Zakari (May 31 - 9:29:06 PM):   Yes .... And I will also keep you as happy as I am.

Rasheed Zakari (May 31 - 9:29:15 PM):   (*Perhaps realizing that Dave suspected she had been manipulating the webcam images, she tried to deflect his suspicions.*) My cam keep giving me problems on my PC.

Rasheed Zakari (May 31 - 9:29:20 PM):   It freezes.

Friends4Dave (May 31 - 9:30:27 PM):   I noticed. Sorry about that. When did your uncle die?

Rasheed Zakari (May 31 - 9:30:42 PM):   About 3 years now.[28]

Rasheed Zakari (May 31 - 9:31:02 PM):   (*Rasheed was pretty good at her schemes. She appealed to Dave's sensibility and emotions.*) I loved him very much.... He used to take good care of me when he was in the U.K.[29]

Friends4Dave (May 31 - 9:31:11 PM):   Accept my condolences. (*Still*

---

[28] Later, however, Rasheed also claimed that she was living with her mother, cousin, and the same uncle she now claimed died three years ago.
[29] Dave thought to himself, "Aha! You have ties to the United Kingdom after all!"

playing along in her game.)

Rasheed Zakari (May 31 - 9:31:19 PM):   Oh ok, I do.

Friends4Dave (May 31 - 9:31:35 PM):   How did he send you the money?

Rasheed Zakari (May 31 - 9:31:57 PM):   (*Jackpot! This was what she had been waiting for… a narrative that will lead her back to her main objective – which was to swindle more some money out of Dave! She responded within seconds.*) Well, open this website here: **WWW.WESTERNUNION.COM.**

Rasheed Zakari (May 31 - 9:33:06 PM):   NAME: HANSON OPARE [30]
COUNTRY: GHANA
CITY: ACCRA NEW TOWN
ZIP CODE: 00233

Rasheed Zakari (May 31 - 9:33:12 PM):   That is my address.

Friends4Dave (May 31 - 9:37:12 PM):   (*Dave now realized, without a doubt, that this was a scam. He hesitated and thought for a while before responding.*) Why did you give me someone else's name, other than yours?

Rasheed Zakari (May 31 - 9:37:28 PM):   This is My Mom's Name …

Rasheed Zakari (May 31 - 9:37:47 PM):   I lost my ID card. So, I now use my Mom's ID card.

Friends4Dave (May 31 - 9:38:06 PM):   (*Dave knew that she was*

---

[30] Now she was exposed for what she really was. Hanson Opare was her accomplice – and he was perhaps her boyfriend. Or, it may be Hanson Opare himself posing as a girl named Rasheed Zakari.

---

lying. Besides, Hanson may be a name for a male, and not her mother's name.) Do you realize that it is a crime to use someone else's ID for any purpose? That is fraud. I will not send you any money in Hanson Opare's name. I will wait. I will send you the money once you get your own ID.

Rasheed Zakari (May 31 - 9:38:25 PM):   I won't get it till next 4 years dear.

Rasheed Zakari (May 31 - 9:38:37 PM):   What's wrong with that?

Friends4Dave (May 31 - 9:38:50 PM):   Everything. I will wait. Goodbye. *(Dave felt insulted that Rasheed would try to scam him like this. He felt stupid and humiliated.)*

Rasheed Zakari (May 31 - 9:39:00 PM):   Why are you quiet? ... Are you wondering?

Rasheed Zakari (May 31 - 9:39:07 PM):   *(She panicked.)* What do you mean Good bye?

Rasheed Zakari (May 31 - 9:39:23 PM):   Why are you leaving me?

Rasheed Zakari (May 31 - 9:39:24 PM):   ??

Friends4Dave (May 31 - 9:39:47 PM):   I do not think you are who you told me you are. Like I said before, I don't like being lied to.

Rasheed Zakari (May 31 - 9:40:22 PM):   Well, how do you mean??? Why do you say I am not who I say I am. Please explain.

Friends4Dave (May 31 - 9:40:32 PM):   I don't lie to people. And I do not want to be lied to.

Rasheed Zakari (May 31 - 9:40:35 PM):   I don't really understand. What you are saying?

Friends4Dave (May 31 - 9:40:42 PM):   (*Dave switched to his investigative mode.*) You know exactly what I mean. What is your real name?

Rasheed Zakari (May 31 - 9:40:52 PM):   My real name is Rasheed.

Rasheed Zakari (May 31 - 9:41:07 PM):   Dear, I never lied to you. (*Rasheed sent Dave romantic "Fallen Hearts" IMVironments to try to mollify him, but Dave knew that it was a ploy and ignored the temptation to be pacified by her. The "Fallen Hearts" romantic IMVironments continued to descend on Dave's computer screen until the very end of their chat.*)

Friends4Dave (May 31 - 9:41:12 PM):   What is your real last name?

Rasheed Zakari (May 31 - 9:41:28 PM):   Oh well, Rasheed Zakari.

Rasheed Zakari (May 31 - 9:41:36 PM):   (*Apparently realizing that Dave knew that Hanson was a male's name, she fished for confirmation.*) Do you think Hanson is a male's name?

Rasheed Zakari (May 31 - 9:41:50 PM):   I lost my ID. That is why I use my Mom's ID.

Friends4Dave (May 31 - 9:42:39 PM):   I know it is a male's name. But it really does not matter whether it is male or female. The point is, you have given me a different name than you told me you are.

Rasheed Zakari (May 31 - 9:42:47 PM):   I told you that I don't want to do something to hurt you. (*This sounded more like a confession – that she was attempting to hurt Dave by defrauding him.*)

Rasheed Zakari (May 31 - 9:43:11 PM):   That does not mean I am not who I said I am. Ok?

Friends4Dave (May 31 - 9:43:43 PM):   As an ex-investigator, I know there are many imposters out there. And you sound fishy.

Rasheed Zakari (May 31 - 9:43:58 PM):   What do you mean??

Friends4Dave (May 31 - 9:44:31 PM):   (*Dave was truly hurt and he felt stupid to have fallen for her scam.*) I don't know if you are real right now. I will have to check you out first before I decide whether to continue with you or not.

Friends4Dave (May 31 - 9:45:05 PM):   And I feel stupid right now. (*Dave became silent, thinking ....*)

Rasheed Zakari (May 31 - 9:45:09 PM):   Oh ok. What shows that am not real? ... Is it my picture or my webcam? (*More confessions.*)

Rasheed Zakari (May 31 - 9:45:15 PM):   Don't feel stupid. Ok?

Rasheed Zakari (May 31 - 9:45:34 PM):   And never feel that.... I am happy, as I talk now, to have a good friend like you. (*Silence still ....*)

Rasheed Zakari (May 31 - 9:46:33 PM):   Talk to me! (*She was now desperate.*)

Friends4Dave (May 31 - 9:47:17 PM):   (*After almost a minute of additional silence, Dave continued.*) I will have to check you out first. Please understand.

Rasheed Zakari (May 31 - 9:48:30 PM):   Oh ok… that is alright.

Rasheed Zakari (May 31 - 9:48:36 PM):   I understand. (*She tried to play it cool in order to change Dave's mind.*)

Rasheed Zakari (May 31 - 9:48:41 PM):   No problem…. Ok?

Rasheed Zakari (May 31 - 9:48:46 PM):   Stop thinking please.

Friends4Dave (May 31 - 9:49:59 PM):   I am a thinker. But it appears I did not think this through this time, which is unusual for me.

Rasheed Zakari (May 31 - 9:50:18 PM):   What do ya mean? (*Dave did not respond.*)

Rasheed Zakari (May 31 - 9:51:03 PM):   Well stop thinking of something too much, it may cause you sickness.

Friends4Dave (May 31 - 9:51:09 PM):   (*Dave did not want to close the door completely shut right now, just in case he needed to communicate with her in order dig more into her background.*) I let my guards down after I saw you briefly on the webcam.

Rasheed Zakari (May 31 - 9:51:25 PM):   I see.

Rasheed Zakari (May 31 - 9:52:26 PM):   Are you there?

Friends4Dave (May 31 - 9:52:45 PM):   Yes.

Rasheed Zakari (May 31 - 9:52:51 PM):   Talk to me!!! (*Very *desperate.*)

Rasheed Zakari (May 31 - 9:52:58 PM):   What is happening?

Friends4Dave (May 31 - 9:53:45 PM):   Can I see your mother on the webcam? Now?

Rasheed Zakari (May 31 - 9:54:00 PM):   She is asleep.

Rasheed Zakari (May 31 - 9:54:29 PM):   You know it's 1 a.m. ... But if you will wait until later then…

Rasheed Zakari (May 31 - 9:54:36 PM):   You will see her on the webcam.

Friends4Dave (May 31 - 9:55:45 PM):   It is 13:00 hrs at night and you are still up? Well …. Fine. But I cannot send you anything or continue to regard you as my friend until I chat with your mother and investigate this through reliable sources. Are you okay with that? (*Dave was obviously upset.*)

Rasheed Zakari (May 31 - 9:56:19 PM):   Oh ok then. You have to chat with My Mom tomorrow then.

Friends4Dave (May 31 - 9:56:49 PM):   What do you think about me?

Rasheed Zakari (May 31 - 9:56:52 PM):   If that is ok…. Well don't let your mind control you…. Ok? I am for real, not just the naked girls' cam.

Rasheed Zakari (May 31 - 9:57:07 PM):   Well that is a good idea and you are an open person.

Friends4Dave (May 31 - 9:57:37 PM):   I don't deal with "naked girl's cam."

Rasheed Zakari (May 31 - 9:58:13 PM):   Well I am not one of them. So don't think I am one of them. Ok?

Friends4Dave (May 31 - 9:59:13 PM):   I can get any girl I want here in the United States. I meet them every day, but I don't want them right now. That's why I remained single since my wife and I divorced even though I am scripturally free to marry again.

Rasheed Zakari (May 31 - 9:59:48 PM):   Oh well that is very good ...

Rasheed Zakari (May 31 - 10:00:14 PM):   Hmmm well, you have to meet a woman get to know the person, trust and see what happens next.

Friends4Dave (May 31 - 10:00:53 PM):   What do you think about me? *(Dave wanted to know if Rasheed thought he was such a fool as to swindle money out of him like this. Even though he did not expect her to tell him that that she thought he was a fool, but he intended to read between the lines.)*

Rasheed Zakari (May 31 - 10:01:29 PM):   Well, I really appreciate you very much. You are a very good man, and you seem to be so quiet...

Rasheed Zakari (May 31 - 10:01:47 PM):   And you are very well-educated, more than I do.

Friends4Dave (May 31 - 10:04:02 PM):   *(Dave read something else ... another meaning to her statement above. Dave felt that Rasheed thought that he was a well-educated fool, who represented a special challenge to her. Therefore, if she was able to scam Dave, that would mean that she has a very special skill. After thinking for a little while, Dave then responded.*) The right woman for me does not have to be very educated. At the same time, she may even be more educated than I am. It does not matter to me. What matters is that we are deeply in love with each other and that she is as God-fearing as I am. Not a schemer.

Rasheed Zakari (May 31 - 10:05:12 PM):   Well I am very God fearing, and a very good Christian as well…

Friends4Dave (May 31 - 10:05:45 PM):   (*Now that Dave knew what Rasheed thought about him, he decided to find out how she felt about him, which was probably very different than what she thought about Dave.*) How do you feel about me?

Rasheed Zakari (May 31 - 10:07:16 PM):   I feel so much happy corresponding with you, ... and so much excited as well… and want to chat with you always, if you like.

Friends4Dave (May 31 - 10:08:07 PM):   Why are you so happy and excited?

Rasheed Zakari (May 31 - 10:09:05 PM):   I like the way you talk ...

Rasheed Zakari (May 31 - 10:09:17 PM):   And do everything. You are an open person.

Friends4Dave (May 31 - 10:10:36 PM):   Please let me see you again on the webcam ... and, please, try to make it stable this time. (*Signaling to her that he was aware that she had been manipulating the webcam images.*)

Rasheed Zakari (May 31 - 10:11:05 PM):   Stable??? what do ya mean?

Rasheed Zakari (May 31 - 10:11:19 PM):   *(She knew now that Dave had figured it out that she had been doctoring up her webcam images, and that she was intentionally shutting off the webcam so that Dave could not get a really good look at her. She decided to end the conversation.)* I need to go to sleep now. Can we make it tomorrow?

Friends4Dave (May 31 - 10:11:40 PM):   I mean try to make it so that it does not freeze or disconnect.

Rasheed Zakari (May 31 - 10:12:03 PM):   Oh ok ...but I need to go to sleep now. Now, what do we do?

Friends4Dave (May 31 - 10:12:06 PM):   Tomorrow will be fine... What time?

Rasheed Zakari (May 31 - 10:12:16 PM):   Can we make this time tomorrow? This same time?

Rasheed Zakari (May 31 - 10:12:17 PM):   Ok?

Rasheed Zakari (May 31 - 10:12:26 PM):   I will meet you at 9 p.m. my time…

Friends4Dave (May 31 - 10:12:43 PM):   Okay. Good night.

Rasheed Zakari (May 31 - 10:13:01 PM):   Good night. *(Relieved.)* See ya later. Bye.

Rasheed Zakari (May 31 - 10:13:06 PM):   I love talking to you.

Rasheed Zakari (May 31 - 10:13:18 PM):   Bye bye. I will chat with you later. Ok?

Rasheed Zakari (May 31 - 10:13:23 PM):   Sweet dreams. (*Dave did not respond. He logged out.*)

CHAPTER 9
IBRAHIM MORO ISSIFU IS AN UNGRATEFUL SCOUNDREL!

Ibrahim Moro Issifu is an ungrateful criminal! On June 1st 2009, Dave went online and immediately noticed that Gracy Isy was already there, and Dave initiated a conversation with her. Dave was impressed that Gracy had not asked him for money. Unlike Rasheed Zakari, Gracy Isy appeared to be genuine. Hence, Dave was interested in having further conversations with Gracy. First, he tried to reach her on the telephone, but the phone kept ringing … no one picked up. So, he began to chat.

Friends4Dave (June 01 - 11:12:39 AM):   Good morning, Gracy.

Talk2bryan2001 (June 01 - 11:13:09 AM):   Hello.

Friends4Dave (June 01 - 11:13:17 AM):   I just tried to call your number. It was ringing but nobody picked up.

Talk2bryan2001 (June 01 - 11:14:38 AM):   Really? It did not ring here. Maybe you try later after chat.

Friends4Dave (June 01 - 11:15:33 AM):   Okay. That's fine. How are you?

Talk2bryan2001 (June 01 - 11:16:50 AM):   I'm great and you?

Friends4Dave (June 01 - 11:18:28 AM):   I'm blessed. Thanks. What are you doing now?

Talk2bryan2001 (June 01 - 11:20:09 AM):   Just got back from school.

Talk2bryan2001 (June 01 - 11:20:30 AM):   Trying to rest.

Friends4Dave (June 01 - 11:22:00 AM):   Okay. I will call you later after you have rested. Is that okay with you?

Talk2bryan2001 (June 01 - 11:24:15 AM): Please do… okay.

* * * * * *

Dave called a few hours later and talked with Gracy on the phone. They spoke freely and seemed to like each other very much. Gracy told Dave that she finds Dave irresistibly attractive and really cares about him, even though she admitted that she didn't know why she likes Dave that much. She also said that she felt very comfortable talking with Dave and that he is a very good listener and with a good sense of humor. Dave, on the other hand, liked Gracy because he thought she was genuine, and he loved the way she laughs. Dave and Gracy went back online to chat after speaking on the phone, as discussed in details in the next chapter.

Meanwhile, Dave responded to Moro Issifu's invitation to chat online. Moro Issifu had come online while Dave was chatting with Gracy. Shortly after Dave ended his conversation with Gracy, and while Dave was doing something else on his computer, Moro initiated a conversation with Dave and Dave responded. Morro's diction was very bad, and Dave had a feeling that he was probably uneducated. Dave had to re-write some of Moro Issifu's conversations in this book, for the purpose of grammar and readability.

Moro.Issifu (June 01 - 11:39:24 AM): Hello dear.

Friends4Dave (June 01 - 11:39:51 AM): Hi. (*Dave still felt uncomfortable about being called "dear" by a man he did not even know, but he also wanted to be polite as usual.*)

Moro.Issifu (June 01 - 11:40:01 AM): How are you doing today dear?

Friends4Dave (June 01 - 11:40:26 AM):   I am fine. And you? (*Dave cringed as he was being called "dear" again by this guy; but, having grown up in Nigeria, he understood that males can show affection towards other males without any erotic intentions. Nevertheless, in Dave's mind, he was hoping that Ibrahim was not a homosexual guy trying to hit on him. Dave is a heterosexual;and based on his religious beliefs, although he was no longer a Jehovah's Witness at the time of this conversation, he finds homosexuality very repulsive – especially if directed towards him; even though he does not discriminate against homosexuals and lesbians, just as he does not discriminate against people of other religions or naitonality. In fact, Dave is opposed to any kind of discrimination against people – including, but not limited to, discriminations against minorities, religious groups, atheists, agnostics, gays/lesbians, and women, etc. Such people have the right to believe and pratice whatever they want; just as he has the right to believe and practice whatever he wants. We are all going to be held accountable someday for our deeds by the Creator of the Universe.*)

Moro.Issifu (June 01 - 11:40:33 AM):   I am fine too.

Moro.Issifu (June 01 - 11:40:38 AM):   Dear where are from you?

Friends4Dave (June 01 - 11:40:43 AM):   (*Dave flinched again when Moro called him "Dear", so Dave ignored the question altogether.*) Good.

Friends4Dave (June 01 - 11:40:51 AM):   How was your weekend?

Moro.Issifu (June 01 - 11:41:04 AM):   Good dear.

Moro.Issifu (June 01 - 11:41:09 AM):   And yours?

Friends4Dave (June 01 - 11:41:23 AM):   It was fair.

Moro.Issifu (June 01 - 11:41:31 AM):   Ok dear.

Friends4Dave (June 01 - 11:41:51 AM):   *(Dave had a feeling that this guy was not using his real name, so he asked Moro for his true identity.)* What is your real name?

Moro.Issifu (June 01 - 11:41:53 AM):   Dear, can I see you on webcam or you can send me pictures of you and tell me a little more about yourself. Ok?

Moro.Issifu (June 01 - 11:42:10 AM):   My real name is Ibrahim.

Moro.Issifu (June 01 - 11:42:23 AM):   And you?

Friends4Dave (June 01 - 11:42:30 AM):   *(Dave now realized that everyone he met online was very much interested in getting Dave's pictures and seeing him live on the webcam but, on the other hand, these same people were not willing to send Dave their own pictures nor been seen on the webcam; and Dave wondered why.)* Do you have a web cam?

Moro.Issifu (June 01 - 11:42:35 AM):   Ohh no. *(Now Dave was suspicious.)*

Moro.Issifu (June 01 - 11:42:39 AM):   And you dear?

Friends4Dave (June 01 - 11:42:41 AM):   I am Dave. By the way, why do you keep calling me "dear"? You don't know me…

Moro.Issifu (June 01 - 11:42:47 AM):   Wowo, nice name! (*He ignored Dave's question.*)

Moro.Issifu (June 01 - 11:42:53 AM):   (*Thinking to himself, "Is this guy trying to say 'wow'? And why the flattery?*) Where are you from Moro?

Friends4Dave (June 01 - 11:42:55 AM):   No, I do not have a webcam either. (*Dave suspected that Moro was lying about not having a webcam, so Dave did not want Moro to see him on the webcam either.*)

Moro.Issifu (June 01 - 11:42:59 AM):   Ok.

Moro.Issifu (June 01 - 11:43:11 AM):   How Old Are U?

Friends4Dave (June 01 - 11:43:13 AM):   I am a Nigerian. (*Dave ignored his question about age.*)

Friends4Dave (June 01 - 11:43:22 AM):   And where are you from?

Moro.Issifu (June 01 - 11:43:31 AM):   I am From Ghana.

Moro.Issifu (June 01 - 11:43:41 AM):   How Old are you?

Friends4Dave (June 01 - 11:43:44 AM):   Why do you want to know how old I am? And what part of Ghana are you from?

Moro.Issifu (June 01 - 11:44:02 AM):   West Africa. (*Ibrahim ignored Dave's question about why he wanted to know Dave's age.*)

Friends4Dave (June 01 - 11:44:34 AM):   I know Ghana is in West

Africa. But what part of Ghana are you from?

Moro.Issifu (June 01 - 11:44:43 AM):   Accra.

Friends4Dave (June 01 - 11:45:02 AM):   I have been to Accra. Where
                in Accra?

Moro.Issifu (June 01 - 11:45:13 AM):   Tema.

Friends4Dave (June 01 - 11:45:33 AM):   Good. How far is Tema from
                Medina?

Moro.Issifu (June 01 - 11:45:53 AM):   2 hours Dave.

Friends4Dave (June 01 - 11:46:06 AM):   I see.

Moro.Issifu (June 01 - 11:46:13 AM):   Ok.

Friends4Dave (June 01 - 11:46:27 AM):   What do you do for a living
                Ibrahim?

Moro.Issifu (June 01 - 11:46:59 AM):   *(Ibrahim saw Dave's question
as an opportunity for him to execute his
scheme to defraud him.)* I am a student but my
father is dead. So I don't have anybody to pay
my school fees for me Dave.

Friends4Dave (June 01 - 11:47:32 AM):   Sorry to hear that. What about
                your mother?

Moro.Issifu (June 01 - 11:47:47 AM):   My mother is old now Dave.

Moro.Issifu (June 01 - 11:47:54 AM):   I have a little brother too.

Friends4Dave (June 01 - 11:47:59 AM):   *(Dave's suspicion was
growing. He could see that this guy was trying*

to scam him, but he decided to play along.) I see.

Moro.Issifu (June 01 - 11:48:03 AM):   My little brother is 9 years old Dave.

Friends4Dave (June 01 - 11:48:37 AM):   Is your little brother by the same mother?

Moro.Issifu (June 01 - 11:48:48 AM):   Ohh yes.

Friends4Dave (June 01 - 11:48:55 AM):   Good.

Moro.Issifu (June 01 - 11:48:55 AM):   And the same father.

Moro.Issifu (June 01 - 11:48:59 AM):   Ok.

Friends4Dave (June 01 - 11:49:17 AM):   When did your father die?

Moro.Issifu (June 01 - 11:49:46 AM):   About 5 years ago Dave.

Friends4Dave (June 01 - 11:50:01 AM):   How old was he when he died?

Moro.Issifu (June 01 - 11:50:23 AM):   He was going to the village and he had an accident Dave.

Friends4Dave (June 01 - 11:50:54 AM):   I am really sorry to hear that. How old was he when he died?

Moro.Issifu (June 01 - 11:51:08 AM):   67 years old.

Friends4Dave (June 01 - 11:51:26 AM):   How old is your mother now?

Moro.Issifu (June 01 - 11:51:37 AM):   54 years old.

Moro.Issifu (June 01 - 11:51:44 AM):   She cannot work Dave.

Friends4Dave (June 01 - 11:52:03 AM):   Your mother is young then?

Moro.Issifu (June 01 - 11:52:13 AM):   Yes Dave.

Moro.Issifu (June 01 - 11:52:26 AM):   Dave, we are suffering.

Friends4Dave (June 01 - 11:52:30 AM):   *(Dave was tempted to say to Ibrahim, "You are not alone. I am suffering here too." But he decided not to do so.)* I thought you said she was old?

Friends4Dave (June 01 - 11:53:13 AM):   Why can't she work Ibrahim?

Moro.Issifu (June 01 - 11:53:44 AM):   She is old.

Moro.Issifu (June 01 - 11:53:53 AM):   *(On second thought, he changed his mother's diagnosis.)* She has a stroke.

Moro.Issifu (June 01 - 11:54:22 AM):   She is very sick.

Friends4Dave (June 01 - 11:54:24 AM):   *(Dave thought to himself, "I got you, you Scoundrel!" But he continued to play Ibrahim's game.)* I am sorry to hear that.

Moro.Issifu (June 01 - 11:54:36 AM):   Ok Dave.

Friends4Dave (June 01 - 11:54:48 AM):   What school do you go to?

Moro.Issifu (June 01 - 11:55:45 AM):   Chemu Secondary School.

Friends4Dave (June 01 - 11:56:00 AM):   How old are you?

Moro.Issifu (June 01 - 11:56:11 AM):   I am 24 years old now.

Friends4Dave (June 01 - 11:57:09 AM):   *(Dave was thinking, "Are you not too old to be in a secondary school? Does this guy really expect me to believe that he is at least six years behind in a high school?" Nevertheless, Dave continued to play Ibrahim's game with him.)*   Good. When will you graduate from Chemu Secondary School?

Moro.Issifu (June 01 - 11:57:20 AM):   This month.

Friends4Dave (June 01 - 11:57:46 AM):   Great!

Moro.Issifu (June 01 - 11:58:01 AM):   Ok.

Friends4Dave (June 01 - 11:58:18 AM):   What are your plans after graduation?

Moro.Issifu (June 01 - 11:58:51 AM):   To make a business so that I will take care of my mom and little brother Dave.

Friends4Dave (June 01 - 11:59:11 AM):   What kind of business?

Moro.Issifu (June 01 - 11:59:25 AM):   I will sell clothes or shoes.

Friends4Dave (June 01 - 11:59:52 AM):   Is that your picture on Flixster?

Moro.Issifu (June 01 - 12:00:11 PM):   Ohh yes.

Friends4Dave (June 01 - 12:01:25 PM):   How long ago did you take that picture?

Moro.Issifu (June 01 - 12:01:48 PM):   4 months ago.

Moro.Issifu (June 01 - 12:02:00 PM):   *(Ibrahim realized that Dave was catching up to his scam; but like most criminals, he thought he could still accomplish his goal.)* Please Dave don't be angry with me. Ok?

Friends4Dave (June 01 - 12:02:33 PM):   *(Dave thought to himself, "This guy knows that I know he is up to something illegal", so Dave decided to defuse Ibrahim's suspicion.)* What makes you think I am angry with you?

Moro.Issifu (June 01 - 12:02:44 PM):   Ok.

Moro.Issifu (June 01 - 12:02:56 PM):   *(His suspicion defused, Ibrahim went for the kill.)* Please can you help me to finish me Graduation?

Friends4Dave (June 01 - 12:03:29 PM):   What do you mean help you to finish your graduation?

Moro.Issifu (June 01 - 12:03:37 PM):   Ok.

Moro.Issifu (June 01 - 12:04:11 PM):   Help me to pay some rich so that every day I will cook for my mom and little brother so that they will eat. Ok Dave?

Friends4Dave (June 01 - 12:05:21 PM):   *(Dave was now feeling impatient with this fool, and he felt insulted that this fool thought he could swindle money from him.)* Those are expensive clothes that you are wearing on your Flixster picture. Didn't you say that you and your family are suffering? How did you get the money to buy those clothes?

Moro.Issifu (June 01 - 12:05:49 PM):   Ohh, it is not mine. (*This crook was fast thinking too! And like most criminals, he was a pathological liar.*)

Moro.Issifu (June 01 - 12:06:05 PM):   I go and borrow from a friend.

Moro.Issifu (June 01 - 12:06:14 PM):   But now my friend is not there.

Moro.Issifu (June 01 - 12:06:21 PM):   He is travel now.

Friends4Dave (June 01 - 12:06:28 PM):   I see. (*Dave was thinking, "This guy must think that he is dealing with a 'stupid American' or something".*)

Moro.Issifu (June 01 - 12:06:34 PM):   Ok.

Moro.Issifu (June 01 - 12:06:47 PM):   So Dave, can you help me to do that for my family?

Friends4Dave (June 01 - 12:07:47 PM):   (*Insulted, Dave clenched his teeth, but decided to continue to play along.*) Let's assume I can help you, what type of business are you going to do when you graduate so that you don't keep asking me for help?

Moro.Issifu (June 01 - 12:08:41 PM):   I want to trade.

Friends4Dave (June 01 - 12:08:51 PM):   What kind of trade?

Moro.Issifu (June 01 - 12:09:08 PM):   Selling dear.

Friends4Dave (June 01 - 12:09:32 PM):   I know that trade means selling. But what do you want to sell?

Moro.Issifu (June 01 - 12:10:35 PM):   I want to make my own boutique so that I can sell clothes.

Friends4Dave (June 01 - 12:10:53 PM):   Good. Now we are getting somewhere.

Moro.Issifu (June 01 - 12:10:57 PM):   Ok.

Friends4Dave (June 01 - 12:12:00 PM):   What are your full names? (First, Middle, and Surname)?

Moro.Issifu (June 01 - 12:12:28 PM):   Full Name… Ibrahim Issifu.

Friends4Dave (June 01 - 12:12:59 PM):   What is your middle name?

Moro.Issifu (June 01 - 12:13:23 PM):   My middle name is Moro.
(Dave noticed that Ibrahim did not mention anything about "Musah", which was the name he used on Flixster.)

Friends4Dave (June 01 - 12:13:41 PM):   Who is Musah?

Moro.Issifu (June 01 - 12:13:55 PM):   Is my little brother name.

Friends4Dave (June 01 - 12:14:15 PM):   So, you use your little brother's name online?

Moro.Issifu (June 01 - 12:14:26 PM):   Ohh yes.

Friends4Dave (June 01 - 12:14:30 PM):   *(Highly offended.)* Why?

Moro.Issifu (June 01 - 12:14:36 PM):   Nothing.

Moro.Issifu (June 01 - 12:14:49 PM):   His name is nice. That is why I use it.

Friends4Dave (June 01 - 12:15:15 PM):   (*Dave has had enough of this numskull. He decided to move on to the last chapter with this criminal and then end the annoying conversation with him.*) What do you want me to do for you now?

Moro.Issifu (June 01 - 12:15:27 PM):   Help me.

Friends4Dave (June 01 - 12:15:54 PM):   You already said that. But, what exactly do you want from me now?

Moro.Issifu (June 01 - 12:16:05 PM):   Money.

Friends4Dave (June 01 - 12:16:11 PM):   How much?

Moro.Issifu (June 01 - 12:16:25 PM):   Any amount set me up. (*This was an indication that this stupid guy was not interested in setting up a boutique as a business. He already ran a business... the business of ripping off innocent and unsuspecting people online. He was definitely a scammer who enjoyed ripping people off. Dave saw this clearly now.*)

Friends4Dave (June 01 - 12:16:57 PM):   Be specific.

Moro.Issifu (June 01 - 12:17:29 PM):   Ok.

Moro.Issifu (June 01 - 12:18:06 PM):   I need 650 dollars... but any amount that you can give me dear.

Friends4Dave (June 01 - 12:19:19 PM):   (*Dave was thinking, "Does this guy really think I am that stupid as to hand over $650.00 to him when I don't even know who he is?" But Dave decided to push him a little further.*) Is that all the money you will need to "finish" your graduation and "set ... up" for your trade?

Moro.Issifu (June 01 - 12:19:56 PM):   No. But I can't ask you for all right now, dear Dave. (*Pretending not to be the greedy type.*)

Friends4Dave (June 01 - 12:21:06 PM):   (*Dave thought to himself, "Unbelievable! So, this guy intends to keep asking me for money in the future!"*) Like I said before, I don't want you to keep asking me for help. So, tell me all the things you need now?

Moro.Issifu (June 01 - 12:21:57 PM):   Please, dear Dave, what is the amount that you can give me?

Moro.Issifu (June 01 - 12:22:23 PM):   Because I don't want to ask more than you can give right now.

Friends4Dave (June 01 - 12:22:29 PM):   (*Now certain that Ibrahim's frequent use of "dear" was just a ploy to rip him off, he decided to put a stop to it.*) Please stop calling me "dear". Now, you tell me what you want me to give to you ... please.

Moro.Issifu (June 01 - 12:23:24 PM):   Please, dear Dave, 1000 dollars.

Friends4Dave (June 01 - 12:24:21 PM):   (*Dave was thinking: "So, this guy wants to swindle $1,000.00 from me. Very convenient! Isn't it?" However, he continued to play Ibrahim's game.*) Okay. No problem. But, there are some things you must do in order for me to help you.

Moro.Issifu (June 01 - 12:24:46 PM):   What do you want me to do, Dear Dave?

Friends4Dave (June 01 - 12:25:31 PM):   *(Dave cringed every time Ibrahim called him "Dear", but he tried so hard not to show his anger and disgust.)* I told you to stop calling me "dear". Now, I just want to make sure that you are real. First, send me a true picture of yourself right now.

Moro.Issifu (June 01 - 12:25:43 PM):   Ok.

Moro.Issifu (June 01 - 12:25:46 PM):   I will do that. Ok.

Friends4Dave (June 01 - 12:26:26 PM):   I am waiting ...

Moro.Issifu (June 01 - 12:26:31 PM):   Ok.

Moro.Issifu (June 01 - 12:27:32 PM):   Dear Dave I don't have many pictures... I have only Two Pics.

Moro.Issifu (June 01 - 12:27:41 PM):   If you will like me to give you. Ok?

Friends4Dave (June 01 - 12:27:58 PM):   Where are the pictures? I don't see any here.

Moro.Issifu (June 01 - 12:28:11 PM):   *(Ibrahim tried to buy some time to think of a plausible excuse not to send the pictures that Dave requested.)* Please wait… ok?

Moro.Issifu (June 01 - 12:29:26 PM):   *(Ibrahim sent Dave two copies the same picture he had on Flixster; the same picture that Dave asked him where he got the money to buy such an expensive clothing, while at the same time claiming to be poor and suffering.)* Have you seen it now, dear Dave?

Moro.Issifu (June 01 - 12:31:32 PM):   Ok.

Friends4Dave (June 01 - 12:31:39 PM):   (*Looking at the two copies of the same profile picture that Ibrahim posted on Flixster.*) Are these the pictures you sent?

Moro.Issifu (June 01 - 12:31:47 PM):   Ohh yes.

Moro.Issifu (June 01 - 12:31:57 PM):   You don't see it on Flixster, dear Dave?

Moro.Issifu (June 01 - 12:35:05 PM):   Please Dave, can I give you my detail to send me the Money?

Friends4Dave (June 01 - 12:35:48 PM):   You realize that you just sent me two copies of the same picture you have on your Flixster profile? This is the same picture I asked you where you got the money from to buy the clothes you were wearing. (*Since this was going to be Dave's next request anyway, Dave agreed.*) Please go ahead. Give me the details now.

Moro.Issifu (June 01 - 12:35:58 PM):   Ok.

Moro.Issifu (June 01 - 12:36:08 PM):   NAME... IBRAHIM ISSIFU.

Moro.Issifu (June 01 - 12:36:13 PM):   COUNTRY... GHANA.

Moro.Issifu (June 01 - 12:36:19 PM):   CITY... TEMA.

Moro.Issifu (June 01 - 12:36:25 PM):   BANK... WESTERN UNION.

Moro.Issifu (June 01 - 12:36:34 PM):   THAT IS ALL DAVE.

Friends4Dave (June 01 - 12:36:43 PM):   Great!

Moro.Issifu (June 01 - 12:36:48 PM):   OK.

Friends4Dave (June 01 - 12:36:55 PM):   Very good. You have one more thing to do before I can help you, as you requested. Next, I want you to take another picture of yourself with your mother. Make sure you hold a big sign that says "I Want $1,000.00 From Dave". Once I receive the email, I will send you more than the money you asked for, and through whatever means you want me to send it to you. Now, is that clear? (*Dave wanted this information in order to use it to expose Ibrahim as a fraud and scammer all over the Internet.*)

Moro.Issifu (June 01 - 12:38:51 PM):   Ohh dear Dave, I don't have money to snap a photo now. (*Ibrahim was determined not to reveal his true identity.*)

Moro.Issifu (June 01 - 12:39:02 PM):   So if you can send me a little money to do that ...

Moro.Issifu (June 01 - 12:39:16 PM):   Then after that you can send me the 1,000.00 dollars.

Moro.Issifu (June 01 - 12:40:55 PM):   (*Dave did not respond and he was thinking to himself, "It is true that criminals are foolishly bold."*) Are you there dear Dave?

Friends4Dave (June 01 - 12:41:23 PM):   (*Dave continued to think to himself: "So, this nincompoop thinks that he can swindle a thousand bucks out of me like this?"*) I will not send you anything until you do what I asked you to do. Go borrow money to do what I asked you to do. You must first send your current pictures to me if you want me to send you the money; especially when I am thinking of sending you a lot more money than the $1,000.00 you are asking. What is the matter with you? Do you want my help or not?

Moro.Issifu (June 01 - 12:42:18 PM):   Dear Dave, please don't say that. I say I will do it. Ok?

Friends4Dave (June 01 - 12:42:22 PM):   Then go do it!

Moro.Issifu (June 01 - 12:42:32 PM):   But I don't have anything to do that now.

Moro.Issifu (June 01 - 12:42:43 PM):   But if you can send me a little money to do that... ok?

Moro.Issifu (June 01 - 12:42:49 PM):   Send me 50 dollars.

Moro.Issifu (June 01 - 12:43:19 PM):   Please I don't have anybody I will go and borrow money from him or her. Dear Dave, trust me. Ok?

Moro.Issifu (June 01 - 12:43:25 PM):   I will not hurt you. (*Dave was thinking, "Trust you? You've got to be kidding! This is incredible! He is telling me he will not hurt me? Doesn't that sound familiar? Didn't a scammer tell me the same thing recently?" Dave recalled that Rasheed had told him the same thing that she will not hurt him, at the same time she was trying to swindle money from him. Dave was wondering if these scamming scoundrels have a Scammer School that they attend to learn how to defraud innocent people online? Dave could see a pattern in the similarities of their terminologies and thought processes.*)

Moro.Issifu (June 01 - 12:43:29 PM):   I promise you. I will not hurt you.

Moro.Issifu (June 01 - 12:43:45 PM):   If I am not serious, I will not chat with you, dear Dave? (*Dave could not believe that this fool was trying to use reverse psychology on him.*)

Moro.Issifu (June 01 - 12:43:51 PM):   I am serious with you. Ok.

Friends4Dave (June 01 - 12:44:02 PM):   I know that you are serious; but the question is, "Serious about what?" You must be out of your mind if you think that I will send you the $50 first. Moreover, what makes you think you can hurt me?

Moro.Issifu (June 01 - 12:44:32 PM):   You are thinking that when you send me the money, I will not do what you say.

Moro.Issifu (June 01 - 12:44:35 PM):   Don't think that. Ok? (*Now Dave has had enough and he did not respond.*)

Moro.Issifu (June 01 - 12:45:51 PM):   (*He was desperate.*) Please dear Dave, talk to me! I don't have much time. My time is coming to an end. So, try to understand me. Ok? Are you thinking that when you send me the money, I will not do what you say?

Friends4Dave (June 01 - 12:47:46 PM):   Is that a confession? If you don't have much time to comply with my request, then I do not have much time to send you the $1,000! (*Dave has had enough.*) When you started with your scam, you failed to realize that you are dealing with the wrong person. I am an ex-Investigator. I used to investigate people like you for years. You said you that want to have a business; but you already have the business, and your business is fraud! (*Dave was now very upset.*) Don't make me mad... because if you do, I can report you to the International Police Organization and have INTERPOL (International Police Organization) pick you up within hours or days. Do you understand me? I saved you from being defrauded by Rose Grand; and now you turned around and try to defraud me? What an ungrateful scoundrel you really are! I am warning you right now.... don't mess with me again! Do you understand? (*Although Dave was trying to scare this bastard from continuing in his criminal enterprise but, at the same time, Dave was also serious.*)

Friends4Dave (June 01 - 12:49:43 PM):   (*Ibrahim did not respond.*) Please do you understand what I just said? You need to respond now!

Ibrahim still did not respond. He remained online for about ten more minutes while Dave continued to observe what he might do next. Then Ibrahim logged out and did not contact Dave for many days. Thereafter, Dave deleted Ibrahim from his "List of Contacts." Dave never heard from Ibrahim again.

CHAPTER 10
DAVE CALLS AND CHATS WITH GRACY IN NIGERIA

𝔄s promised earlier in the day, and as indicated briefly in the previous chapter, Dave called a few hours later and talked with Gracy on the phone. They spoke freely and seemed to like each other very much. Gracy told Dave that she finds Dave irresistibly attractive and really cares about him, even though she admitted that she did not know why she likes Dave that much. She also said that she felt very comfortable talking with Dave and that he is a very good listener and with a good sense of humor. Dave, on the other hand, liked Gracy because he thought she was genuine, and he loved the way she laughs. Now, as they finished their telephone conversation, they agreed to go online and chat some more, before Gracy apparently fell asleep.

Talk2bryan2001 (June 01 - 4:26:38 PM):   Hello, are you there?

Talk2bryan2001 (June 01 - 4:27:49 PM):   Nice talking to you on the phone.

Talk2bryan2001 (June 01 - 4:28:15 PM):   I mean nice speaking with you on the phone.

Friends4Dave (June 01 - 4:28:16 PM):   Yes, I am here. My computer is very slow.

Friends4Dave (June 01 - 4:28:38 PM):   It was a pleasure speaking with you, too.

Friends4Dave (June 01 - 4:29:12 PM):   I liked it when you laughed. I really did.

Friends4Dave (June 01 - 4:30:14 PM):   Are you still there, Gracy?

Talk2bryan2001 (June 01 - 4:30:40 PM):   Okay well, I must say that I
                                            had fun chatting with you.

Friends4Dave (June 01 - 4:30:57 PM):   So did I.

Friends4Dave (June 01 - 4:32:09 PM):   I would love to see a picture of
                                         you, so that I can have a picture of you in my
                                         mind and heart.

Friends4Dave (June 01 - 4:34:27 PM):   *(After about two minutes of no
                                         response, Dave sensed Gracy may be tired and
                                         he decided to end the conversation.)* Good
                                         night for now...

Talk2bryan2001 (June 01 - 4:34:35 PM):   So, have you had lunch?

Talk2bryan2001 (June 01 - 4:34:35 PM):   Dave?

Talk2bryan2001 (June 01 - 4:34:36 PM):   Are you there?

Friends4Dave (June 01 - 4:35:23 PM):   I was just leaving. Yes, I have
                                         eaten, which is usual for me at this hour.
                                         Thanks. What about you?

Friends4Dave (June 01 - 4:39:58 PM):   *(Gracy did not respond. Dave
                                         thought that perhaps she was tired and asleep,
                                         since it was late at night in Nigeria at the time.
                                         Or, was she perhaps chatting with someone
                                         else ...? He couldn't be sure. After about four
                                         and a half minutes of no response from Gracy,
                                         he ended the conversation.)* I guess you are
                                         not available, or sleeping. Good night ....

CHAPTER 11
RASHEED IS FULLY EXPOSED!

On May 31ˢᵗ 2009, after Rasheed tried unsuccessfully to swindle more money from Dave, the following were the last conversations they had before they parted that night:

Friends4Dave (May 31 - 10:10:36 PM):   Please let me see you again on the webcam ... and, please, try to make it stable this time. (*Signaling to her that he was aware that she had been manipulating the webcam images.*)

Rasheed Zakari (May 31 - 10:11:05 PM):   Stable??? what do ya mean?

Rasheed Zakari (May 31 - 10:11:19 PM):   (*She knew now that Dave had figured it out that she had been doctoring up her webcam images, and that she was intentionally shutting off the webcam so that Dave could not get a really good look at her. She decided to end the conversation.*) I need to go to sleep now. Can we make it tomorrow?

Friends4Dave (May 31 - 10:11:40 PM):   I mean try to make it so that it does not freeze or disconnect.

Rasheed Zakari (May 31 - 10:12:03 PM):   Oh ok ...but I need to go to sleep now. Now, what do we do?

Friends4Dave (May 31 - 10:12:06 PM):   Tomorrow will be fine... What time?

Rasheed Zakari (May 31 - 10:12:16 PM):   Can we make this time tomorrow? This same time?

Rasheed Zakari (May 31 - 10:12:17 PM):   Ok?

Rasheed Zakari (May 31 - 10:12:26 PM):   I will meet you at 9 p.m. my
                                         time...

Friends4Dave (May 31 - 10:12:43 PM):   Okay. Good night.

Rasheed Zakari (May 31 - 10:13:01 PM):   Good night. (*Relieved.*) See ya
                                         later. Bye.

Rasheed Zakari (May 31 - 10:13:06 PM):   I love talking to you.

Rasheed Zakari (May 31 - 10:13:18 PM):   Bye bye. I will chat with you
                                         later. Ok?

Rasheed Zakari (May 31 - 10:13:23 PM):   Sweet dreams. (*Dave did not
                                         respond. He logged out.*)

* * * * * * *

Today, June 1st 2009, Dave went online early to wait there for Rasheed to come online at 21:00 hrs in Ghana (Rasheed's time) as previously arranged, which was 17:00 hrs EST in the United States (Dave's time). But Rasheed did not show up. Even though Rasheed was the one that set up the appointment yesterday for them to meet again at 21:00 hrs today, June 1st, she did not come online as scheduled. So, Dave waited another forty minutes for Rasheed before he decided to post the message below.

Friends4Dave (June 01 - 5:40:23 PM):   Rasheed, you set this
                                          appointment up, but you did not show up. Why
                                          is that? I waited for you for 40 minutes from
                                          the time you scheduled. I will not wait any
                                          longer. I have to go now. You just missed a
                                          very great opportunity. (*Dave was obviously
                                          very upset with Rasheed.*)

* * * * * * *

Nevertheless, approximately 50 minutes after Dave left the message above, Rasheed called Dave on the telephone, but when Dave picked up the phone, she hung up after saying: "hello, how are you doing?" The call was from a Ghanaian phone number – in fact, it was from the same phone number that Rasheed had given to Dave; but the voice sounded American or Canadian. So, Dave went back online and left this message below for Rasheed.

Friends4Dave (June 01 - 6:29:23 PM):   You just called me. What do you want?

* * * * * * *

About six minutes thereafter, Rasheed came online and she began to chat with Dave.

Rasheed Zakari (June 01 - 6:35:50 PM):   Hello well, what do you mean? I just called you and ask you whether you are online or not … but why are you doing this dear??

Rasheed Zakari (June 01 - 6:36:51 PM):   Let me Explain.

Rasheed Zakari (June 01 - 6:37:23 PM):   Why are you upset with me?

Friends4Dave (June 01 - 6:37:34 PM):   *(Dave wanted to give Rasheed the benefit of doubt and an opportunity to explain herself as she requested.)* Go ahead, please explain.

Rasheed Zakari (June 01 - 6:38:24 PM):   Why are you upset with me?

Friends4Dave (June 01 - 6:38:47 PM):   What makes you think I am upset?

Rasheed Zakari (June 01 - 6:39:54 PM):   The way you left me the other day. You went offline with a temper, and why did you said I lost a big Opportunity?

Rasheed Zakari (June 01 - 6:40:00 PM):   How does that mean?

Rasheed Zakari (June 01 - 6:40:01 PM):   ??

Friends4Dave (June 01 - 6:41:10 PM):   I said good night last night before I signed off. You told me you wanted to go to sleep and I did not have any problem with that. So, I said good night.

Rasheed Zakari (June 01 - 6:41:37 PM):   Oh ok. So, how are you doing and how was your day ?????

Friends4Dave (June 01 - 6:42:13 PM):   I did not have any temper yesterday. If I have a temper, you will definitely notice it.

Friends4Dave (June 01 - 6:42:37 PM):   My day was blessed. And yours?

Rasheed Zakari (June 01 - 6:43:02 PM):   Mine was also good, thank you so much.

Friends4Dave (June 01 - 6:43:18 PM):   *(Dave wanted to ascertain once and for all whether Rasheed had really been manipulating her webcam images so that Dave could not get a clear look at who she really was.)* Please turn on your webcam.

Rasheed Zakari (June 01 - 6:43:44 PM):   Oh ok. Hold on... turn yours on. *(Dave refused to turn his webcam on.)*

Rasheed Zakari (June 01 - 6:48:11 PM):   Turn yours on.

Friends4Dave (June 01 - 6:48:54 PM):   I asked you to turn on your webcam. You want me to turn mine on first before you turn yours on?

Rasheed Zakari (June 01 - 6:49:09 PM):   Wait a minute? (*Dave accidentally logged out and could not log back in for a few minutes.*)

Rasheed Zakari (June 01 - 6:57:29 PM):   Why did you go offline?

Friends4Dave (June 01 - 6:59:00 PM):   (*Dave was finally able to log in and return to the chat.*) I accidentally logged off ... sorry.

Rasheed Zakari (June 01 - 6:59:18 PM):   Oh ok, did you see me?

Friends4Dave (June 01 - 6:59:32 PM):   No, please turn it on.

Rasheed Zakari (June 01 - 6:59:53 PM):   So, you didn't see me for the long time when I turn on my webcam? (*She is good at this game ... really good.*)

Friends4Dave (June 01 - 7:00:19 PM):   No, it was trying to load when I was logged out.

Rasheed Zakari (June 01 - 7:00:36 PM):   Oh ok.

Rasheed Zakari (June 01 - 7:01:17 PM):   Can you see my picture.

Friends4Dave (June 01 - 7:01:29 PM):   (*It was a fuzzy image of a painting ... impossible to tell whether the painting was that of a male or female.*) Ok, I see a painting of a portrait now.

Friends4Dave (June 01 - 7:01:50 PM):   Whose portrait is this?

Friends4Dave (June 01 - 7:02:04 PM):   You are blank.

Friends4Dave (June 01 - 7:02:47 PM):   It is completely off again.
                         What is going on?

Rasheed Zakari (June 01 - 7:04:16 PM):   (*She did not answer Dave's
                         question about whose painting she showed to
                         Dave through the webcam.*)   Can you still see
                         me?

Friends4Dave (June 01 - 7:04:28 PM):   It is frozen.

Friends4Dave (June 01 - 7:04:47 PM):   Do you see me?

Rasheed Zakari (June 01 - 7:05:12 PM):   Yes, I can see you now.

Rasheed Zakari (June 01 - 7:05:17 PM):   Handsome you are today.

Friends4Dave (June 01 - 7:05:50 PM):   Thank you. (*Then Dave saw
                         an image of Rasheed's dog, Leo.*)

Rasheed Zakari (June 01 - 7:05:53 PM):   My puppy.

Friends4Dave (June 01 - 7:06:07 PM):   Hi Leo!

Friends4Dave (June 01 - 7:06:54 PM):   (*Dave wanted to know if the
                         image of the dog he was seeing was live or
                         perhaps doctored.*) Now wave your puppy's
                         hand toward me like he is saying "Hi."

Friends4Dave (June 01 - 7:07:28 PM):   (*As soon as Dave asked
                         Rasheed to wave the dog's hand, the dog's
                         image immediately disappeared.*) What
                         happened?

Rasheed Zakari (June 01 - 7:10:36 PM):   Sorry I got disconnected when I opened my cam.

Friends4Dave (June 01 - 7:10:49 PM):   That's okay.

Rasheed Zakari (June 01 - 7:11:21 PM):   I hope you are not upset.

Friends4Dave (June 01 - 7:11:32 PM):   About what?

Rasheed Zakari (June 01 - 7:12:15 PM):   About my DC...

Friends4Dave (June 01 - 7:12:53 PM):   What is a DC?

Rasheed Zakari (June 01 - 7:13:23 PM):   Disconnected.

Rasheed Zakari (June 01 - 7:13:28 PM):   Ok.

Friends4Dave (June 01 - 7:14:11 PM):   Oh no! It was not your fault. I got disconnected too, remember? I may even get disconnected again, who knows. (*Dave still gave Rasheed the benefit of the doubt.*)

Rasheed Zakari (June 01 - 7:14:52 PM):   Oh ok, that is cool.

Friends4Dave (June 01 - 7:14:54 PM):   (*Dave tried again to establish if Rasheed was deliberately concealing her video images from him.*) I really would like to be seeing you when I chat with you.

Rasheed Zakari (June 01 - 7:15:52 PM):   Yes, and my webcam totally gives this PC problem whenever I get it on. (*Now, Dave did not believe her.*)

Friends4Dave (June 01 - 7:16:19 PM):   Do it again, please.

Rasheed Zakari (June 01 - 7:17:07 PM):   Can you now see me?

Friends4Dave (June 01 - 7:18:01 PM):   No, it says, "This person's webcam is not available", and when I click "OK" it disappeared.

Rasheed Zakari (June 01 - 7:18:29 PM):   Oh what happened.

Rasheed Zakari (June 01 - 7:18:43 PM):   I am really sorry my webcam don't work. Please forgive me...

Friends4Dave (June 01 - 7:19:10 PM):   No problem. (*Dave was now convinced that Rasheed had been deliberately tempering with the web cam images.*)

Friends4Dave (June 01 - 7:20:00 PM):   You asked me to let you "explain" something earlier. Now, what is it?

Rasheed Zakari (June 01 - 7:21:24 PM):   Well because you said I called you ... I tried to call you to verify whether you are online or not.

Rasheed Zakari (June 01 - 7:21:28 PM):   So I came on.

Friends4Dave (June 01 - 7:21:43 PM):   Okay. (*Dave did not believe what she said.*)

Friends4Dave (June 01 - 7:22:07 PM):   Why were you about 1 hour 30 minutes late?

Rasheed Zakari (June 01 - 7:23:03 PM):   Sorry, I was not able to connect with you... my internet link went off. So, I tried to call the company and look it up for me ... sorry once more.

Friends4Dave (June 01 - 7:25:04 PM):   (*Dave decided to forgive her because she said she was sorry.*) Okay.

Enough of that then.

Friends4Dave (June 01 - 7:25:13 PM):   Where is your Mom?

Rasheed Zakari (June 01 - 7:25:49 PM):   Mom went to her friend.

Friends4Dave (June 01 - 7:26:11 PM):   I see. Did you tell her about me?

Rasheed Zakari (June 01 - 7:26:31 PM):   Yes, I did. I told her about you, and she will really like to meet you.

Friends4Dave (June 01 - 7:26:43 PM):   When?

Rasheed Zakari (June 01 - 7:27:26 PM):   I told her when we were at the market.

Friends4Dave (June 01 - 7:28:02 PM):   When does she want to meet me? I would like to meet and speak with her too.

Rasheed Zakari (June 01 - 7:29:32 PM):   Wow, that is great.... Well, when this relationship works between us, then I think you can speak and meet her. (*Dave thought to himself, "She is definitely a scammer."*)

Friends4Dave (June 01 - 7:30:21 PM):   Why can't I at least speak with her before we proceed with the relationship?

Rasheed Zakari (June 01 - 7:31:25 PM):   Oh ok. Do you wanna speak with her on the Phone?

Friends4Dave (June 01 - 7:31:52 PM):   Nope. On a webcam, please. (*Dave did not want to speak to anyone who may be pretending to be Rasheed's mother.*)

Rasheed Zakari (June 01 - 7:32:45 PM):   I think I have to try and get a new webcam.

Friends4Dave (June 01 - 7:33:08 PM):   I want to see her and I want her to see me when we speak with each other. She needs to see who is going to have a relationship with her daughter, and then give her approval and blessing before, before you and I can proceed any further with this potential relationship.

Rasheed Zakari (June 01 - 7:33:37 PM):   Yes you are right.

Friends4Dave (June 01 - 7:34:03 PM):   I also want to hear your voice.

Rasheed Zakari (June 01 - 7:34:38 PM):   But it seems my cam have a problem. So I need to get a new one... and for the call, I will try and call you. Ok? Don't worry.

Friends4Dave (June 01 - 7:35:27 PM):   I can call you now, if you don't mind.

Rasheed Zakari (June 01 - 7:36:27 PM):   Oh ok, but the phone is in my Uncle's bedroom. He is asleep.

Rasheed Zakari (June 01 - 7:36:30 PM):   Can we make it tomorrow?

Friends4Dave (June 01 - 7:37:34 PM):   Your uncle? (*Dave knew that Rasheed was lying and trying to evade anything that would reveal her true identity.*) You just called me with the same phone before we started chatting. Right?

Rasheed Zakari (June 01 - 7:38:35 PM):   Yes I did... but I left it over in my uncle's bedroom when I was coming to the

Computer.

Friends4Dave (June 01 - 7:38:47 PM):   So, you live with your uncle? I thought you said that your uncle was dead?

Rasheed Zakari (June 01 - 7:39:39 PM):   No, I live with my Mom, uncle and cousin.

Friends4Dave (June 01 - 7:40:32 PM):   Does anybody else live with you besides your Mom, Uncle, and Cousin?

Rasheed Zakari (June 01 - 7:41:10 PM):   Oh no.

Friends4Dave (June 01 - 7:41:48 PM):   What about your little sister whom you told me yesterday that you gave your computer's speakers to?

Rasheed Zakari (June 01 - 7:43:02 PM):   *(She mulled the question over before she answered.)* Oh ok... well you see, I am the only daughter to my Mom but I have one sister and one brother with different Mom. They now live with my Dad in South Africa. *(She is good at her scams... really good; – at least that's what she thought.)*

Friends4Dave (June 01 - 7:43:40 PM):   Where are you originally from?

Rasheed Zakari (June 01 - 7:44:17 PM):   I am originally from Ghana as I told you.

Friends4Dave (June 01 - 7:44:36 PM):   Ok.

Rasheed Zakari (June 01 - 7:45:05 PM):   I am from Ghana, born and raised in Ghana.

Friends4Dave (June 01 - 7:45:25 PM):   What about your parents?

Rasheed Zakari (June 01 - 7:46:12 PM):   My dad is born and raised in Ghana but now he lives in South Africa.

Friends4Dave (June 01 - 7:46:40 PM):   That's good .... and your Mom?

Rasheed Zakari (June 01 - 7:47:05 PM):   From Australia.

Friends4Dave (June 01 - 7:47:11 PM):   *(Dave found it hard to believe that Rasheed's father, who is a full-blooded Ghanaian, lives in South African while at the same time her mother, who is a full-blooded Australian, lives in Ghana; nevertheless, Dave thought that it was possible though highly improbable.)* Ok.

Rasheed Zakari (June 01 - 7:47:32 PM):   I hope you are trying to understand me very well.

Friends4Dave (June 01 - 7:48:23 PM):   Yes. I want to know who I opened my heart to yesterday. This is what I should have done first.

Rasheed Zakari (June 01 - 7:48:47 PM):   Yes ... you are right.

Friends4Dave (June 01 - 7:49:42 PM):   Tell me, why do you want a relationship with me? Tell me the real reason … good or bad .... Remember, I do not like lies.

Rasheed Zakari (June 01 - 7:50:44 PM):   I don't like Lies Either …

Rasheed Zakari (June 01 - 7:51:16 PM):   Well nothing. Well I am just trying to have a friend and if something comes in, then fine. I can handle it.

Friends4Dave (June 01 - 7:51:41 PM):   That is very good. So, we are on the same page. Therefore, this is your chance to really tell me why.

Rasheed Zakari (June 01 - 7:52:15 PM):   How you mean?

Friends4Dave (June 01 - 7:53:54 PM):   I want you to tell me exactly why you want me to become your friend. Tell me why you contacted me in the first place. Tell me why you allowed me to pour out my heart to you yesterday. Tell me what you really think and how you truly feel. That's what I mean.

Friends4Dave (June 01 - 7:55:34 PM):   Consider my questions as a job interview; an interview for the job that you really want and that will give you many benefits.

Rasheed Zakari (June 01 - 7:56:14 PM):   Well at first, I saw your profile on Flixster. So I decided to email you because I liked your profile... (*She changed the subject.*) ... and let me ask, did you Pour your heart to me yesterday, if so that is really good. I did too ...

Friends4Dave (June 01 - 7:56:41 PM):   Yes, I did.

Friends4Dave (June 01 - 8:00:10 PM):   I have never showed my apartment to anybody I do not know very well. But I showed it to you. That was really very foolish of me; but there is nothing I cannot correct, by the grace of God, if I want to, though. You probably saw a minimum of eight security cameras and other security systems last night when I panned over the rooms.

Those are just the ones that are visible to the eyes. I do not discuss the invisible ones; those are classified information. (*It was true that Dave's apartment had many security surveillance cameras and other security systems. Eight of the cameras were strategically placed where they could be seen, but there were hidden cameras too. There were also placards with "Electronic Surveillance" and "Security: 24-Hours Protected" written on the placards. There were other security equipments and apparatus that Dave just does not discuss with anyone.*)

Rasheed Zakari (June 01 - 8:01:30 PM):   I see.

Friends4Dave (June 01 - 8:02:00 PM):   So, for someone whom I just opened my heart to, don't you think that I have the right to ask the person some personal questions?

Rasheed Zakari (June 01 - 8:02:50 PM):   Yes, you have the right to, and I can see that is why you asked me many question, and I think that is very good of you.

Friends4Dave (June 01 - 8:03:19 PM):   What is it about me or my profile did you like?

Rasheed Zakari (June 01 - 8:03:39 PM):   All about you.

Friends4Dave (June 01 - 8:04:05 PM):   Please be specific.

Rasheed Zakari (June 01 - 8:04:28 PM):   Yes I a...

Rasheed Zakari (June 01 - 8:04:30 PM):   I am... (*Rasheed was unable to be specific.*)

Friends4Dave (June 01 - 8:05:12 PM):   How many people did you send such invitations to before you sent it to me? (*Earlier today before coming online, Dave did some background investigation on Rasheed. One of the things he found out was that Rasheed had posted the following message on the profiles of many Flixster members.*)

"RasheedZakari

My name is Rasheed 30 years of age single with no kids and a student studying accounting[31] who is now searching for the right man to spend the rest of her life with and i will like to know more about u and so if u have access to yahoo instant messenger then u can add me there as rasheed_zakari@yahoo.com so that we can chat there and know more about each other."

Rasheed Zakari (June 01 - 8:07:18 PM):   Oh well, few. I joined that site few days ago and after we chatted yesterday, I took my account off from there. (*She just lied again. She joined Flixster months ago, and her account was still active as of August 20th, when Dave checked her profile again at a much later date – more than two months after the statement she just made.*)

Friends4Dave (June 01 - 8:08:05 PM):   When exactly did you close the account?

Rasheed Zakari (June 01 - 8:08:35 PM):   Yesterday when we finished chatting. (*She was lying. Her account was still very active as of August 20th. According to her profile page, Rasheed "last logged in" on her Flixster.com account on August 16th, and the*

---

[31] Here, she claims to be a student studying Accounting. But she told Dave that she studied Journalism. At one time she even claimed that she had a Journalism degree; but later, she claimed that she could not continue her education. Dave noticed the conflicting stories.

account remained active as of the last time that Dave checked it out.)

Friends4Dave (June 01 - 8:09:46 PM):   Ok. How many people have you sent your invitations to after you and I were sending messages to each other, but before we chatted yesterday?

Rasheed Zakari (June 01 - 8:11:38 PM):   I sent to about 15 peoples but they showed no interest. (*She sent her invitations to a lot more than fifteen people, and many of them showed interest and were communicating with her and had exchanged email addresses with her. So, here was another lie.*)

Friends4Dave (June 01 - 8:13:04 PM):   Fine, no problem. How many people have you called "handsome" since you and I started corresponding with each other?

Rasheed Zakari (June 01 - 8:14:49 PM):   Hhahah Lol... Honestly many people. (*She finally told the truth.*)

Friends4Dave (June 01 - 8:15:16 PM):   Okay, not bad.

Friends4Dave (June 01 - 8:15:39 PM):   Do you know why I am asking you the last set of questions?

Rasheed Zakari (June 01 - 8:16:09 PM):   Oh no, I don't know. Tell me.

Friends4Dave (June 01 - 8:16:23 PM):   As a matter of fact, do you know why I am asking you all these questions?

Rasheed Zakari (June 01 - 8:17:29 PM):   No.

Friends4Dave (June 01 - 8:17:55 PM):   Did you notice on my profile that I am an experienced Ex-Investigator?

Rasheed Zakari (June 01 - 8:18:26 PM):   Not really.

Friends4Dave (June 01 - 8:19:46 PM):   Okay. Yesterday, I told you that I will investigate you... and I did. Furthermore, I am still conducting an investigation on you.

Rasheed Zakari (June 01 - 8:20:54 PM):   Oh yes, I guess so.

Friends4Dave (June 01 - 8:22:25 PM):   Like I told you yesterday, I say what I mean and mean what I say. I also keep my promises. There are things I have found out, some of which I asked you questions about. But, I will not discuss the other information with you.

Rasheed Zakari (June 01 - 8:23:26 PM):   I understand. I see you are a great man.

Friends4Dave (June 01 - 8:27:08 PM):   No. I am not a great man. But I like you already. It does not matter whether you are a man or woman, I am willing to have compassion on you and perhaps try to be your friend, not romantically, though; but you must tell me the whole truth. If I did not like you when I got upset, I would have reported you to the FBI and/or the INTERPOL. I just might still do that, depending on what you do from here on; and they can have you picked up where ever you are. Believe me, they can find anyone that they really want to get. All I need to do is send them the information I already have and they will do the rest. Do you understand what I am saying?

Rasheed Zakari (June 01 - 8:28:40 PM):   Yes, I am trying to understand what you are saying my dear, I think you are a

big man then, and may I ask you a question??
Do you deal with the government?

Friends4Dave (June 01 - 8:29:42 PM):   I will not answer that.
Remember that I just said I couldn't discuss
certain information with you?

Rasheed Zakari (June 01 - 8:30:18 PM):   Yes, you did… and I do
understand by the way. Sorry for asking.

Friends4Dave (June 01 - 8:31:20 PM):   I like you. Please do not try to
deceive me again. Is that okay with you?

Rasheed Zakari (June 01 - 8:32:13 PM):   Yes, no problem, and I won't
try to deceive you my dear... I am honest and
I'll try to tell you all the truth. Ok?

Friends4Dave (June 01 - 8:34:30 PM):   Fine then. I will not report you
and you will not be picked up. But tell me,
who really are you? I already know, but I want
you to tell me. That will not affect our
friendship; as long as you stop doing whatever
illegal activities that you have been involved in
until now. I can advice you on what not to do
henceforth – meaning, you must refrain from
doing anything which constitutes a crime – so
that you can avoid getting into trouble in the
future.

Friends4Dave (June 01 - 8:34:59 PM):   I just want to hear it from your
mouth. (*Dave was trying to get her to reveal
her true identity. But, it appeared someone
may have been watching over her and,
therefore, she could not really tell me the truth
about her real identity. Could the person
watching her be Hanson Opare ... her
boyfriend and accomplice in her scams?*)

Rasheed Zakari (June 01 - 8:35:00 PM):   I see.

Rasheed Zakari (June 01 - 8:35:34 PM):   Well dear .... to be honest I
                                            am who I say I am ... (*Rasheed threw Dave's
                                            phrase back at him.*)

Friends4Dave (June 01 - 8:36:11 PM):   Why do you prowl the
                                         Internet?

Rasheed Zakari (June 01 - 8:36:20 PM):   (*She ignored Dave's last
                                           question.*)   And I am me. I am not trying to lie
                                           to you or something ... All am saying it true ...
                                           please try to understand me. Ok ? I am not here
                                           for games or to play with someone's feelings
                                           ...

Friends4Dave (June 01 - 8:37:14 PM):   (*Dave was upset that she still
                                         refused to fully admit that she is a scammer.*)
                                         That will be all for today. Good night...

Rasheed Zakari (June 01 - 8:37:36 PM):   (*Alarmed.*)   Please what are
                                           you doing ??

Rasheed Zakari (June 01 - 8:37:37 PM):   Why ??

Friends4Dave (June 01 - 8:37:45 PM):   I have to go. (*Dave logged
                                         out. He did not see Rasheed's messages below
                                         until the next time he logged on to Yahoo!
                                         Messenger.*)

Rasheed Zakari (June 01 - 8:38:00 PM):   (*She panicked.*)   Please what
                                           do you want me to tell you? I will!

Rasheed Zakari (June 01 - 8:38:09 PM):   Please you don't have to do
                                           this!

Rasheed Zakari (June 01 - 8:38:55 PM):   Well, do you want the truth from me or what ???????????//

Rasheed Zakari (June 01 - 8:39:31 PM):   Talk to me! I know you are not gone! Ok!

Rasheed Zakari (June 01 - 8:41:17 PM):   Well I will talk to you tomorrow. Ok?

Rasheed Zakari (June 01 - 8:41:27 PM):   Bye if you need to go then. Ok?

Rasheed Zakari (June 01 - 8:41:50 PM):   Please try and talk with me tomorrow so I can tell you my secrets. Ok?

Rasheed Zakari (June 01 - 8:41:51 PM):   *<ding>* *(She buzzed Dave but he was already gone and did not respond.)*

Rasheed Zakari (June 01 - 8:41:56 PM):   Bye bye then. *(She logged out.)*

* * * * * * *

Some of the information about Rasheed Zakari were from the web links below. But the pictures were that of a man, not a woman. The pictures also indicated that it was the same person in Ghana.

Websites: http://www.Facebook.com/people/Rasheed-Zakari
http://www.idolbin.com/fprofile/1499791815
https://www.Facebook.com/Rashmatazz
http://crumbel.com/search/rashpyjamaz/
https://twitter.com/rashpyjamaz
https://www.Facebook.com/ebenezer.bassaw.54

Nevertheless, the image that Dave observed on the unsteady webcam, during his conversations with Rasheed, was that of a young lady. She was a brunette and possibly from India, Pakistan, Lebanon, Australia, or the Middle Eastern diasporas. But her voice sounded like an American or a Canadian. She also wrote more like an American or Canadian, except when she informed Dave that she told her mother about him when they were in the "market." That is a common terminology used in West African, including Ghana. Therefore, Dave suspected that Rasheed Zakari was possibly an American or Canadian, perhaps currently living in Ghana, and that the real person may be a male, not female. Or perhaps it was really a female, and she has a male accomplice.

Alternatively, the pictures on these websites may belong to a person who is totally innocent, and the person chatting with Dave online may have used this guy's name and image fraudulently. It is also possible that this guy (whose pictures are on the websites above) may have nothing to do with the Rasheed Zakari on Flixster.com. These were the possibilities, but the truth remained elusive.

Now let's briefly switch to Abigail Osei in the next chapter.

CHAPTER 12
ABIGAIL AND DAVE EXCHANGE EMAILS

𝕭elow are more email correspondences between Dave and Abigail:

"From: Abigail Osei [mailto:loveangle200@yahoo.com]
Sent: June 04, 2009 - 5:36 AM
To: Friends4Dave *(This email address was substituted.)*
Subject: MISS YOU

Hello Dave,

How are you doing?? And if I may ask, how is work?? I believe everything is fine and it is a long time since I heard from you and I wanted to know how you are doing…. I will like to hear from you... Abigail."

* * * * * * *

Dave send a reply email to Abigail that same day, and he included two of his pictures:

"Hi Abigail:

Thanks for your email. I really do appreciate it. Quite frankly, I have been thinking of you also … almost every day. I would like us to chat and see each other on the webcam. Please let me know when you would like us to do that. Hope to hear from you soon.

Be blessed,
Dave."

* * * * * * *

On June 6th 2009, Abigail sent another email to Dave:

"From: Abigail Osei [mailto:loveangle200@yahoo.com]
Sent: June 06, 2009 - 5:31 AM
To: Friends4Dave (*This email address was substituted.*)
Subject: THX FOR THE MAIL.

Hello Dave,

I am glad to hear from you and, if I may ask, how are doing?? I
hope you are fine as I am here. You have nice pictures. Wow,
you are so cute and let's find a time to view each other on cam if
you will like that... Until then, bye and have a nice day ...
Abigail."

CHAPTER 13
RASHEED'S DESPERATE ATTEMPTS TO CONTACT DAVE

𝔜esterday (June 1ˢᵗ), Dave went offline upset because Rasheed did not fully and expressly admit that she was a scammer. Since then, Rasheed had been making desperate attempts to contact Dave. The last set of conversations between Dave and Rasheed yesterday is reprinted below:

Friends4Dave (June 01 - 8:36:11 PM):   Why do you prowl the Internet?

Rasheed Zakari (June 01 - 8:36:20 PM):   (*She ignored Dave's last question.*) And I am me. I am not trying to lie to you or something ... All am saying it true ... please try to understand me. Ok ? I am not here for games or to play with someone's feelings ...

Friends4Dave (June 01 - 8:37:14 PM):   (*Dave was upset that she still refused to admit that she was a scammer.*) That will be all for today. Good night...

Rasheed Zakari (June 01 - 8:37:36 PM):   (*Alarmed.*) Please what are you doing ??

Rasheed Zakari (June 01 - 8:37:37 PM):   Why ??

Friends4Dave (June 01 - 8:37:45 PM):   I have to go. (*Dave logged out. He did not see Rasheed's messages below until the next time he logged back into Yahoo! Messenger.*)

Rasheed Zakari (June 01 - 8:38:00 PM):   (*She panicked.*) Please what do you want me to tell you? I will!

Rasheed Zakari (June 01 - 8:38:09 PM):   Please you don't have to do this!

Rasheed Zakari (June 01 - 8:38:55 PM):   Well, do you want the truth from me or what ???????????//

Rasheed Zakari (June 01 - 8:39:31 PM):   Talk to me! I know you are not gone! Ok!

Rasheed Zakari (June 01 - 8:41:17 PM):   Well I will talk to you tomorrow. Ok?

Rasheed Zakari (June 01 - 8:41:27 PM):   Bye if you need to go then. Ok?

Rasheed Zakari (June 01 - 8:41:50 PM):   Please try and talk with me tomorrow so I can tell you my secrets. Ok?

Rasheed Zakari (June 01 - 8:41:51 PM):   *<ding>* (*She buzzed Dave but he was already gone and did not respond.*)

Rasheed Zakari (June 01 - 8:41:56 PM):   Bye bye then. (*She logged out.*)

* * * * * * *

For the next few days, Rasheed tried to get in touch with Dave so that they could talk more, but Dave was not interested. He ignored Rasheed until the fourth day when he sent a reply message agreeing to chat with Rasheed in three days' time at 15:00 hrs. Meanwhile, Rasheed continued to try to contact Dave before the time scheduled by Dave. He just ignored her messages:

Rasheed Zakari (June 02 - 6:43:58 PM):   Hello. How are you doing?

Rasheed Zakari (June 03 - 7:07:41 PM):   Hello Dave. How are you doing? Hope you are well? Why did you do so, and why didn't you come online since we chatted last? Please come online so we can talk.

Rasheed Zakari (June 03 - 7:08:58 PM):   *<ding>* *(Rasheed buzzed Dave, but he was not online.)*

Rasheed Zakari (June 03 - 7:09:06 PM):   Are you there?

Rasheed Zakari (June 03 - 7:09: 13 PM):   *<ding>* *(She buzzed Dave again, but there was no response.)*

* * * * * *

Friends4Dave (June 04 - 1:56:33 PM):   *(Dave decided to respond on June 4th.)* Hi Rasheed. I will chat with you on June 07 at about 15:00 hrs (3:00 p.m.) my time, that is about 19:00 hrs (7:00 p.m.) your time. I am upset with you, but we can talk then.

* * * * * *

Rasheed Zakari (June 05 - 5:25:01 PM):   Please what made you upset with me? Please tell me when we meet on Sunday. Try and tell me what I did, so I can correct my Mistake… ok? Hope to chat with ya soon.

Rasheed Zakari (June 05 - 5:25:01 PM):   *<ding>* *(Rasheed buzzed Dave in desperation to get him to chat with him. But Dave did not respond.)*

* * * * * *

As promised, Dave went online at 15:00 hrs on June 7th but, again, Rasheed was late by one hour thirteen minutes.

Friends4Dave (June 07 - 3:01:10 PM):   Hi Rasheed, I am here as promised. (*Rasheed was not online yet. And Dave waited.*)

While still waiting for Rasheed, Dave noticed that Gracy came online at about 15:19 hrs, Dave's local time, and he initiated a conversation with her. See the next chapter for details.

* * * * * * *

Rasheed Zakari (June 07 - 4:13:49 PM):   (*Rasheed was 1 hour, 13 minutes late.*) Hi and how are you doing today honey?

Friends4Dave (June 07 - 4:14:55 PM):   (*Dave was thinking to himself: "Does she really think that she can woo me with her dangerous and poisonous sweet 'honey'?"*) I am fine, and you?

Rasheed Zakari (June 07 - 4:15:07 PM):   I am also fine honey.

Rasheed Zakari (June 07 - 4:15:14 PM):   I have really missed you a lot honey.

Friends4Dave (June 07 - 4:15:30 PM):   Please wait. I will be with you in a minute. (*Dave got up from his chair to stretch and walk around for a little while because his back was hurting really badly. Dave has serious back and neck problems that make it difficult for him to sit, stand, or walk for more than 15 minutes at a time without greatly exacerbating his back and neck pains. So, Dave had to get up from his chair to stretch frequently when chatting online. And in most cases, he used his laptop while sitting in a reclining position on his recliner, and he sometimes also chatted online using his Blackberry phone while lying down on a comfortable couch or the recliner, in order to minimize his pains as much as possible.*)

Rasheed Zakari (June 07 - 4:15:47 PM):   Okay.

Friends4Dave (June 07 - 4:17:23 PM):   Thanks for missing me.

Friends4Dave (June 07 - 4:17:39 PM):   Are you always late?

Rasheed Zakari (June 07 - 4:17:59 PM):   No honey, but I am sorry for today.

Friends4Dave (June 07 - 4:18:10 PM):   What happened?

Rasheed Zakari (June 07 - 4:18:50 PM):   Honey, it is just that I just went out to search for something to eat.

Friends4Dave (June 07 - 4:19:03 PM):   I see.

* * * * * * *

Dave's simultaneous conversation with Gracy ended amicably. See next chapter for details. However, Dave's conversation with Rasheed below did not end well.

Friends4Dave (June 07 - 4:20:09 PM):   How was your week?

Rasheed Zakari (June 07 - 4:20:24 PM):   Fine honey, but I have really missed you a lot.

Rasheed Zakari (June 07 - 4:20:38 PM):   So honey, what are you doing about the $100 that you said you were going to send?

Friends4Dave (June 07 - 4:22:23 PM):   I remember correctly what I said. I told you that I will not send you anything until I am satisfied about who you really are.

Rasheed Zakari (June 07 - 4:23:11 PM):   Okay but I hope you saw me on webcam.

Rasheed Zakari (June 07 - 4:23:31 PM):   So what more will you need as a verification?

Friends4Dave (June 07 - 4:23:33 PM):   You mean your doctored webcam?

Friends4Dave (June 07 - 4:24:09 PM):   Turn on your webcam, please.

Friends4Dave (June 07 - 4:24:41 PM):   (*He repeated his request.*) Turn on your webcam please.

Friends4Dave (June 07 - 4:24:55 PM):   I will turn mine on, too.

Rasheed Zakari (June 07 - 4:25:26 PM):   (*Rasheed stalled to buy herself more time to think about her next move.*) I will do that later today please.

Rasheed Zakari (June 07 - 4:25:31 PM):   Because a friend of mine came for the cam.

Friends4Dave (June 07 - 4:25:50 PM):   Okay. (*Dave sensed that Rasheed was lying to him again.*)

Friends4Dave (June 07 - 4:26:28 PM):   What secrets did you say you want to tell me?

Friends4Dave (June 07 - 4:30:16 PM):   (*After about four minutes of no response from Rasheed, Dave continued.*) If you are not prepared to chat, please let me know so that I can leave right now. I do not like to waste my time.

Rasheed Zakari (June 07 - 4:32:44 PM): (*Rasheed waited additional two minutes before responding.*) Hi Dave.

Friends4Dave (June 07 - 4:33:47 PM): (*Dave was now getting exasperated.*) I know you can see me now.

Rasheed Zakari (June 07 - 4:33:50 PM): You are looking so handsome today. (*Dave recognized Rasheed's comments as mere flattery intended to mollify him.*)

Rasheed Zakari (June 07 - 4:34:06 PM): (*She tried to steer him away from the real issues at stake with her poisonous ivy flattery.*) So tell me what has made you so handsome?

Friends4Dave (June 07 - 4:34:52 PM): (*Dave tactfully evaded her question.*) Thanks for the compliment.

Rasheed Zakari (June 07 - 4:35:09 PM): Do you love me Dave?

Friends4Dave (June 07 - 4:36:49 PM): I like you. But how can I love someone who does not want to tell me the truth? I want to love you, but I can't until you tell me the whole truth, which I already know anyway.

Rasheed Zakari (June 07 - 4:37:31 PM): So what do you want to know?

Friends4Dave (June 07 - 4:39:22 PM): The truth. I stopped chatting with you the last time because, even though some of your answers were truthful, you lied about what really matters. I want to hear the truth from you. I cannot continue as your friend unless and until you tell me the whole truth.

Rasheed Zakari (June 07 - 4:40:32 PM):   And what truth do you want me to tell you now?

Friends4Dave (June 07 - 4:41:25 PM):   Start with the "secrets" you said you wanted to tell me after I had logged off that day.

Rasheed Zakari (June 07 - 4:42:26 PM):   Is just that I love you and that I will want you to love me also.

Rasheed Zakari (June 07 - 4:42:39 PM):   And that I promise never to ever break your heart honey. (*Dave was thinking to himself, "Is that not what you promised just before you tried to swindle money from me?"*)

Rasheed Zakari (June 07 - 4:42:52 PM):   Because I really love you and I really want to spend the rest of my life with you.

Rasheed Zakari (June 07 - 4:43:10 PM):   And now you are telling me that there is something that I am not telling you the truth.

Rasheed Zakari (June 07 - 4:43:28 PM):   You are making me feel more worried and it makes me feel like you don't want me.

Rasheed Zakari (June 07 - 4:43:57 PM):   Just ask me about the truth that you will want to know.

Rasheed Zakari (June 07 - 4:44:02 PM):   And I am ready to tell you. Okay?

Rasheed Zakari (June 07 - 4:44:14 PM):   Because I am really confused now.

Friends4Dave (June 07 - 4:48:19 PM):   You probably did not believe me when I told you I know much about you already. For one thing, I know that you do not have an Accounting or Journalism degree as you claimed. I will not discuss the other pieces of information on you, which I obtained from other sources. I mean everything that I say, and I say exactly what I mean. If I did not like you, you would perhaps be arrested soon for trying to defraud me. Do you understand me? I am giving you the very last chance if you want to be my friend. You probably do not believe me when I told you before that I used to be an Investigator. So, let me show you something. *(Dave showed Rasheed the gold shields that he used when he was the Compliance Agent and Chief Investigator of his Investigative Agency, and his law enforcement shield had "Investigator: Chief" inscribed on it.)*

Rasheed Zakari (June 07 - 4:49:17 PM):   *(She became defensive again.)* Well I don't know what you are talking about. *(Dave knew from his past experiences with his ex-wife that when people say, "I don't know what you are talking about," it was usually an indication of their admission of guilt while at the same time lying to their teeth.)*

Rasheed Zakari (June 07 - 4:49:19 PM):   I will want to go for the webcam now. Okay? So, please be online and wait for me. I will be with you soon. I promise you. *(She immediately logged out.)*

Friends4Dave (June 07 - 4:49:43 PM):   Okay.

Friends4Dave (June 07 - 8:20:12 PM):   *(Dave waited for Rasheed for about 3 hours and 30 minutes, but Rasheed never returned. This further confirmed Dave's suspicions about her.)* Just as I thought .... I waited for you for about three-and-a-half hours. If you ever contact me again in any manner, I may report you to the FBI and/or the INTERPOL for them to investigate you further and possibly have you arrested. That is a promise!

Friends4Dave (June 07 - 8:22:28 PM):   In pursuit of your schemes to try to defraud me, you failed to realize that you were dealing with the wrong person. I investigated criminals like you for years in the past. No doubt, you probably think that you are very smart; and perhaps you are. But do you really think that someone cannot find you because you hide behind the computer at home or at Internet Cafés? Then I hate to tell you, you are very wrong! Please don't make me mad ... because if you do, I may report you to the FBI and/or the INTERPOL (International Police Organization), and you may be arrested by the FBI or INTERPOL at any time. So, watch yourself! I am warning you ..., please don't mess with me again! *(Obviously very upset.)*

Friends4Dave (June 07 - 8:25:06 PM):   I strongly suggest that you, Hanson Opare, and any of your other accomplices must stop defrauding people immediately. If you keep defrauding people, you will defraud the wrong person one of these days, and that person will find you wherever you are and then kill you. Remember that... you will get killed one of these days if you don't stop scamming people now. Not everyone will forgive you the same way I just did. You may not be so fortunate next time. Like I said previously, do not try to contact me again in anyway (chat, email, phone, etc.); otherwise, you and your accomplice(s) will eventually be arrested! I promise you that! *(Dave was really ticked off.)*

CHAPTER 14
GRACY MISSES DAVE

𝕯ave and Gracy have not talked with each other since June 1ˢᵗ 2009. Gracy came online while Dave was still waiting for Rasheed to show up for their scheduled chat. Dave immediately decided to initiate a conversation with Gracy and they chatted for a while. It was obvious that they missed each other very much, and it appeared that their affection for each other was growing stronger. Dave chatted with both Rasheed and Gracy simultaneously, until his conversation with Gracy ended amicably and he continued to chat with Rasheed alone (as presented in the preceding chapter).

Friends4Dave (June 07 - 3:19:13 PM):   Hi Grace! How are you?

Talk2bryan2001 (June 07 - 3:20:29 PM):   I miss you so... so... much. Honey what happened?

Talk2bryan2001 (June 07 - 3:20:59 PM):   Well sorry, don't mind my language. (*On second thought, Gracy did not want to appear too openly affectionate. As of the time Dave left Nigeria decades ago, it was not customary for a Nigerian female to be perceived as running after a Nigerian male. Most Nigerians also believe that the man was "supposed to pursue" the woman. Perhaps things have changed in Nigeria ... Dave was not sure.*)

Friends4Dave (June 07 - 3:21:05 PM):   I missed you, too. I had a busy week. Did you get my email?

Talk2bryan2001 (June 07 - 3:21:32 PM):   Did you get mine? (*Gracy had sent Dave an email with two pictures. Gracy's pictures basically showed her head. Dave evidently appreciated her sending the pictures*

149

to him, and he sent her a reply email thanking him for the pictures she sent.)

Friends4Dave (June 07 - 3:21:44 PM):   That's okay. Your language is fine with me.

Friends4Dave (June 07 - 3:22:26 PM):   I got your pictures and I responded. You are beautiful!

Talk2bryan2001 (June 07 - 3:24:07 PM):   You got me worried. I did not hear from you. You have no idea how that makes me feel.

Talk2bryan2001 (June 07 - 3:24:21 PM):   Thanks.

Friends4Dave (June 07 - 3:25:41 PM):   I am very sorry you were worried about me. I appreciate it though. The week did not go well with me, but I am blessed though. How was your week, my dear?

Talk2bryan2001 (June 07 - 3:27:19 PM):   Well, my week was great and my exams are starting tomorrow, by his grace.

Friends4Dave (June 07 - 3:28:00 PM):   That's good. I wish you the very best on your exams.

Talk2bryan2001 (June 07 - 3:30:33 PM):   Thanks. I tried calling.

Friends4Dave (June 07 - 3:30:52 PM):   I did not get any call from you.

Talk2bryan2001 (June 07 - 3:30:58 PM):   It was not going through.

Friends4Dave (June 07 - 3:31:17 PM):   Sorry about that.

Friends4Dave (June 07 - 3:31:55 PM):   Have you prepared for your exams?

Talk2bryan2001 (June 07 - 3:32:16 PM):   Yeah.

Friends4Dave (June 07 - 3:32:47 PM):   That's good. I wish you the best.

Talk2bryan2001 (June 07 - 3:33:20 PM):   Are you alone?

Friends4Dave (June 07 - 3:33:34 PM):   Yes, I am.

Talk2bryan2001 (June 07 - 3:33:46 PM):   Ok.

Friends4Dave (June 07 - 3:34:04 PM):   Why did you ask?

Talk2bryan2001 (June 07 - 3:36:51 PM):   Just asking. Okay?

Friends4Dave (June 07 - 3:37:07 PM):   That's fine.

Talk2bryan2001 (June 07 - 3:37:32 PM):   When can you call me?

Talk2bryan2001 (June 07 - 3:37:51 PM):   I sent two pictures.

Friends4Dave (June 07 - 3:38:36 PM):   I received the two pictures, and I sent you a reply. They are beautiful. Did you not get my reply?

Friends4Dave (June 07 - 3:39:05 PM):   Like I said, you are beautiful.

Talk2bryan2001 (June 07 - 3:39:24 PM):   I haven't checked.

Talk2bryan2001 (June 07 - 3:39:41 PM):   Thanks dear.

Friends4Dave (June 07 - 3:40:21 PM):   You are welcome, my dear. I will try and call you on Wednesday or

Thursday. I do not have enough credit to call you right now. (*Dave did not want to call Nigeria direct from his home phone because it was too expensive to do so. He didn't want his home phone to be disconnected later for non-payment. Therefore, he usually bought and used Internet Calling Cards to make calls to Nigeria.*)

Talk2bryan2001 (June 07 - 3:41:37 PM):   Well, I don't want to call you names. Just being conscious.

Talk2bryan2001 (June 07 - 3:42:10 PM):   Well, that's okay.

Friends4Dave (June 07 - 3:42:31 PM):   Go ahead... What names do you want to call me?

Talk2bryan2001 (June 07 - 3:42:56 PM):   Call me anytime. I will be glad you called.

Friends4Dave (June 07 - 3:43:28 PM):   I wish I could call you every day.

Friends4Dave (June 07 - 3:43:54 PM):   I will be glad to speak with you every day, if I could.

Friends4Dave (June 07 - 3:45:21 PM):   (*Gracy did not respond.*) Are you still there?

Talk2bryan2001 (June 07 - 3:45:48 PM):   Well, nice names, you know.

Friends4Dave (June 07 - 3:46:26 PM):   Go ahead ... my dear. Let me hear the names, please.

Talk2bryan2001 (June 07 - 3:46:37 PM):   Nice names, you know.

Friends4Dave (June 07 - 3:47:29 PM):   Tell me at least one or two.

Talk2bryan2001 (June 07 - 3:49:25 PM):   Hi dear.

Friends4Dave (June 07 - 3:49:59 PM):   Okay.

Friends4Dave (June 07 - 3:50:42 PM):   By the way, were you able to see my pictures, which I sent to you before?

Talk2bryan2001 (June 07 - 3:51:33 PM):   Sorry I am kind of slow. Well it's network. Ok?

Friends4Dave (June 07 - 3:52:00 PM):   That's okay. Please take your time, my dear.

Talk2bryan2001 (June 07 - 3:52:38 PM):   Yeah, I saw your videos also on the YouTube website you gave me.

Talk2bryan2001 (June 07 - 3:52:49 PM):   Nice.

Friends4Dave (June 07 - 3:53:09 PM):   That's good.... Thanks.

Friends4Dave (June 07 - 3:54:14 PM):   There are about 18 videos on that site. How many of them were you able to see and watch?

Talk2bryan2001 (June 07 - 3:55:16 PM):   Five of them.

Friends4Dave (June 07 - 3:55:49 PM):   That's good. Whenever you have the time, check out the rest of them, if you don't mind.

Talk2bryan2001 (June 07 - 3:57:34 PM):   Those pictures I sent are old pictures; but anyway, That was GRACY.

Friends4Dave (June 07 - 3:58:27 PM):   Okay. (*Gracy had told Dave on the phone the last time he called her that her real name is GRACE.*) Now, how does the new Grace look?

Talk2bryan2001 (June 07 - 3:58:44 PM):   Do you have them on your PC?

Friends4Dave (June 07 - 3:59:19 PM):   Yes, I saved them, and I look at them almost every day. (*Dave opened his Photo-Viewer and pulled up the two pictures.*)

Talk2bryan2001 (June 07 - 4:00:19 PM):   Really?

Friends4Dave (June 07 - 4:01:06 PM):   Yes, really. I am even opening them up now as I write.

Talk2bryan2001 (June 07 - 4:01:34 PM):   What game do like, honey?

Friends4Dave (June 07 - 4:01:51 PM):   Bowling ... but I have not been able to bowl for years now.

Friends4Dave (June 07 - 4:02:11 PM):   I also like to play Chess.

Talk2bryan2001 (June 07 - 4:02:27 PM):   Nice.

Friends4Dave (June 07 - 4:02:30 PM):   What about you?

Talk2bryan2001 (June 07 - 4:05:08 PM):   Well, I like watching football and like Chess too. (*Nigerian Football is called Soccer here in the United States.*)

Friends4Dave (June 07 - 4:06:22 PM):   I also like watching Football (American Football) and sometimes Soccer (Nigerian Football). You and I will play chess when we meet.

Friends4Dave (June 07 - 4:07:24 PM):   (*Dave sent Gracy the two pictures that she had previously sent to Dave.*) I just sent you two pictures. Check them and tell me what you see.

Talk2bryan2001 (June 07 - 4:07:30 PM):   That will be nice.

Talk2bryan2001 (June 07 - 4:08:26 PM):   I will, but not now. Okay?

Friends4Dave (June 07 - 4:10:11 PM):   Okay. I thought you could see them right on your screen. You will not be able to see them after we end the chat because they will be deleted automatically when one of us logs out. (*Dave did not realize that she could not view files sent while chatting on the mobile phone screen.*)

Talk2bryan2001 (June 07 - 4:10:44 PM):   Okay.

Friends4Dave (June 07 - 4:11:07 PM):   Just click on "accept" on your screen, please.

Talk2bryan2001 (June 07 - 4:11:53 PM):   Honey, I am mobile.

Friends4Dave (June 07 - 4:12:14 PM):   Okay, my dear, I forgot.

Friends4Dave (June 07 - 4:12:23 PM):   I am sorry.

Friends4Dave (June 07 - 4:12:48 PM):   The pictures I just sent you are yours, which you had sent to me.

Friends4Dave (June 07 - 4:13:26 PM):   I just wanted you to know that I really saved them on my computer.

Friends4Dave (June 07 - 4:14:37 PM):   I am sorry, I need to go. I have to be somewhere in about one hour 30 minutes.

I will talk to you later. Is that okay? (*Dave wanted to finalize his conversation with Rasheed with whom he was simultaneously chatting on Yahoo! Messenger.*)

Talk2bryan2001 (June 07 - 4:14:42 PM):   Well, I am planning to get a PC but the money I have is not enough. Hope to get a PC soon. Ok.

Talk2bryan2001 (June 07 - 4:15:26 PM):   Okay then.

Friends4Dave (June 07 - 4:15:57 PM):   Thanks a lot, my dear. I will keep thinking of you as usual.

Talk2bryan2001 (June 07 - 4:19:39 PM):   Me too.

Talk2bryan2001 (June 07 - 4:19:41 PM):   Bye dear.

Dave logged out and returned to chatting with Rasheed Zakari alone. (*See preceding chapter for details.*)

CHAPTER 15
DAVE INVESTIGATES ABIGAIL OSEI

The following morning, Abigail sent a message to Dave on the *Yahoo! Messenger*. Dave responded later in the day and requested that she send him her pictures, just as Dave had sent her his pictures. But Abigail never did. Dave then decided to investigate Abigail Osei.

Abigail Osei (June 08 - 7:05:45 AM): How are you doing?? and i have really miss you a lot and hope everything is moving on well out there. (*Dave was not available at the time Abigail left this message.*)

Friends4Dave (June 08 - 6:59:04 PM): Hi Abigail. (*Dave left the message below for her.*)

Friends4Dave (June 08 - 7:00:58 PM): I got your message. Please give me a date and time for you and me to chat online. Remember that I am about five or six hours behind your time in Ghana. Hope to talk with you soon; but in the meantime, please send me some pictures of yourself. Thanks. .... Dave.

A few days after Dave sent Abigail the above message, he decided to dig into Abigail's background before proceeding further with her. Dave explored Flixster and other websites on the Internet, as well as other sources of background information on her. He found out that Abigail had been soliciting dating relationships from other Flixster members, and the information from other sources seemed to indicate that she is a dating scammer using different identities on the Internet. The facts and data below are just some of the information Dave found, which may be about the same person who calls herself "Mandy Klimmy Anderson" on Flixster and who identified herself as "Abigail Osei" in her email to Dave. The information below also includes dating scammers in general and not necessarily related to Abigail Osei. Due credits for the information below are hereby given to http://www.delphifaq.com, which is the website where the information was obtained.[32]

"Dating scammer Osei Kwesi Accra Ghana kind_osei@hotmail.com **from Accra, Ghana:**

>Email: kind [mailto:kind_osei@hotmail.com]
>Osei Kwesi Box ms 395,
>Mile Seven-Achimota,
>Accra Ghana 00233."

* * * * * * *

The following comment was posted by an anonymous writer, who also included a picture of a Caucasian lady who claims to be Abigail Osei:

>"Alright i am here to help all of you guys. i work with the internet security department of an underground **security network** in Ghana and other [A]frican countries. we are eager to investigate such issues if the scammer gave you any phone number and then called you to confirm it, then just get me all necessary info about her and i will fish her out. Send all info to supportspeed@gmail.com."

Below are more website links to Abigail Osei's fraudulent accounts on Flixter.com alone:

>http://www.flixster.com/user/abigailnyarko31?lsrc=USR-PRO-URL.
>http://www.flixster.com/user/abigail4u2009?lsrc=USR-PRO-URL.
>http://www.flixster.com/user/biggles22gh?lsrc=USR-PRO-URL.
>http://www.flixster.com/user/sexzyabi?lsrc=USR-PRO-URL.
>http://www.flixster.com/user/abigailnyarko21?lsrc=USR-PRO-URL.
>http://www.flixster.com/user/abrahamofosuhene?lsrc=USR-PRO-URL.
>http://www.flixster.com/user/sweetberrycherrydiva?lsrc=USR-PRO-URL.

---

[32] The information can be found at this web address: http://www.delphifaq.com/faq/ russian_marriage. It should be noted that the information (including pictures) on this have changed over the years since Dave retrieved the data.

Below, you will find the warning message that someone, who calls himself "Agent 86 Maxwell Smart" from Salem in the United States, posted on www.delphifaq.com. Agent 86 Maxwell Smart, one of thousands of people who have apparently been scammed online, posted this warning message at http://www.delphifaq.com/faq/russian_ marriage. (The message below was edited a little bit for punctuation, grammar, and style only;[33] but most of the errors have been left intact):

"Anyone who will read this !!!!!!!!!!!!!!!!!!!!!!!

I would write to each individual posting here but that would take forever besides writing the very same thing that would get real old. Well, I see Sheep ready for the slaughter here.

Everyone one of you is connected to a scammer. That's right, all of you, if you are connected online to anyone at all from Ghana, Nigeria, Dakar, Senegal, Refugee Camp, Gold Coast, Ivory Coast, all of West Africa, you are hooked up with a scammer. NO EXCEPTIONS !!

There isn't a single Girl online from West Africa no matter if they are White or Black, Woman or Man, it's a 100% certainty it's a scammer.[34] Not only are you hooked up with a scammer,

---

[33] It was necessary to edit it a little with punctuations only because one could really not make much sense reading it the way it was originally written. Other errors have been left intact.

[34] Agent 86 Maxwell Smart's claims that anyone "online" in West Africa is "a 100% certainty it's a scammer" are ridiculous and completely false. His statement is also based on his greedy quest to exploit West Africans, and he is angry because he failed woefully. His foolish claim that all West Africans online are "scammers" and his use of the term "Black Guy" are racist and very offensive. If he felt that way about all West Africans, then what was he doing in West Africa anyway? Was he trying to defraud West Africans (like Western countries have historically done to African countries for centuries)? Has he succeeded in defrauding Africans, or did he only succeed in finding himself been scammed in West Africa? While there is no justification for what the real scammers in West Africa (and anywhere else for that matter) do, is Agent 86 Maxwell Smart angry because he failed in his own attempts to defraud West Africans? Yes, they are scammers in West Africa, but not all of them. Similarly, there are scammers in Europe, Asia, Middles East, and North and South Americas; but not all of them. Besides, investigation into online scamming indicates that some unscrupulous scammers in Russia and China pose as Nigerians and Ghanaians in their fraudulent schemes. Would it be fair to conclude that all Russians and all Chinese are scammers? Would that not be a ridiculous and false conclusion?

---

nearly 100% of those are men. It is completely impossible that you are not talking to a scammer. Get over all the Love talk, Your He / She is telling you. Scammers use Fake names. They can appear on webcam as a Girl, They can fake the voice on a phone, They have many e mail addresses, and they have many phone numbers.

They use stolen photos. You can try to chase down the fictional person made up by the scammer all you want, it won't do anything except delay you finding out it's a scammer. If you knew to delete anyone that contacted you from West Africa, then thousands of scams would be prevented. It should take you less than one second to tell if it's a scammer. When, I first came to this site, I was just like you are. I would not listen to warnings either. Well, You can fallow in my footsteps if you want to. LOL. I did not listen and now, I'm Homeless. You can lose your Ass if you want to. But, I am telling you the truth. There isn't any chance at all you're hooked up with anyone other than a Black Guy sitting on His Butt in an Internet Café if your Sweetie has any connection to West Africa. Well if you listened to me then stop all contact with the scammer now. Never tell a scammer about this site. Never post your email address on this site.

If you have made that mistake then contact Peter the site administrator: ptiemann_2000@yahoo.com. Tell, Him the name of this thread. Page # 52 if it's this page. Give the Date and time also. You need to get your e mail address removed before hundreds of scammers fill you inbox. Scammers watch this site constantly. Never tell any scammer how you learned the truth. They only lie more as they have been confronted before. It also helps teach them how to scam someone else better. Remember there is not a single person online from West Africa that's not a scammer. Well, I hope the best for you. Post everything you have on your scammer to help others.

Kind Regards Agent 86 Maxwell Smart \\'^o^'//"

* * * * * * *

The warning above by "Agent 86 Maxwell Smart" is a helpful reminder to potential victims of online scams that the consequences of being scammed can be disastrous. In his case, he became homeless, which is very sad and unfortunate. There is no justification whatsoever for what the scammer(s) did to Agent 86 Maxwell Smart. What happened to him can also happen to you too, if you are not careful. Having said that, it is important also to note that Agent 86 Maxwell Smart's conclusions are grossly erroneous and racist, and indicated in the footnote.

Let's turn now to another scammer, Rasheed Zakari, whom Dave met online. To Dave, the warning by another victim of online scams below seemed to describe Rasheed Zakari's *modus operandi*. The warning was posted on http://www.delphifaq.com by Jerry, from the United States, who was defrauded by an online dating scammer. As an online scam victim, Jerry was trying to warn another potential victim not to fall prey to the scammer:

> "Hello Anonymous from the United States:
>
> Do not, Repeat, Do not send money for any reason. You are hooked up with a scammer. It is almost 100% positive that if you were contacted by her first somehow. Plus if she is white at all. There are no white woman[35] in Ghana Africa online. Just guys using stolen photo's of models. I was contacted on Christianmingle. These people have no problem using Christianity.
>
> If you stay hooked up with this scammer, don't be surprised if you [are] not made to feel guilty for not sending money. They play on your emotions. They have done this for years and

---

[35] Jerry's assertion that there "are no white woman in Ghana Africa online" is not true. The fact is, that there are many White people (men and women) living in West African, including Ghana and Nigeria. Some are even citizens of their respective West African countries. Some are businessmen and businesswomen. Some are diplomats. Some are spies. Some are there just because they love to live there. With so many White people living in Nigeria and Ghana in today's global technology World, it is inconceivable that "no white woman" would be "online". These are the facts. If Jerry still does not believe these facts, then he needs to visit Ghana and Nigeria.

know exactly what to say. They also make mistakes. Your gut must be telling you something is wrong. Your gut is right. I Lost over $1500.00 USD to most likely the same scammer. Do not be surprised when she wants to masturbate while you talk to her. Just remember you [are] most likely talking to a guy. That should wake you up. Yes they have girls help them. But the voice never matches the photo. She or He will get very angry if you press for answers to simple questions.

Never post your email address on this site and never tell your scammer where you got your information from. Try running the photo you most likely got through the picture search at the bottom of this page. I bet even if you don't find it if you post it, I can find plenty of the same girl for you. I have a very big collection of pictures from many scammers. I keep getting contacted by them. They try everything to stop me. From helping someone like you. I bet *she loves to talk with falling hearts on Yahoo messenger.*

Please contact me direct if you want to. I am not afraid to post my email address as they haven't been able to do anything to me. But, I'm always ready for them. I have several new scammers to post myself. I gave my scammer the nick name of Angel and have noticed it has been used ever since.

Please do not send money to a stranger. There is no way she could Love You. You just met. They will tell any lie they have to in order to get money from you. Try demanding they appear live on cam. I bet they say they don't have a cam. Or they want you to pay for it. There are Internet Cafés all over Accra, Ghana. They are filled with scammers that work 24 - 7 The Cafés don't close. They are mostly guys in their 20's doing this. Well, I hope, I have said enough. Please save yourself from losing money for nothing and getting your feelings trashed by a heartless ass hole.

Kind Regards Jerry \\'^o^'//"

* * * * * * *

Sad. Isn't it? Anyway, Dave found out later when he looked deeper into Abigail Osei's background that she has posted dating messages on several other Flixster members' profiles, soliciting dating relationships from them. Below are just a few examples of her solicitations, before and after she contacted Dave for a relationship with him. She preyed on men abroad and didn't want to deal with men from Ghana. Due credits for the information below are given to http://www.Flixster.com.

For example, below was a message Abigail Osei posted on Emery Rebelclass' profile at: http://www.flixster.com/user/rebelclass/comments.

lovemandycare:

"Hello Dear,

How are you today? and how is things moving with you? hope fine and you are in good health. My name is Abigail Osei, I am looking for a very nice person of love, caring, sincere, easy going, matured, and understanding, then after going through your profile now on this site (flixter.com) i pick interest in you, so i will like you to write me via my email address which is as follow (Loveangle200@yahoo.com) so that i will give you my picture for further discussion, because i am really looking forward for a serious friendship with you.

Yours New Friend Abigail."

* * * * * * *

It was also obvious to Dave that Abigail has been preying on innocent people who live abroad (outside of Ghana). Here was her response posting on a fellow Ghanaian's profile (Samuel Lartey) on Flixster at http://www. flixster.com/user/lsamuel71, because Samuel Lartey asked for dating relationship with Abigail:

Lovemandycare:

"I don't need any male friends from Ghana and i am engaged ok."

Yet, Abigail Osei continued to post dating invitations like the one below for many people; including someone called Tom Chaberlain, on his online Flixster.com profile at: http://www.flixster.com/user/toma1mac?lsrc= USR-PRO-URL.

Lovemandycare:

"Hello I am Abigail and i will like us to be friends and know each other if you don't mind. This is my email address Loveangle200@ yahoo.com and i will like you to send me a mail and tell me more about you. I will be happy to hear from you.... Abigail"

Furthermore, at the time of this investigation, Abigail Osei had several accounts on Flixster at http://www.flixster.com. There was also an "Abigail Osei" that recently signed up at the Minekey dating site. This Abigail Osei is also from Ghana, the same country that the one on Flixster is from, too. The picture posted on her profile, on the Minekey website, had two black girls, one of whom was supposed to be Abigail Osei. None of the girls in the picture on the Minekey website had any semblance to Abigail Osei's pictures in any of her profiles on Flixster.com. There was not much background information in her profile on the Minekey website at the time of this inquiry: http://minekey.com/user/mk/abigail-osei/?id=50157.

There was yet another Abigail Osei with a different picture (in a pink dress) who was prowling the dating site called Friendster. This Abigail's information was somewhat similar to that posted on Flixster. Both are from Ghana. But the picture is totally different from all the other pictures seen so far, which include several Caucasians and Blacks. This time, Abigail's profile on Friendster at http://www.friendster.com/photos/ 29480995/ 298692539/14975, states: [36]

---

[36] As with all the comments of the people involved in this book, Dave did not edit what was said, except in very few occasions when it was absolutely necessary to improve the

"**About Me:** I am a young African lady of 30 yrs of age and single..I am black in complexsion and am a fashion designer by profession..I am 5 ft 6 inches tall..I am a Christian and love to swim and play with kids in my free time.

Who I Want to Meet: I am here looking for a trust and a honest man that is ready for a long time relationship. I want any man around the globe...who is loving and caring."

* * * * * * *

Based on the information gathered online about Abigail Osei, who also called herself "Mandy Klimmy Anderson" on Flixster.com, Dave decided not to proceed with his relationship with her. Granted, the people with the name Abigail Osei on the different websites (many of which are not included in this book) may or may not be the same Abigail that Dave met on Flixster, but Dave did not want to take any chances on her. The fact that Abigail did not send Dave her true pictures, as Dave repeatedly requested from her, did not sit well with him. In Dave's opinion, it was best to end the relationship before his feelings get hurt by another scammer.

---

readability. So, Dave wrote Abigail's comments (including the typographical errors) exactly as she had originally written them, without any corrections.

CHAPTER 16
THE AFFECTION BETWEEN DAVE AND GRACY GROWS STRONGER

It has been exactly one week since Dave and Gracy chatted online, even though Dave called her a few days ago and spoke with her on the telephone. The affection between them appeared to be growing deeper and stronger.

Talk2bryan2001 (June 14 - 5:47:15 PM):   Helloooooww....

Friends4Dave (June 14 - 5:49:27 PM):   Hi Grace!

Talk2bryan2001 (June 14 - 5:50:29 PM):   Gracy is cool. And you?

Friends4Dave (June 14 - 5:50:33 PM):   I'm so sorry. My computer is very slow when it is downloading updates. I saw you, but I could not type anything as I signed onto Yahoo!

Friends4Dave (June 14 - 5:50:57 PM):   I'm blessed, thank you.

Friends4Dave (June 14 - 5:51:31 PM):   My computer has finished downloading security updates. Now I can type normally.

Talk2bryan2001 (June 14 - 5:51:59 PM):   Ok.

Friends4Dave (June 14 - 5:52:16 PM):   How was your week?

Talk2bryan2001 (June 14 - 5:52:29 PM):   But it shows you are offline.

Talk2bryan2001 (June 14 - 5:52:31 PM):   Why?

Friends4Dave (June 14 - 5:52:59 PM):   I am online. Does it show that
                                        I am offline?

Talk2bryan2001 (June 14 - 5:53:17 PM):   Yes.

Friends4Dave (June 14 - 5:53:27 PM):   Hummmnn .... (*Dave
                                        wondered why that was.)*

Friends4Dave (June 14 - 5:53:44 PM):   Let me check something.
                                        (*Dave checked his online status, and it showed
                                        that he was logged in as "Invisible to Others.
                                        So, he changed the status to "Visible to All".)*

Talk2bryan2001 (June 14 - 5:54:34 PM):   Ok now it shows you are
                                        online. You signed in invisible, right?

Friends4Dave (June 14 - 5:54:56 PM):   It shows here that I am online
                                        now. There may be some problem with my
                                        computer or something ... if it is still showing
                                        that I am offline on your screen.

Friends4Dave (June 14 - 5:55:36 PM):   I may have inadvertently
                                        signed in as invisible.

Friends4Dave (June 14 - 5:55:55 PM):   But it shows here that I am
                                        visible.

Talk2bryan2001 (June 14 - 5:55:56 PM):   It shows you are online now.

Friends4Dave (June 14 - 5:56:05 PM):   Ok good.

Friends4Dave (June 14 - 5:56:25 PM):   Have you completed all your
                                        exams?

Talk2bryan2001 (June 14 - 5:57:05 PM):   (*She missed Dave's question.)*
                                        Hope you are having a great weekend.

Talk2bryan2001 (June 14 - 5:57:21 PM):   (*She now answers Dave's question about her exams at school.*) Yes, I have.

Friends4Dave (June 14 - 5:57:42 PM):   Yes, I am having a great weekend. Thanks for asking. That is great that you have finished all your exams!

Talk2bryan2001 (June 14 - 5:57:52 PM):   I finished on Friday.

Friends4Dave (June 14 - 5:58:34 PM):   My weekend was quiet. But my friend and his wife just lost their unborn baby. I found out today, and that has made me very sad.

Talk2bryan2001 (June 14 - 5:58:47 PM):   (*She missed Dave's comment about his friend's loss of their unborn baby.*) I care a lot about you, you know.

Friends4Dave (June 14 - 5:59:26 PM):   I appreciate that. I think about you a lot, too.

Talk2bryan2001 (June 14 - 5:59:45 PM):   (*Gracy now responded to Dave's comment about the loss of the baby.*) Oh I am so sorry dear.

Friends4Dave (June 14 - 6:00:04 PM):   Me too, I am so sorry about it. I feel so bad for them. They wanted the baby so badly, and she was only a couple of months left before she could have delivered the baby, at least prematurely.

Friends4Dave (June 14 - 6:01:17 PM):   I feel like calling you every day, but I cannot due to funds. Nevertheless, I periodically check to see if you are online so that I could chat with you, but I didn't see you whenever I came online.

Talk2bryan2001 (June 14 - 6:01:24 PM):   Do you think you were going to meet me online?

Friends4Dave (June 14 - 6:02:04 PM):   I mostly come online now to see if you are there.

Talk2bryan2001 (June 14 - 6:02:35 PM):   Okay.

Talk2bryan2001 (June 14 - 6:03:46 PM):   I missed talking with you, my ....

Friends4Dave (June 14 - 6:04:54 PM):   I missed you, too, my dear.

Friends4Dave (June 14 - 6:05:20 PM):   *(Dave reminisced on how pleasant he felt each time she laughed during their telephone conversations in the past.)* I love your laughs...

Talk2bryan2001 (June 14 - 6:05:44 PM):   Honey, I sent you a request on Skype. Did you get it?

Friends4Dave (June 14 - 6:06:13 PM):   No, I did not. When did you send it? I checked Skype, my email, and *Yahoo! Messenger* about three days ago.

Talk2bryan2001 (June 14 - 6:06:46 PM):   2 days ago.

Friends4Dave (June 14 - 6:07:36 PM):   Okay. Let me check it now. Please be patient ... my computer is going to be slow again now that I am opening another program ...

Talk2bryan2001 (June 14 - 6:08:09 PM):   Ok.

Talk2bryan2001 (June 14 - 6:08:25 PM):   Maybe you should do that
                   later.

Talk2bryan2001 (June 14 - 6:08:49 PM):   Sweetheart!

Friends4Dave (June 14 - 6:08:53 PM):   Alright then ...

Friends4Dave (June 14 - 6:09:24 PM):   I wish you were closer to me
                   here ...

Talk2bryan2001 (June 14 - 6:09:40 PM):   Well. Hope you don't mind
                   the names?

Friends4Dave (June 14 - 6:10:06 PM):   No, I don't mind at all.

Talk2bryan2001 (June 14 - 6:10:23 PM):   Because that's what I feel like
                   calling you.

Friends4Dave (June 14 - 6:10:57 PM):   That is fine with me, my
                   sweetheart.

Friends4Dave (June 14 - 6:11:39 PM):   You may call me that anytime
           ... (*Dave was pleased that Gracy was
           affectionate.*)

Talk2bryan2001 (June 14 - 6:12:23 PM):   If it's ok by you.

Friends4Dave (June 14 - 6:12:36 PM):   Yes.

Talk2bryan2001 (June 14 - 6:13:38 PM):   Honey, do you still go to
                   work?

Talk2bryan2001 (June 14 - 6:14:19 PM):   How is your baby girl?

Friends4Dave (June 14 - 6:14:49 PM):   (*Dave still did not want to tell
          her yet that he is currently disabled and unable*

to work currently.) I have not gone to work for a while. My daughter is fine, thanks you.

Talk2bryan2001 (June 14 - 6:15:04 PM):   Hope you heard from her.

Friends4Dave (June 14 - 6:15:10 PM):   (*Dave missed her last comment.*) How are your parents?

Friends4Dave (June 14 - 6:15:34 PM):   (*Dave responded to Gracy's question about whether he has heard from his daughter.*) Yes, I spoke to her a few days ago.

Friends4Dave (June 14 - 6:15:51 PM):   I appreciate that, sweetheart.

Friends4Dave (June 14 - 6:16:01 PM):   Do you mind me calling you "my dear", and "my sweetheart"?

Talk2bryan2001 (June 14 - 6:16:59 PM):   (*Gracy responded to Dave question about how her parents are.*) Fine but they both traveled. So I am home alone now.

Talk2bryan2001 (June 14 - 6:18:06 PM):   (*She now responded to Dave's question about whether she minds if Dave calls her "my dear" and "my sweetheart".*) If that's what you wish to call me, well it's ok then.

Friends4Dave (June 14 - 6:18:57 PM):   If you don't like it, I will not call you that. You just let me know what you prefer I call you.

Talk2bryan2001 (June 14 - 6:20:07 PM):   Honey, I am fine with that. Okay?

Friends4Dave (June 14 - 6:20:28 PM):   Okay then.

Friends4Dave (June 14 - 6:21:01 PM):   (*Dave changed the subject.*)

So, you are back in Lagos?

Talk2bryan2001 (June 14 - 6:21:14 PM):   No.

Friends4Dave (June 14 - 6:21:40 PM):   In what state is Delta State University?

Friends4Dave (June 14 - 6:21:52 PM):   I mean in what city is Delta State University?

Talk2bryan2001 (June 14 - 6:22:12 PM):   (*She misunderstood Dave's question.*) My family house in Delta.

Talk2bryan2001 (June 14 - 6:23:25 PM):   Sweetheart, are you there?

Friends4Dave (June 14 - 6:23:53 PM):   Ok. What city is your university located in? (*Dave now responded to her last comment.*) Yes, I am here, sweetheart.

Talk2bryan2001 (June 14 - 6:24:40 PM):   (*She answered Dave's question about the location of her university.*) Agbor.

Friends4Dave (June 14 - 6:24:47 PM):   Ok.

Friends4Dave (June 14 - 6:24:55 PM):   Thanks dear. (*Glad that she finally answered his question.*)

Friends4Dave (June 14 - 6:25:12 PM):   I really missed you.

Talk2bryan2001 (June 14 - 6:25:15 PM):   And I was in Benin yesterday. (*Benin City is the city where Dave was born and grew up.*)

Talk2bryan2001 (June 14 - 6:25:30 PM):   Me too, I really missed you very much.

Friends4Dave (June 14 - 6:25:46 PM): Oh, you were in Benin. How was it?

Friends4Dave (June 14 - 6:26:08 PM): I haven't been there since 2001.

Talk2bryan2001 (June 14 - 6:26:32 PM): Okay.

Friends4Dave (June 14 - 6:27:22 PM): How long did you stay in Benin City?

Friends4Dave (June 14 - 6:30:16 PM): (*Dave's computer was slowing down again.*) My computer is acting up again.

Friends4Dave (June 14 - 6:31:43 PM): (*Gracy did not answer Dave last question, but Dave asked her another question.*) When you sent me the request on Skype, what screen name did you use?

Friends4Dave (June 14 - 6:35:20 PM): (*After about eight minutes of no response from Gracy, Dave wondered what was going on.*) Are you there?

Talk2bryan2001 (June 14 - 6:36:58 PM): I lost my connection.

Talk2bryan2001 (June 14 - 6:37:16 PM): Well, I am back now.

Friends4Dave (June 14 - 6:37:20 PM): (*Happy that she was back online and responding.*) Ok. I was concerned.

Talk2bryan2001 (June 14 - 6:37:51 PM): I know sweetheart.

Friends4Dave (June 14 - 6:38:29 PM): What screen name did you use to send me the request on Skype? I just checked, your request did not come through.

Talk2bryan2001 (June 14 - 6:39:09 PM):   I used "Gracy."

Friends4Dave (June 14 - 6:39:42 PM):   I mean what did you type in as my screen name?

Friends4Dave (June 14 - 6:40:11 PM):   You will need to type in my name for it to come to me.

Talk2bryan2001 (June 14 - 6:41:01 PM):   I typed in "Dave-Washington".[37]

Talk2bryan2001 (June 14 - 6:41:37 PM):   I guess so.

Friends4Dave (June 14 - 6:42:17 PM):   That is the correct one. I wonder why it did not come through. And I searched again three days ago for your screen name that you gave me, but I could not find anyone with the screen name of "Gracy" in Nigeria or the United States that matches your name.

Friends4Dave (June 14 - 6:43:16 PM):   Please would you kindly check it again and send me the request one more time. I really would like us to be able to call each other very often and for free on Skype.

Talk2bryan2001 (June 14 - 6:44:50 PM):   Ok dear, I will but not now. I am mobile that's why I really need a PC.

Talk2bryan2001 (June 14 - 6:45:49 PM):   I used "swtisy" as the search name.[38] Ok?

---

[37] This screen name has been substituted.
[38] Dave wondered why she would use a different name "Swtisy" on Skype, and why she said a moment ago that she used "Gracy" on Skype.

Friends4Dave (June 14 - 6:46:19 PM):   That is fine. Or, if you would like me to sign you up for another account and then link my account and yours together, I will be happy to do so.

Friends4Dave (June 14 - 6:46:42 PM):   Ok. Let me try search for "Swtisy" now. (*Dave logged in to his Skype account and searched for "Swtisy". He found it. He added her to his Contacts. Then he returned to Yahoo! Messenger to continue his chat with Gracy.*)

Friends4Dave (June 14 - 6:48:03 PM):   Yes! That's it! I just added you, sweetheart!

Talk2bryan2001 (June 14 - 6:48:23 PM):   Okay.

Friends4Dave (June 14 - 6:48:58 PM):   All you need to do now is accept my request and you can call me free anytime on Skype-to-Skype!

Friends4Dave (June 14 - 6:49:48 PM):   As soon as you have accepted my request, I will also call you.

Talk2bryan2001 (June 14 - 6:50:27 PM):   Okay, but like I said, not now because I am using my phone. (*She became impatient with Dave.*)

Talk2bryan2001 (June 14 - 6:50:39 PM):   Okay.

Talk2bryan2001 (June 14 - 6:51:53 PM):   Sweetheart?

Friends4Dave (June 14 - 6:52:08 PM):   Okay. I am sorry. I forgot that you are using a mobile phone. I just thought your mobile phone has Skype built-in, just as it is in the United Kingdom and in Italy.

Friends4Dave (June 14 - 6:52:37 PM):   I was just excited that we can finally connect and communicate on Skype... that's all.

Friends4Dave (June 14 - 6:53:31 PM):   You see, I feel the same way you feel about me....

Talk2bryan2001 (June 14 - 6:55:04 PM):   Yeah, I have Skype on my phone,[39] but that's not the phone I am using at the moment to chat.

Friends4Dave (June 14 - 6:55:24 PM):   Oh, I see.

Friends4Dave (June 14 - 6:56:02 PM):   *(Dave decided to change the subject.)* When will your school resume again?

Talk2bryan2001 (June 14 - 6:56:24 PM):   *(Seemed happy that Dave changed the subject.)* Next month.

Friends4Dave (June 14 - 6:56:36 PM):   Next month?

Friends4Dave (June 14 - 6:56:54 PM):   Don't you have the summer off?

Talk2bryan2001 (June 14 - 6:57:35 PM):   Emmm... yeah, but... *(She did not want to complete the sentence.)*

Friends4Dave (June 14 - 6:58:29 PM):   But what, dear?

Talk2bryan2001 (June 14 - 7:00:11 PM):   Well, we do honey.

Friends4Dave (June 14 - 7:01:06 PM):   *(Dave began to wonder*

---

[39] Dave noticed that many people in Nigeria have multiple mobile phones with multiple carriers, and he wondered why that was. Here in the United States, people have usually have just one cell phone with a single carrier.

whether she was really a university student; and, if she was truly a student, why was her university resuming just one month after its end of academic year major exams?) If you do have the summer off, then why are you going back to school next month?

Talk2bryan2001 (June 14 - 7:03:21 PM):   (*She mulled over the question for about two minutes before she responded.*) Honey, it's Nigeria we are talking about, not USA.

Friends4Dave (June 14 - 7:03:51 PM):   (*Dave thought, "She's got a good point." Since Dave had not lived in Nigeria for about twenty years now, he thought that she might be right.*) Okay. I'm sorry.

Friends4Dave (June 14 - 7:04:20 PM):   What time is it now there?

Talk2bryan2001 (June 14 - 7:04:22 PM):   Our system of education here in Nigeria is quite different from yours in the United States.

Talk2bryan2001 (June 14 - 7:05:23 PM):   12:10 a.m.

Talk2bryan2001 (June 14 - 7:06:09 PM):   What's the time there?

Friends4Dave (June 14 - 7:06:25 PM):   Oh, I am really sorry for keeping you up that late. Do you want to go? We can chat again tomorrow sometime, if you like?

Friends4Dave (June 14 - 7:06:52 PM):   It is 19:06 hrs here. That's 7:06 p.m.

Friends4Dave (June 14 - 7:08:57 PM):   Would you like us to end our conversation now and then chat again tomorrow?

Talk2bryan2001 (June 14 - 7:09:36 PM):   Hey honey, I'm doing this because I _____ you.

Friends4Dave (June 14 - 7:10:13 PM):   You can complete the sentence ....

Talk2bryan2001 (June 14 - 7:10:41 PM):   Hey.

Friends4Dave (June 14 - 7:11:02 PM):   I am waiting....

Talk2bryan2001 (June 14 - 7:11:28 PM):   Honey?

Talk2bryan2001 (June 14 - 7:11:47 PM):   Sweetheart?

Friends4Dave (June 14 - 7:11:51 PM):   Yes, sweetheart?

Friends4Dave (June 14 - 7:12:51 PM):   Please complete the sentence you started: "I'm doing this because I ___ you".[40]

Talk2bryan2001 (June 14 - 7:13:39 PM):   I care so much about you.[41] Okay? Please you do have that in mind.

Friends4Dave (June 14 - 7:15:09 PM):   I am honored. I feel the same way about you. That is why I think about you almost all the time. And I wish you were closer to me here. But I know that with time, you and

---

[40] Dave sensed that she wanted to say "because I love you." However, Dave also knew, at least as of the time he left Nigeria, that it was not customary for a woman to be that straightforward when she is dating a man. That was supposed to be the man's obligation until the couple's relationship was well established.

[41] This was as far as Gracy could go; which was essentially a confession that she was deeply in love with Dave.

I shall meet, if our relationship continues in its current direction.

Talk2bryan2001 (June 14 - 7:16:04 PM):   Yeah, I know that too.

Talk2bryan2001 (June 14 - 7:16:28 PM):   My dearest Dave.

Friends4Dave (June 14 - 7:16:52 PM):   The way I feel about you is like you and I have already met, my sweetheart.

Talk2bryan2001 (June 14 - 7:17:36 PM):   Same here, you know...

Friends4Dave (June 14 - 7:18:13 PM):   (*Dave was now determined to do dating chats only with Gracy and to work towards a lasting relationship with her, if possible.*) That is good. I need you to be patient, please. With time, everything will be alright.

Talk2bryan2001 (June 14 - 7:19:40 PM):   Yeah, I know and I will keep praying for you. Okay?

Friends4Dave (June 14 - 7:20:11 PM):   I appreciate that. And I will pray for you, too.

Talk2bryan2001 (June 14 - 7:20:11 PM):   Honey, it's well... late.

Talk2bryan2001 (June 14 - 7:20:35 PM):   It's well... okay.

Friends4Dave (June 14 - 7:21:21 PM):   Alright, Sweetheart. With that, you may go to bed and we shall chat again tomorrow. Is that okay?

Talk2bryan2001 (June 14 - 7:22:45 PM):   I love you! [42]

---

[42]   There it was. She finally said it!

Friends4Dave (June 14 - 7:22:55 PM):   I love you, too. (*Dave reciprocated.*)

Friends4Dave (June 14 - 7:23:55 PM):   What time do you want us to chat tomorrow? Your time.

Talk2bryan2001 (June 14 - 7:24:14 PM):   Well, that's okay by me. We will chat tomorrow.

Friends4Dave (June 14 - 7:25:05 PM):   What time?

Talk2bryan2001 (June 14 - 7:25:07 PM):   8:00 p.m.

Talk2bryan2001 (June 14 - 7:25:31 PM):   I miss you.

Friends4Dave (June 14 - 7:26:03 PM):   Okay. I will see you at 18:00 hrs your time tomorrow. I'll miss you, too. Goodnight Sweetheart!

Friends4Dave (June 14 - 7:26:38 PM):   I meant to say 20:00 hrs (8:00 p.m.) your time.

Talk2bryan2001 (June 14 - 7:26:46 PM):   Have a good night's rest.

Friends4Dave (June 14 - 7:27:04 PM):   And may you have sweet dreams ....

Friends4Dave (June 14 - 7:27:25 PM):   Sweet dreams, Sweetheart .... (*Dave fell in love. Dave and Gracy went offline.*)

CHAPTER 17
JEALOUSY AND UNCERTAINTY CAUSE A STRAIN IN THE RELATIONSHIP

Gracy chatted with Dave until late in the night (her local time) last night. Dave could not wait to resume chatting with her today. Dave was truly falling in love with Gracy, and he believed that she was in love with him, too. At least, Gracy had indicated a few times during chats and on the telephone that she cared so much about Dave and that she loved Dave. And Dave believed her. So, today, they continued from where they left off last night. However, jealousy caused a strain in their relationship.

Friends4Dave (June 15 - 2:58:18 PM):   Hi Sweetheart!

Talk2bryan2001 (June 15 - 2:58:57 PM):   Hello Dear!

Friends4Dave (June 15 - 2:59:10 PM):   How was your day?

Talk2bryan2001 (June 15 - 2:59:22 PM):   Good day!

Friends4Dave (June 15 - 2:59:30 PM):   Wonderful.

Talk2bryan2001 (June 15 - 2:59:34 PM):   Fine.

Friends4Dave (June 15 - 3:00:10 PM):   *(Dave confessed.)* I missed you. I have been thinking about you since last night.

Talk2bryan2001 (June 15 - 3:02:17 PM):   Me too honey.

Friends4Dave (June 15 - 3:02:36 PM):   Good.

Friends4Dave (June 15 - 3:02:59 PM):   What did you do today?

Talk2bryan2001 (June 15 - 3:08:41 PM):   It has rained all through today, and right now it's so cold down here.[43]

Talk2bryan2001 (June 15 - 3:09:54 PM):   Sweetheart.

Friends4Dave (June 15 - 3:10:46 PM):   *(Dave stood up for a moment to stretch his aching back and neck.)* Yes. I'm back, sorry.

Friends4Dave (June 15 - 3:10:59 PM):   How cold is it?

Talk2bryan2001 (June 15 - 3:11:36 PM):   My dear, very cold.

Friends4Dave (June 15 - 3:11:40 PM):   Do you have the A/C on?

Talk2bryan2001 (June 15 - 3:11:58 PM):   Nope.

Friends4Dave (June 15 - 3:12:49 PM):   It is surprising that Nigeria could be that cold, except in Jos, of course. I know Jos can be really cold for Nigeria's standard. My brother used to live there, and I visited there a few times when I lived in Nigeria. But now, that would be a perfect weather for me.

Friends4Dave (June 15 - 3:13:20 PM):   I meant Jos Plateau State can be really cold for most Nigerians.

Friends4Dave (June 15 - 3:14:00 PM):   Hope you have enough plankets to cover yourself?

Friends4Dave (June 15 - 3:14:13 PM):   I meant "blankets", not "plankets." Sorry.

---

[43] What Gracy considered "so cold" was likely a perfect weather for Dave since he had lived in the United States now for about two decades.

Talk2bryan2001 (June 15 - 3:14:27 PM):   Yeah.

Friends4Dave (June 15 - 3:14:36 PM):   What is wrong with me today? I am misspelling words.

Talk2bryan2001 (June 15 - 3:14:40 PM):   I do have some blankets.

Friends4Dave (June 15 - 3:14:50 PM):   Great then!

Friends4Dave (June 15 - 3:15:30 PM):   I hope you get warm very soon.

Talk2bryan2001 (June 15 - 3:15:36 PM):   Hey, but I can read it because I know what you mean. So don't worry about it. Ok?

Friends4Dave (June 15 - 3:16:00 PM):   I appreciate that, and thanks sweetheart.

Talk2bryan2001 (June 15 - 3:16:04 PM):   I hope so too; that I get warm soon.

Friends4Dave (June 15 - 3:16:45 PM):   What are you doing right now?

Talk2bryan2001 (June 15 - 3:17:39 PM):   Eaten.

Talk2bryan2001 (June 15 - 3:17:59 PM):   Eating.

Friends4Dave (June 15 - 3:18:12 PM):   (*Apologetically.*) I'm sorry. Maybe you should finish eating before we chat ….

Friends4Dave (June 15 - 3:18:40 PM):   I will wait ...

Talk2bryan2001 (June 15 - 3:19:19 PM):   Hey, no! I am fine chatting with you.

Friends4Dave (June 15 - 3:20:45 PM):   I admire you. When I eat, I concentrate on my eating and do not do anything else.

Talk2bryan2001 (June 15 - 3:21:56 PM):   Oh really! But you should know that I am doing this for you.

Friends4Dave (June 15 - 3:23:22 PM):   I appreciate that ... But I can and should also do something for you by waiting for you to finish eating before we chat. I will be willing to wait for you. Please, I insist.

Talk2bryan2001 (June 15 - 3:24:28 PM):   Can I call you Babee! Well, not this kind of little "baby".

Talk2bryan2001 (June 15 - 3:24:39 PM):   You know.

Friends4Dave (June 15 - 3:24:53 PM):   You can call me whatever you like.

Talk2bryan2001 (June 15 - 3:27:56 PM):   Okay then, I will like to call you that.

Friends4Dave (June 15 - 3:28:22 PM):   Fine.

Talk2bryan2001 (June 15 - 3:28:42 PM):   That's what I would like to call my Dave.

Friends4Dave (June 15 - 3:30:13 PM):   I like all the names you have called me: Honey, Sweetheart, Dear, and Babee! They are all fine with me, my sweetheart.

Friends4Dave (June 15 - 3:31:58 PM):   You are a romantic lady. And I like that very much.

Talk2bryan2001 (June 15 - 3:33:30 PM):   I am glad you are okay with it.

Friends4Dave (June 15 - 3:33:58 PM):   I am okay with them all, my sweet lady.

Friends4Dave (June 15 - 3:35:12 PM):   What name do you prefer I call you? Sweetheart, Dear, Honey, Sweet Lady ...?

Talk2bryan2001 (June 15 - 3:37:35 PM):   Emm.... well, the one you prefer. Ok?

Friends4Dave (June 15 - 3:39:21 PM):   They are all good to me. But I would like you to pick your favorite.

Talk2bryan2001 (June 15 - 3:42:54 PM):   Babee and honey.

Friends4Dave (June 15 - 3:44:34 PM):   That's fine, Honey. I will call you these two names Babee.

Talk2bryan2001 (June 15 - 3:45:54 PM):   Okay. So tell me the once you prefer I call you.

Friends4Dave (June 15 - 3:46:27 PM):   *(Dave missed Gracy's last request.)* One of these days, I will be able to hold you close in my arms, and go on long walks holding each other's hands.

Friends4Dave (June 15 - 3:47:45 PM):   Actually, I prefer Honey, Baby, or Sweetheart; especially Honey.

Talk2bryan2001 (June 15 - 3:47:58 PM):   Really? Well, that will be nice.

Friends4Dave (June 15 - 3:48:22 PM):   Yes. Really.

Talk2bryan2001 (June 15 - 3:49:51 PM):   Okay honey!

Friends4Dave (June 15 - 3:50:34 PM):   Have you been to the movies?

Talk2bryan2001 (June 15 - 3:52:38 PM):   Emm... not really.

Friends4Dave (June 15 - 3:53:07 PM):   I would love to take you to the movies.

Talk2bryan2001 (June 15 - 3:53:32 PM):   I feel like I am not interested.

Talk2bryan2001 (June 15 - 3:53:51 PM):   Okay babe.

Friends4Dave (June 15 - 3:54:02 PM):   You are not interested in movies?

Friends4Dave (June 15 - 3:55:16 PM):   Don't you like watching movies on television?

Talk2bryan2001 (June 15 - 3:57:11 PM):   Of course, I like movies. But going to the movie house? Nope, I prefer watching movies at home.

Friends4Dave (June 15 - 3:57:55 PM):   Okay then. We will watch them at home.

Friends4Dave (June 15 - 3:58:35 PM):   I am a home person myself; but sometimes, I like to go out once in a while.

Friends4Dave (June 15 - 4:00:34 PM):   The movie theatres here are really nice.

Talk2bryan2001 (June 15 - 4:01:07 PM):   Babee!

Friends4Dave (June 15 - 4:01:22 PM):   Yes, honey?

Talk2bryan2001 (June 15 - 4:04:34 PM):   Okay.

Friends4Dave (June 15 - 4:06:03 PM):   I didn't realize it is 16:00 hrs already. I will need to get back to what I was doing. When shall we chat again?

Talk2bryan2001 (June 15 - 4:06:43 PM):   What kind of work.

Friends4Dave (June 15 - 4:07:21 PM):   I need to make a phone call.

Friends4Dave (June 15 - 4:08:07 PM):   Plus, there are some documents I have to prepare and send to the U.S. Department of Education.

Talk2bryan2001 (June 15 - 4:08:43 PM):   What's your kind of job honey?

Friends4Dave (June 15 - 4:09:15 PM):   I am not working right now; but I used to be an investigator, law enforcement officer, a Realtor, and a businessman. I thought I told you before. I apologize if I didn't.

Friends4Dave (June 15 - 4:09:33 PM):   As a Realtor, I used to help people with home purchase. I still have my license; but I just don't work right now.

Talk2bryan2001 (June 15 - 4:10:14 PM):   Okay.

Friends4Dave (June 15 - 4:10:33 PM):   A Realtor gets paid commission only if the person finally buys the house. It takes months for one transaction to complete.

Talk2bryan2001 (June 15 - 4:10:45 PM):   Do you have a house in Nigeria?

Friends4Dave (June 15 - 4:11:04 PM):   No. Not yet. But I plan to in the future.

Talk2bryan2001 (June 15 - 4:12:09 PM):   Okay, do you have a house in USA?

Friends4Dave (June 15 - 4:13:09 PM):   I did. But I left that for my ex-wife when we ended our marriage in 2008 due to adultery and after our separation in 2005. I have not purchased another yet. I cannot afford it right now. Houses are very expensive in the United States.

Friends4Dave (June 15 - 4:14:14 PM):   I currently rent a three-bedroom apartment.

Talk2bryan2001 (June 15 - 4:14:35 PM):   Why did you leave the house for her?

Talk2bryan2001 (June 15 - 4:15:57 PM):   Is that one of the Constitution of the United States?

Friends4Dave (June 15 - 4:16:59 PM):   We bought it together. Plus, my daughter lives with her. It was the right thing to do. If I had insisted on selling the house, it would also adversely affect my own daughter. Besides, my ex-wife stood by me while I was going to school. I cannot forget the good things she did in the past; and I do not want to talk about the negatives about her. I left the house for her because I believe that it was the right thing to do.

Friends4Dave (June 15 - 4:18:21 PM):   (*Dave now responded to her question about whether his decision to leave the house for his ex-wife, when they separated, had any relationship with the United States' Constitution.*) No, my decision has nothing to do with the Constitution of the United States.

Friends4Dave (June 15 - 4:20:01 PM):   And by God's grace, I will buy another house again.... It's just a matter of time.

Talk2bryan2001 (June 15 - 4:20:25 PM):   Okay.

Talk2bryan2001 (June 15 - 4:20:25 PM):   Why did you break up?

Friends4Dave (June 15 - 4:23:19 PM):   There were just too many lies, mischief, and many irreconcilable differences that lasted for almost throughout the marriage; and she was not willing to change. I hate such things. Anyway, I was wrong too, because I committed adultery. She asked for a divorce three years after our last separation because of the adultery. I was also increasingly becoming miserable and angry. I don't like to be angry. Before our separation, I gave her a five-year deadline to change; or else, I would leave. Things did not change; if fact, things got much worse.[44] It was time to separate again in 2005, and the marriage ended in 2008 on the grounds of adultery when she demanded a divorce.

Friends4Dave (June 15 - 4:38:03 PM):   (*After about 15-minutes.*) You didn't respond after I answered your questions why my marriage ended. And you signed out without saying goodbye? Did you get offended because I answered your question?

Friends4Dave (June 15 - 4:39:02 PM):   Goodbye then .... (*Dave was upset and he logged out too.*)

---

[44] That was as far as Dave could go on describing how terrible his marriage was. He did not want to give any details that would reveal how treacherous, vicious and malicious his ex-wife was to him. On the other hand, she was sometimes very kind and supportive; but always with some ulterior motives.

CHAPTER 18
DAVE IGNORES GRACY FOR TWO WEEKS

Dave ignored Gracy for two weeks because he was so upset about Gracy logging out without saying goodbye on June 15th. Giving Grace the benefit of doubt that perhaps there was a good reason for why she logged out last night, he went online periodically all day June 16th, but Gracy did not come online. Dave figured that Gracy's going offline the previous day was therefore not accidental but rather deliberate. So, for the next couple of weeks, he ignored Gracy's phone calls and chat messages, including the chat messages on June 17th below:

Talk2bryan2001:   Honey, are you there?

Talk2bryan2001:   BUZZ!!! (*She tried to buzz Dave.*)

Talk2bryan2001:   Are you there?

* * * * * *

After about two weeks of not speaking to Gracy, Dave decided to accept her invitation to chat on July 03. Gracy was already online when Dave logged in.

Talk2bryan2001 (July 03 - 2:42:58 PM):   Hi.

Talk2bryan2001 (July 03 - 2:43:10 PM):   Are you there?

Friends4Dave (July 03 - 2:43:25 PM):   Hi.

Talk2bryan2001 (July 03 - 2:44:37 PM):   Why have you kept silent all
                           this while?

Friends4Dave (July 03 - 2:44:51 PM):   You know why.

Talk2bryan2001 (July 03 - 2:45:04 PM):   *(She missed Dave's last comment.)* Anyway, how are you?

Talk2bryan2001 (July 03 - 2:45:21 PM):   Why?

Friends4Dave (July 03 - 2:45:28 PM):   *(Dave missed her question about why he had been silent.)* I'm fine. And you?

Talk2bryan2001 (July 03 - 2:45:33 PM):   Please dear, tell me.

Talk2bryan2001 (July 03 - 2:45:54 PM):   *(She answered Dave's question about how she was doing.)* I'm great.

Friends4Dave (July 03 - 2:46:00 PM):   *(Dave responded to Gracy's request for him to tell her why he had been silent for the past two weeks.)* You broke my heart.

Talk2bryan2001 (July 03 - 2:46:18 PM):   I missed you.

Friends4Dave (July 03 - 2:46:39 PM):   Thanks. But I was trying to forget you.

Talk2bryan2001 (July 03 - 2:46:46 PM):   But honey, it is not what you think. Ok?

Friends4Dave (July 03 - 2:47:12 PM):   What was it then?

Talk2bryan2001 (July 03 - 2:50:10 PM):   My connection was slow the last time we chatted online. So that's why I left like that. Ok? It's not because of anything else. I'm really sorry. I never knew you took it that far and I was so worried about you.

Talk2bryan2001 (July 03 - 2:50:51 PM):   Honey.

Talk2bryan2001 (July 03 - 2:51:15 PM):   I'm sorry okay.

Friends4Dave (July 03 - 2:51:21 PM):   *(Dave forgave her.)* Okay. I thought you logged off because I told you the truth.

Friends4Dave (July 03 - 2:52:38 PM):   And I was hoping that you would leave me a message the following day or so if it was a connection problem that you had. Nevertheless, your apology is accepted.

Talk2bryan2001 (July 03 - 2:53:18 PM):   And I am glad you told me the truth. Okay?

Friends4Dave (July 03 - 2:53:40 PM):   I am sorry, too, for not keeping in touch with you since then.

Talk2bryan2001 (July 03 - 2:54:56 PM):   Although I never expected it for you, but it's okay.

Talk2bryan2001 (July 03 - 2:55:12 PM):   But it's okay.

Friends4Dave (July 03 - 2:55:42 PM):   What did you not expect for me, dear?

Talk2bryan2001 (July 03 - 2:56:24 PM):   How you handled it.

Friends4Dave (July 03 - 2:56:55 PM):   I know some people may not agree; but I thought it was the right thing to do.

Talk2bryan2001 (July 03 - 2:56:59 PM):   You never called.

Friends4Dave (July 03 - 2:57:56 PM):   I'm sorry I didn't call. I really was trying to forget you, but I could not. I truly care about you.

Talk2bryan2001 (July 03 - 2:58:09 PM):   Really? Well it's okay.

Friends4Dave (July 03 - 2:58:42 PM):   How have you been since I last chatted with you?

Talk2bryan2001 (July 03 - 2:58:59 PM):   (*She responded to Dave's comment that he truly cares about her.*) You should know that I do too.

Talk2bryan2001 (July 03 - 2:59:33 PM):   I've been doing great.

Friends4Dave (July 03 - 2:59:45 PM):   Wonderful!

Friends4Dave (July 03 - 3:00:02 PM):   I missed you.

Talk2bryan2001 (July 03 - 3:00:52 PM):   Me too.

Friends4Dave (July 03 - 3:01:44 PM):   Are your grades out yet at school?

Talk2bryan2001 (July 03 - 3:02:42 PM):   No.

Talk2bryan2001 (July 03 - 3:03:07 PM):   How is work?

Friends4Dave (July 03 - 3:03:10 PM):   I hope you aced it all!

Friends4Dave (July 03 - 3:03:21 PM):   Fine, thank you.

Talk2bryan2001 (July 03 - 3:03:47 PM):   By his grace.

Friends4Dave (July 03 - 3:04:18 PM):   I went to New York with my daughter for a few days. Came back on Tuesday afternoon.

Talk2bryan2001 (July 03 - 3:05:04 PM):   Hope you had fun.

Friends4Dave (July 03 - 3:05:19 PM):   Yes, moderately so. (*Dave did not want to tell her that he went for medical reasons to consult his neurosurgeon in New York.*)

Talk2bryan2001 (July 03 - 3:05:21 PM):   And how is your daughter?

Friends4Dave (July 03 - 3:05:32 PM):   She is fine, thank you.

Talk2bryan2001 (July 03 - 3:06:03 PM):   Nice.

Friends4Dave (July 03 - 3:06:20 PM):   Are you hearing from your parents? How are they doing?

Talk2bryan2001 (July 03 - 3:07:12 PM):   Just hold on for me. I will be back. Okay? They are fine, thanks.

Talk2bryan2001 (July 03 - 3:07:40 PM):   I will be right back. (*Dave did not know where she was going.*)

Talk2bryan2001 (July 03 - 3:13:53 PM):   (*She returned.*)   Honey?

Friends4Dave (July 03 - 3:14:01 PM):   Yes, dear.

Talk2bryan2001 (July 03 - 3:14:05 PM):   I am back now.

Friends4Dave (July 03 - 3:14:17 PM):   Alright.

Friends4Dave (July 03 - 3:14:41 PM):   Are you still in Agbor, or are you now in Lagos?

Talk2bryan2001 (July 03 - 3:17:12 PM):   Agbor. Just trying to do one or two things so that I can get myself a PC.

Talk2bryan2001 (July 03 - 3:17:13 PM): Because honey I really need a PC.

Friends4Dave (July 03 - 3:17:15 PM): (*Dave signed back in after he was temporarily logged out.*) Are you there?

Friends4Dave (July 03 - 3:17:55 PM): I understand.

Friends4Dave (July 03 - 3:18:12 PM): What does a PC cost in Nigeria?

Talk2bryan2001 (July 03 - 3:18:15 PM): Ok.

Talk2bryan2001 (July 03 - 3:19:53 PM): 95,000 Naira, but I already have 60,000 Naira with me now.

Friends4Dave (July 03 - 3:22:37 PM): I will try and send you something in August, even though it will not cover the balance you need. My funds for July are already depleted.

Talk2bryan2001 (July 03 - 3:25:23 PM): Okay, thanks.

Talk2bryan2001 (July 03 - 3:26:03 PM): How can you send it?

Friends4Dave (July 03 - 3:26:23 PM): MoneyGram.

Talk2bryan2001 (July 03 - 3:26:32 PM): Honey.

Friends4Dave (July 03 - 3:26:47 PM): Yes?

Talk2bryan2001 (July 03 - 3:28:00 PM): Okay, that's nice. Thanks.

Friends4Dave (July 03 - 3:28:40 PM): Please don't thank me yet. Get the money first before any thanks.

Talk2bryan2001 (July 03 - 3:30:06 PM): Why? Or are you not sure about that?

Friends4Dave (July 03 - 3:30:43 PM): I am sure. I am a person of my word.

Friends4Dave (July 03 - 3:31:26 PM): I don't say what I will not do.

Friends4Dave (July 03 - 3:32:36 PM): But get the money first before you thank me; otherwise, you will be given me too many gratitude.

Friends4Dave (July 03 - 3:35:09 PM): What is the official exchange rate for the dollar now in Nigeria?

Talk2bryan2001 (July 03 - 3:35:59 PM): Oh okay. But please do know that I appreciate you a lot just as a person, and not anything. Okay?

Friends4Dave (July 03 - 3:36:21 PM): I know that. (*Dave believed that, and that was why he fell in love with Gracy.*)

Friends4Dave (July 03 - 3:37:11 PM): And that is why I think I am falling in love with you.

Talk2bryan2001 (July 03 - 3:39:01 PM): Really?

Friends4Dave (July 03 - 3:39:11 PM): Yes, really.

Talk2bryan2001 (July 03 - 3:43:56 PM): Baby!

Talk2bryan2001 (July 03 - 3:43:56 PM): Honey!

Talk2bryan2001 (July 03 - 3:43:57 PM): Sweetheart!

Talk2bryan2001 (July 03 - 3:43:57 PM):   Are you all in one?

Friends4Dave (July 03 - 3:44:56 PM):   (*Dave did not want to blow his trumpet.*) Perhaps. I know what I say is true.

Talk2bryan2001 (July 03 - 3:45:49 PM):   Sweetheart, are you there?

Friends4Dave (July 03 - 3:46:11 PM):   That is why I could not forget you even when I tried to for the past two weeks. I really think that I am falling in love with you, honey.

Talk2bryan2001 (July 03 - 3:48:36 PM):   Wow... what can I say! I am just being short of words to say.

Friends4Dave (July 03 - 3:49:13 PM):   That is alright. You don't have to say anything for now.

Talk2bryan2001 (July 03 - 3:50:03 PM):   I really care about you, you know.

Talk2bryan2001 (July 03 - 3:50:16 PM):   So much.

Friends4Dave (July 03 - 3:50:56 PM):   Thanks. I truly appreciate that and I appreciate you very much.

Friends4Dave (July 03 - 3:52:34 PM):   When I wake up in the morning, I often think about you. During the day, I think about you a lot. And before I go to sleep, I think about you also.

Friends4Dave (July 03 - 3:54:23 PM):   And I come online only to see if you are there, in most cases.

Talk2bryan2001 (July 03 - 3:54:24 PM):   Thanks.

Friends4Dave (July 03 - 3:54:48 PM):   You are welcome.

Friends4Dave (July 03 - 3:55:49 PM):   Anyway, how is the weather now there.

Talk2bryan2001 (July 03 - 3:56:18 PM):   Your number is not going through? Please get a new line.[45]

Friends4Dave (July 03 - 3:56:41 PM):   What number did you call?

Talk2bryan2001 (July 03 - 3:57:27 PM):   I will be glad if you do so, so that I will be able to reach you.

Talk2bryan2001 (July 03 - 3:57:53 PM):   I called the number you gave me.

Friends4Dave (July 03 - 3:58:36 PM):   It is working fine. What number did you call?

Friends4Dave (July 03 - 3:59:04 PM):   Let me log on to Skype and call you from there.

Talk2bryan2001 (July 03 - 3:59:56 PM):   I called +1-760-748-4126. That was the number you gave me.

Friends4Dave (July 03 - 4:00:52 PM):   No, that's not my number. *(Dave was thinking: "Perhaps she is mistaking me for someone else who might have given her that number. I know that I couldn't have given her that wrong number.")* That was not the phone number I gave to you. My number is +1-757-271-6756. [46]

---

[45] Dave thought to himself: "This is now Nigeria where you can just get a new phone line anytime you feel like it or where people get multiple phone lines just to show off." Besides, Dave does not like showing off.

[46] This number no longer belongs to him.

Talk2bryan2001 (July 03 - 4:01:53 PM):   Are you there?

Friends4Dave (July 03 - 4:01:54 PM):   I don't know the number you just stated. (*Dave wondered if she was confusing him with someone else.*)

Friends4Dave (July 03 - 4:02:34 PM):   I'm here. Try my number. It is +1-757-271-6756.

Friends4Dave (July 03 - 4:03:20 PM):   I will wait for you to call; but if you can't, then I will log on to Skype and call you. (*Dave was inadvertently logged out by the system.*)

Talk2bryan2001 (July 03 - 4:08:55 PM):   But you gave it to me.

Friends4Dave (July 03 - 4:13:01 PM):   (*Dave was able to log back in after about ten minutes of no connection. As usual, Dave used the time to stretch his back, shoulders, and neck that were hurting so badly, as usual, for sitting more than about 15 minutes at a time.*) Sorry, I was logged off. I am having some connection problems, I suppose. I'm afraid that was not the number I gave to you. It must be a mistake. I don't even know which state in the United States that number is from.

Friends4Dave (July 03 - 4:13:41 PM):   My number is 1-757-271-6756.

Friends4Dave (July 03 - 4:14:01 PM):   Try to call it and I will pick up.

Friends4Dave (July 03 - 4:15:40 PM):   (*After waiting for about a minute and his phone did not ring.*) Are you going to try calling my number now, or do you want me to call you?

Friends4Dave (July 03 - 4:20:02 PM): *(Gracy did not respond.)* Are you there?

Talk2bryan2001 (July 03 - 4:27:15 PM): I will call but not now honey. Is that ok?

Friends4Dave (July 03 - 4:27:34 PM): That is fine.

Talk2bryan2001 (July 03 - 4:28:07 PM): Okay.

Friends4Dave (July 03 - 4:28:57 PM): If you are busy now, that's okay by me. We can log off and then you can call me when you are ready. Is that okay with you?

Talk2bryan2001 (July 03 - 4:29:30 PM): Baby, I am feeling sleepy now. It's my bed time.

Friends4Dave (July 03 - 4:30:10 PM): Alright. Call me tomorrow. Good night.

Talk2bryan2001 (July 03 - 4:30:22 PM): I am feeling sleepy now. It's my bedtime.

Friends4Dave (July 03 - 4:30:53 PM): That's fine, honey. Call me tomorrow.

Friends4Dave (July 03 - 4:31:05 PM): Good night.

Talk2bryan2001 (July 03 - 4:31:14 PM): Okay my honey.

Talk2bryan2001 (July 03 - 4:32:36 PM): LOVE FROM ME TO YOU. *(Then Gracy called Dave. He picked up but she did not speak before hanging up.)*

Friends4Dave (July 03 - 4:39:56 PM): I just got your call; but you did not speak when I answered. Please call me back when you can. (*Gracy logged out. When Dave did not get another call from her, he figured that she just called his number to make sure it is a valid number. Dave logged out too.*)

CHAPTER 19
HUMOR IS UPLIFTING!

𝔜es, humor is uplifting! The following day, July 4th 2009, when Gracy did not call by the afternoon (Dave's time) as expected, Dave then called Gracy on the phone as promised. He also called her the next day, too (July 5th). They had very lively and friendly conversations. They laughed out loud those two days, and they even joked about one of them being the President of Nigeria and the other being the Vice President so that they can both clean up the corrupt practices in Nigeria. Nevertheless, they also recognized the dangers of trying to rid Nigeria of corruptions because of the fact that many disgruntled and corrupt people in Nigeria would stop at nothing to prevent any real progress in the country.

A day after their last telephone conversation on July 5th, Dave and Gracy met online again and chatted below, as arranged during their last telephone conversation the day before:

Friends4Dave (July 06 - 3:05:29 PM):   Hi Honey! Are you there?
                                         (*Even though Gracy was online, she did not respond for about twenty minutes. Dave thought that she was perhaps very busy doing something else and did not know that he was online; so he waited for her.*)

Talk2bryan2001 (July 06 - 3:25:49 PM):   HI DEAR

Friends4Dave (July 06 - 3:26:14 PM):   Hi!

Friends4Dave (July 06 - 3:26:19 PM):   How are you?

Talk2bryan2001 (July 06 - 3:26:53 PM):   I'M GREAT.

Talk2bryan2001 (July 06 - 3:26:59 PM):   AND YOU?

Friends4Dave (July 06 - 3:27:24 PM):   I'm blessed! Thanks. (*Dave noticed that she was shouting, and he wondered why.*)

Talk2bryan2001 (July 06 - 3:28:05 PM):   HOW HAS YOUR DAY BEEN?

Friends4Dave (July 06 - 3:28:08 PM):   I thought maybe you forgot we were meeting here at 15:00hrs (my time) and 20:00hrs (your time).

Friends4Dave (July 06 - 3:28:51 PM):   Oh, my day has been busy, thank you very much. How has your day been?

Talk2bryan2001 (July 06 - 3:29:24 PM):   BUSY TOO.

Friends4Dave (July 06 - 3:29:59 PM):   Okay. What did you do today, honey?

Talk2bryan2001 (July 06 - 3:31:11 PM):   A lot, my dear.

Friends4Dave (July 06 - 3:31:55 PM):   That's good.

Friends4Dave (July 06 - 3:32:03 PM):   How is the weather?

Talk2bryan2001 (July 06 - 3:33:06 PM):   Well, it's much better today.

Friends4Dave (July 06 - 3:34:14 PM):   That's good. It is bright and sunny here. Really nice.

Talk2bryan2001 (July 06 - 3:34:50 PM):   That's good.

Friends4Dave (July 06 - 3:35:08 PM):   I missed you. And I enjoyed talking with you yesterday.

Talk2bryan2001 (July 06 - 3:35:56 PM):   Me too.

Friends4Dave (July 06 - 3:36:20 PM):   I appreciate you.

Talk2bryan2001 (July 06 - 3:37:05 PM):   Do you watch a programme titled "CHEATERS"?

Friends4Dave (July 06 - 3:37:46 PM):   *(Not knowing why she asked that question, he answered honesty.)* Not really. But I have heard about it and come across bits and pieces of the program on TV in the past.

Talk2bryan2001 (July 06 - 3:38:45 PM):   OKAY.

Friends4Dave (July 06 - 3:38:59 PM):   I used to do many such investigations in the past, when I was Private Investigator. I really liked catching the cheaters and bad guys in the act.

Talk2bryan2001 (July 06 - 3:40:04 PM):   REALLY? *(She heartily inserted a laughing emoticon.)*

Friends4Dave (July 06 - 3:40:15 PM):   Yes. Really.

Friends4Dave (July 06 - 3:40:59 PM):   The job was dangerous sometimes, but very gratifying.

Talk2bryan2001 (July 06 - 3:41:48 PM):   WOW...

Friends4Dave (July 06 - 3:42:32 PM):   It was dangerous because the investigator could be shot and killed anytime; just like it was with my law enforcement job.

Talk2bryan2001 (July 06 - 3:43:11 PM):   WOW.... *(She inserted a surprise emoticon.)*

Friends4Dave (July 06 - 3:43:42 PM):   The program CHEATERS is for TV, but mine was for real. No TV.

Friends4Dave (July 06 - 3:44:31 PM):   You are very funny with your emoticons. I love them. (*He inserted a love-struck emoticon.*)

Friends4Dave (July 06 - 3:46:16 PM):   I wish you were here with me now. I would take you on a long walk through the parks, holding hands.

Talk2bryan2001 (July 06 - 3:48:44 PM):   NICE. (*She inserted clapping hands emoticon.*)

Friends4Dave (July 06 - 3:49:13 PM):   Do you like taking walks?

Talk2bryan2001 (July 06 - 3:51:33 PM):   Emm...yeah.

Friends4Dave (July 06 - 3:52:43 PM):   You don't sound like you like taking walks. Okay, what do you like to do?

Talk2bryan2001 (July 06 - 3:54:53 PM):   Yeah I do.

Friends4Dave (July 06 - 3:55:21 PM):   What else do you like doing?

Talk2bryan2001 (July 06 - 3:56:28 PM):   Please dear, send me your pictures.

Friends4Dave (July 06 - 3:57:03 PM):   I do not have any new pictures besides the ones I sent you before.

Talk2bryan2001 (July 06 - 3:57:57 PM):   Well, I did not see them. Please resend them. Ok?

Friends4Dave (July 06 - 3:58:45 PM):   Alright.

Talk2bryan2001 (July 06 - 3:59:00 PM):   Thanks.

Friends4Dave (July 06 - 3:59:13 PM):   Do you want me to send them here right now?

Talk2bryan2001 (July 06 - 4:00:15 PM):   Yes you can send them to my email. Ok?

Talk2bryan2001 (July 06 - 4:00:50 PM):   swtisy@hotmail.com.

Friends4Dave (July 06 - 4:01:03 PM):   I just sent them here. Click on "Accept" on your screen.

Talk2bryan2001 (July 06 - 4:01:59 PM):   Please send it to me at this email address: swtisy@hotmail.com.

Talk2bryan2001 (July 06 - 4:02:36 PM):   I'm mobile. Remember?

Friends4Dave (July 06 - 4:07:08 PM):   I just re-sent the pictures to your email address: swtisy@hotmail.com.

Talk2bryan2001 (July 06 - 4:08:01 PM):   That's my Dave. (*Dave doesn't like flattery, but he said nothing.*)

Talk2bryan2001 (July 06 - 4:08:13 PM):   Thanks dear. (*Dave was thinking: "That's more like it; not the flattery."*)

Friends4Dave (July 06 - 4:08:30 PM):   You are welcome. I need you to send me clear pictures of yourself. One close-up and one full-figured.

Friends4Dave (July 06 - 4:09:08 PM):   I want to print them out and put them on my desk at home where I will see them every day.

Talk2bryan2001 (July 06 - 4:12:00 PM):   But you can use that other one
I sent you first.

Talk2bryan2001 (July 06 - 4:12:21 PM):   Ok dear. I will. Ok?

Friends4Dave (July 06 - 4:12:53 PM):   Thanks. The other two you
sent me are not clear.

Friends4Dave (July 06 - 4:13:40 PM):   Can you see me on webcam?

Talk2bryan2001 (July 06 - 4:14:27 PM):   I'm mobile. (*Dave kept
forgetting that she said many times that she
was mobile. Is old age creeping in?*)

Talk2bryan2001 (July 06 - 4:14:40 PM):   I can't see you.

Friends4Dave (July 06 - 4:15:09 PM):   Okay. I was not sure if you
could see me on your mobile or not.

Friends4Dave (July 06 - 4:17:33 PM):   Are you there, honey?

Talk2bryan2001 (July 06 - 4:17:42 PM):   Yeah.

Friends4Dave (July 06 - 4:19:11 PM):   I would love for you to be able
to see me on the webcam and I will be able to
see you via the same. I know that is not
possible now until you get your PC.

Talk2bryan2001 (July 06 - 4:20:52 PM):   Yes, that will be when I get
my PC. Okay? Then we can both see each
other.

Talk2bryan2001 (July 06 - 4:22:24 PM):   Baby?

Friends4Dave (July 06 - 4:22:32 PM):   Yes, my dear.

Friends4Dave (July 06 - 4:22:51 PM):   I agree with you.

Friends4Dave (July 06 - 4:23:40 PM):   What do you normally do during your free time?

Talk2bryan2001 (July 06 - 4:26:38 PM):   Well, nothing in particular. Anything can keep me busy.

Friends4Dave (July 06 - 4:26:58 PM):   I see.

Talk2bryan2001 (July 06 - 4:27:20 PM):   Yes.

Friends4Dave (July 06 - 4:27:39 PM):   That's not bad.

Talk2bryan2001 (July 06 - 4:28:14 PM):   Have you had lunch?

Friends4Dave (July 06 - 4:28:44 PM):   Yes, sweetheart. I ate rice with stew.[47]

Friends4Dave (July 06 - 4:29:03 PM):   What about you?

Friends4Dave (July 06 - 4:29:15 PM):   Have you had your dinner?

Talk2bryan2001 (July 06 - 4:29:49 PM):   Nice. You prepared it yourself?

Talk2bryan2001 (July 06 - 4:30:09 PM):   Yeah, I have had dinner.

Friends4Dave (July 06 - 4:30:53 PM):   Yes. I like to cook almost all the foods I eat. I really do not like eating in the restaurants, unless when I am away from home for a few days or so.

---

[47] That was usual for Dave because he does not like to eat breakfast and lunch. He only eats dinner everyday.

Talk2bryan2001 (July 06 - 4:32:58 PM):   That's good.

Friends4Dave (July 06 - 4:33:28 PM):   I like to cook if I could. Do
                you like to cook?

Talk2bryan2001 (July 06 - 4:35:28 PM):   Yes, very much.

Friends4Dave (July 06 - 4:36:09 PM):   Uhmnnnnn! That's very good!
                *(Dave was impressed but not surprised
                because most Nigerian women can cook very
                well.)*

Talk2bryan2001 (July 06 - 4:37:03 PM):   In fact, I love cooking.

Friends4Dave (July 06 - 4:39:13 PM):   That's great. If and when you
                live in a big city in the United States or
                Canada, you will not miss Nigeria that much
                because you can find any foodstuff in Nigeria
                here too. 😊 *(He inserted a big grin
                emoticon.)*

Talk2bryan2001 (July 06 - 4:39:57 PM):   Okay.

Friends4Dave (July 06 - 4:41:02 PM):   *(Dave's back, shoulders, and
                neck were hurting so badly that he could not
                even think straight anymore. He was also
                having a terrible migraine. He needed to end
                their conversation fast and then go and lie
                down on the bed for a while.)* Honey, if you
                don't mind, I need to go now.

Talk2bryan2001 (July 06 - 4:43:44 PM):   You've got something doing?

Friends4Dave (July 06 - 4:45:06 PM):   *(Dave did not want to give her
                any cause for alarm; so, he gave her a
                different excuse.)* Yes, honey. I wanted to chat
                with you at 15:00hrs before it got too late for

you. But I still have things I need to do before the businesses close for today.

Talk2bryan2001 (July 06 - 4:46:27 PM):   How many of your pictures did you send to me?

Friends4Dave (July 06 - 4:46:39 PM):   Two.

Talk2bryan2001 (July 06 - 4:47:39 PM):   Ok.

Talk2bryan2001 (July 06 - 4:47:48 PM):   Thanks, bye.

Friends4Dave (July 06 - 4:48:18 PM):   Shall we chat tomorrow or in a couple of days please?

Talk2bryan2001 (July 06 - 4:49:02 PM):   When do you think dear?

Friends4Dave (July 06 - 4:49:19 PM):   You pick a time, please.

Talk2bryan2001 (July 06 - 4:50:27 PM):   Same time. Tomorrow.

Friends4Dave (July 06 - 4:50:48 PM):   Alright. Goodbye love.

CHAPTER 20
DAVE GOES MOBILE!

On July 7th 2009, Dave decided to use his new cell phone to chat. Unlike his old cellular phone, this new *Blackberry 8800* phone, surprisingly to Dave, has several instant messengers, including the *Blackberry Messenger* and *Yahoo! Messenger*. When he logged in to his *Yahoo!* account, he found Gracy already online. There are no date and time stamps below because Dave used his *Blackberry* mobile phone to chat with Gracy. Dave was watching Michael Jackson's memorial[48] on TV when he began to chat with Gracy.

Participants:[49] Friends4Dave and Talk2bryan2001.

Talk2bryan2001:   Hi dear!

Friends4Dave: Hi Baby!

Friends4Dave: How was your day?

Talk2bryan2001:   (*Gracy missed Dave's question.*) How are you doing?

Friends4Dave: I'm blessed, thanks.

Friends4Dave: How are you? And how was your day?

Talk2bryan2001:   I am fine, I had a stress free day.

Friends4Dave: Great!

Talk2bryan2001:   Hope you are having a great day too?

---

[48]   The music legend, Michael Jackson, recently passed away. Today was his memorial, which was being broadcast live on CNN.
[49]   There are no time stamps in these conversation because Dave was chatting with his mobile phone.

Friends4Dave:	Not really. I am watching Michael Jackson's memorial on TV.
Talk2bryan2001:	Oh yes, it's today.
Friends4Dave:	Yes.
Friends4Dave:	Sad ... isn't it?
Talk2bryan2001:	Yes, it is. 🙁 *(She pouted sadly.)*
Friends4Dave:	Anyway .... What did you do today, honey?
Talk2bryan2001:	Well, I was just indoors.
Friends4Dave:	Relaxing?
Talk2bryan2001:	Yes.
Friends4Dave:	Great!
Friends4Dave:	I have been thinking about you all day today.
Talk2bryan2001:	So how are you spending your day?
Talk2bryan2001:	Wow... really?
Friends4Dave:	Thinking about you mostly. But I also made some important calls. Then, I started watching the Michael Jackson memorial.
Talk2bryan2001:	Okay, so what were you thinking of me?
Friends4Dave:	Good things, of course. And what the future holds for us.

Talk2bryan2001:	Oh, I see!
Friends4Dave:	Do you think about me?
Talk2bryan2001:	Yes, I do!
Friends4Dave:	What do you think about me?
Talk2bryan2001:	(*Gracy ignored Dave's question, and she asked him a question instead.*) When is your birthday dear?
Friends4Dave:	(*Dave was thinking, "Didn't I already answer that question?" But Dave was not sure whether he really told Gracy his birth date or not.*) Already passed. In February.
Talk2bryan2001:	HELLO DEAR, ARE YOU THERE FOR ME?
Talk2bryan2001:	BUZZ!!! (*She buzzed Dave when he didn't respond on time; but he had inadvertently been logged out.*)
Friends4Dave:	(*Dave was able to log back in.*) I'm here. I was logged off.
Friends4Dave:	When is your birth day?
Talk2bryan2001:	The date please.
Friends4Dave:	February 1st. When is yours?
Talk2bryan2001:	SEPTEMBER 10.
Friends4Dave:	Good.
Friends4Dave:	What were you thinking about me?

Talk2bryan2001:   WELL I KNOW YOU GUYS "WITNESS" DON'T CELEBRATE BIRTHDAY. RIGHT? (*Dave had previously told Gracy during one of their telephone conversations that he used to be a Jehovah's Witness; and that even though he was no longer a Jehovah's Witness at the moment, to a large extent, he still strived to live his life in accordance with the beliefs and practices of Jehovah's Witnesses. Gracy, on the other hand, had told Dave that she has friends and relatives who are Jehovah's Witnesses, including her uncle, and that she was familiar with some of their beliefs and practices. Dave also made it clear during their phone conversations that he preferred his future wife to be a Jehovah's Witness because he was trying to get back into Jehovah's organization; and that he had begun attending their meetings again in recent years, even though he was still currently disfellowshipped.*)

Friends4Dave: That's right.

Friends4Dave: You know Jehovah's Witnesses very well, then.

Talk2bryan2001:   BUZZ!!! (*She buzzed Dave for attention.*)

Friends4Dave: BUZZ!!! (*He buzzed Gracy back.*)

Friends4Dave: (*Dave realized that Gracy still did not answer his question about what she had been thinking about him.*) You have not told me what you were thinking about me...

Friends4Dave: (*Gracy still did not answer Dave's questions for several minutes, so Dave buzzed her for her attention to his last question.*) BUZZ!!!

Friends4Dave: (*Gracy still did not answer for several minutes. Dave was getting irritated by her ignoring his questions often.)* Are you there?

Talk2bryan2001: *(Gracy finally responded to Dave's question.)* Some good stuff about you. The first time we will meet... how it's gonna be like.

Friends4Dave: Me too. *(Dave had also thought about that in the past.)*

Friends4Dave: *(Optimistically.)* I think it's gonna be great.

Talk2bryan2001: How is it going to look like?

Friends4Dave: I can't say exactly yet until we actually meet; but I know it is going to be great!

Talk2bryan2001: When we meet what will you do to me? *(Gracy wanted some specifics. But Dave did not respond because he did not know. Besides, Dave was not the type that wanted sex the first time. He also does not want to have sex until marriage, just as it was when he married his ex-wife; because, even though he was disfellowshipped and no longer a Jehovah's Witness, he was hoping to be reinstated some day.)*

Talk2bryan2001: What will you do to me? *(Gracy insisted.)*

Talk2bryan2001: Hug or....

Talk2bryan2001: Smart... *(After a few more minutes of Dave not responding to her question, she changed the tone a little bit.)*

Talk2bryan2001: Okay?

Friends4Dave:	*(Dave finally responded.)* First, I will hug you tightly. What happens next will happen naturally.
Talk2bryan2001:	*(She just missed Dave's response by a few seconds)* Are you there?
Friends4Dave:	I am here, honey.
Friends4Dave:	*(Dave decided to switch places with her. He wanted to know what exactly she was thinking about… about how she wanted to be treated when they first meet.)* What do you think our first meeting is going to be like? What will you do to me?
Friends4Dave:	*(Gracy did not respond for several minutes but Dave did not want to say anything else until she answered his question; so he buzzed her.)* BUZZ!!!
Talk2bryan2001:	*(She finally responded, but she only regurgitated what Dave had said back to him.)* Give you a very Big Hug and then anything can follow. *(She inserted a kissing love affection emoticon.)*
Friends4Dave:	Okay. *(He thought to himself, "She is smart".)*
Talk2bryan2001:	Yeah.
Talk2bryan2001:	That's it.
Friends4Dave:	*(Dave's affection for Gracy was evidently growing stronger as the days went by.)* I wish you were here with me.
Friends4Dave:	*(Dave just remembered that he did not really know what Gracy's last name was because the email she sent to him previously had a different last name than the last name she used on Flixster. So, Dave decided to ask*

her what her real last name is.) What is your surname?

Talk2bryan2001: (*Gracy was evidently away or logged out without Dave knowing it. She did not respond for several minutes. After a long hiatus, she returned.*) I am back now!

Talk2bryan2001: Sorry it's the network.

Talk2bryan2001: (*Dave was unable to respond because he too was inadvertently logged out. He had been using his new Blackberry phone to chat and he was unable to log back in using the phone. So, Gracy buzzed Dave when he failed not respond.*) BUZZ!!!

****

Friends4Dave (July 07 - 3:56:00 PM): [50] (*Dave then decided to login using his computer instead of his Blackberry phone; and he was finally able to log back in. Now that he was again using the computer to chat, the date and time stamps started to appear in their chats.*) I'm very sorry, honey. I was logged out and couldn't log back in on time with my phone.

Friends4Dave (July 07 - 3:56:22 PM): (*Gracy ignored Dave momentarily; perhaps she was upset because Dave did not respond to her for several minutes when he was accidentally logged out; or perhaps she may be having some network issues.*) Are you still there?

Talk2bryan2001(July 07 - 3:56:54 PM): Okay I understand. Yeah I am here.

---

[50] Dave returned to chatting on his laptop computer.

217

Friends4Dave (July 07 - 3:57:27 PM):   What is your surname?

Talk2bryan2001(July 07 - 4:02:29 PM):   Nwaokoro.

Talk2bryan2001(July 07 - 4:02:29 PM):   Have you heard of the name
                                                before?

Friends4Dave (July 07 - 4:02:51 PM):   No.

Friends4Dave (July 07 - 4:03:16 PM):   I only knew your first name.

Friends4Dave (July 07 - 4:04:18 PM):   *(Dave was still having*
problems with his connection. He was logged
out again; however, he was able to log back in
almost immediately.) Something must be
wrong with *Yahoo!* server today; because I
keep getting logged out.

Friends4Dave (July 07 - 4:05:03 PM):   What does Nwoakoro mean?

Friends4Dave (July 07 - 4:05:25 PM):   I mean Nwaokoro ... sorry.

Friends4Dave (July 07 - 4:10:08 PM):   *(Gracy did not respond for*
about five minutes.) Halo! Anybody home?
(Dave's intended humor did not have any
positive effect on Gracy. Gracy did not
respond for an additional ten minutes.)

Friends4Dave (July 07 - 4:20:05 PM):   Honey, if you are not in the
mood to chat right now, that's okay.... we can
chat some other time. *(It appeared that Gracy*
continued to ignore Dave. He thought to
himself: "Or could it be that, perhaps, her
network was completely down?")

Friends4Dave (July 07 - 4:32:33 PM):   *(An additional silent period of twelve minutes passed and Gracy still did not respond even though Dave could see that she was still online. He suspected that she was busy chatting with someone else. Therefore, Dave ended the conversation and logged out.)* Goodbye, my dear .... We'll talk some other time. *(Gracy never responded after Dave logged out.)*

CHAPTER 21
PAINS AND RESERVATIONS

On July 8th, Dave went online with the intention of chatting with Gracy. But she was not available online. Therefore, he left the message below for her that he would be chatting with her in two days' time. The fact was that Dave did not want to chat for the next two days because his back, neck, and shoulder pains have been so severe since he woke up this morning that he did not want to talk to anybody.

As a direct result of the tensions from Dave's physical pains, his frequent debilitating migraines also resurfaced. Whenever he had these migraines, which happened very often, he really could not even think straight. The migraines literally exert so much pressure in his head to the point Dave often feels his head would explode. At such times, he also feels that his eyes are going to pop out of their sockets. In most cases, his medications had little to no effects whatsoever. Anyway, the chats below do not have date and time stamps because Dave was using his mobile phone.

Friends4Dave: (*The date and time stamps were not shown because Dave used his Blackberry phone to log in to his Yahoo! Messenger account.*) I was indisposed today, and tomorrow will be the same. But I hope to chat with you on Friday at about 21:00 hrs (9:00pm) your time. Love you!

Two days later, on July 10, Dave was still having very serious back, shoulder, and neck pains, as well as his migraines, but the intensity was not as it was on July 08. Even though Dave thought his pains and migraines were not as bad as they were two days ago, the level of pains that Dave always experienced on a daily basis would make most pain sufferers rush to the emergency room.

In Dave's case, going to the emergency room was pointless because he did not have any health insurance. Even if he had health insurance, it still would be a useless trip to the emergency room, because all that the doctor could do would be to prescribe yet another pain medication which would probably be less powerful than the medications that Dave was already taking. None of these sp-called powerful pain medications was able to relieve Dave's pains, including Vicodin and Skelaxin. Dave was so frustrated and upset sometimes because these pain medications had little to no effect on his pains and migraines that he refused to take the medications at times, because of his fears of over-medicating himself or becoming addicted to these so-called powerful pain killers.[51]

Despite his excruciating pains and migraines as usual, Dave decided to go online to chat with Gracy as he promised. But he was too frail to put his laptop on his lap on the recliner as usual to chat online. He sometimes chatted while sitting on his ergonomically comfortable office chair at his desk in his Study, but he usually chatted while reclining in his ultra-comfortable recliner because sitting straight up put too much pressure on his back, which in turn exacerbated his pains. Therefore, Dave decided to chat with his mobile phone while reclining. And since he was using his Blackberry phone to chat, there were no date and time stamps.

* * * * * * *

Participants:[52] __Friends4Dave__ and __Talk2bryan2001__:

Friends4Dave: Hi Baby!

Talk2bryan2001:   Hello Honey.

Friends4Dave: I'm blessed. How are you doing?

Talk2bryan2001:   Fine.

---

[51] Dave decided to stop taking Skelaxin altogether because it was not helping and the medication was just too dangerous. He also stopped using Vicodin later for the same reasons. He later settled on Ibuprofen, Lyrica, and Fentanyl patch as substitute prescriptions by his physicians. Even then, his excruciating pains continued. Later on, he also stopped using Fentanyl and then settled more on using natural remedies that now seem to work better, even though his pains remain but to a lesser degree.

[52] As usual, there were no time stamps because Dave was using his mobile phone.

Friends4Dave:	Great. How have your week been?
Talk2bryan2001:	Well not too bad.
Talk2bryan2001:	How has your day been?
Friends4Dave:	Very busy the past three days. (*But aside to himself, he said: "Oh yeah, you're right, very busy being in severe pains!"*) Thanks.
Talk2bryan2001:	With work?
Friends4Dave:	(*Dave was thinking, "Why do you have to ask that?", but he answered differently to her. On the one hand, Dave did not want to lie to her but, on the other hand, he also did not want to complain about his pains. Dave did not want to tell her yet that he did not currently work due to his disability. He believed that there was no need to complain about his unfortunate condition.*) Mostly something else.
Talk2bryan2001:	Okay.
Friends4Dave:	(*Dave changed the subject.*) I missed you very much.
Talk2bryan2001:	Me too.
Friends4Dave:	Thanks.
Friends4Dave:	What have you been up to the last couple of days?
Talk2bryan2001:	Nothing much.
Talk2bryan2001:	And you?
Friends4Dave:	Busy somewhat. (*To himself, he says, "Yes, busy doing*

nothing basically, but mired in severe pains.)

Friends4Dave: What happened the last time we chatted? I waited for you for about 30 minutes without any response before I decided to log out.

Talk2bryan2001:   I am so... so sorry about that. Okay? Just that I had a stressful day, so I slept off. When I woke up, you had logged out. Please dear, forgive me.

Friends4Dave: (*Dave forgave.*) Okay. No problem.

Friends4Dave: How are your parents?

Talk2bryan2001:   They are fine.

Friends4Dave: Are your school results out yet?

Talk2bryan2001:   Nope.

Talk2bryan2001:   Not yet.

Friends4Dave: When do you expect the results?

Talk2bryan2001:   (*It took more than twenty minutes for her to respond.*) When we resume.

Friends4Dave: Okay.

Friends4Dave: (*Dave was silent and after about fifteen more minutes, he resumed.*) Are you sleepy?

Talk2bryan2001:   No...

Talk2bryan2001:   Not at all sweetheart.

Friends4Dave: Okay, but if you are, please let me know. (*Dave's phone rang.*) Sorry, I've got to answer a phone call.

Talk2bryan2001:   Okay dear. (*Dave talked on the phone few minutes.*)

Friends4Dave: (*Dave hung the phone up.*) Sorry. But I'm back now.

Talk2bryan2001:   Okay.

Friends4Dave: I think about you a lot.

Talk2bryan2001:   Oh

Talk2bryan2001:   I do too.

Talk2bryan2001:   I can't wait to have your picture on my phone.

Friends4Dave: Great. I sent them to you the other day. Did you not get them?

Talk2bryan2001:   I will be going to the Internet café on Sunday. Then I can download it to my phone. It would have been a lot more easier if I had my own computer.

Friends4Dave: I agree.

Friends4Dave: (*Dave began to remember his friendship with Mitchell, who got pregnant and gave birth to another man in Nigeria, and he was now reluctant to earnestly proceed with a serious relationship with Gracy for fear that she might do what Mitchell did.*) I care so much about, but I am also afraid.

Talk2bryan2001:   Why? (*Dave was inadvertently logged out and it was not able to log back in until about ten minutes later.*)

Talk2bryan2001:   Why are you afraid?

Talk2bryan2001:   For what?

Talk2bryan2001:   *(She had become impatient as she buzzed Dave for attention.)* BUZZ!!!

Talk2bryan2001:   Please tell me dear. *(She pleaded with Dave, not knowing that Dave was logged out and not able to login on time to respond to her questions.)*

Talk2bryan2001:   Afraid of what? Talk to me please!

Talk2bryan2001:   *(In panic mode, it appeared.)* BUZZ!!!

Friends4Dave: *(Dave was finally able to log back in.)* In 2001 when I visited Nigeria last, I met a very beautiful girl who is a sister of my former friend here in the US. I was there when their father died, and I helped her very much with doctor's bills and some funeral expenses. Later, she wrote me to thank me for all I did for them. I was not interested in her romantically at the time because I was married.

Talk2bryan2001:   So? *(She did not get it.)*

Talk2bryan2001:   I still don't understand. *(She was wondering what did that got to do with her?)*

Friends4Dave: *(Dave explained further.)* She told me she was interested in me. Later, after my wife and I separated and agreed to get a divorce, I accepted Mitchell's dating proposal. We continued to talk until her mother told me, while visiting me at my home, that the Mitchell just gave birth to twins. Mitchell's mother knew what I had done for their family during her husband's sickness and funeral. She also knew that Mitchell and I were in a long-distance dating relationship. So, she broke the news to me because he did not want me to continue to wait for her to come to the United States. See why I am afraid about you? I know the twins were not mine because I never kissed nor had sex with Mitchell.

Talk2bryan2001: Please.

Friends4Dave: Please what?

Talk2bryan2001: Everyone is different. Okay?

Friends4Dave: I know that, but I think about how hurt I was when I found out. I just do not want to get hurt like that again.

Talk2bryan2001: We are friends... right? And I care so much about you. (*Dave was accidentally logged out again.*)

Talk2bryan2001: So you left your wife because of her?

Talk2bryan2001: (*After a few minutes of no response from Dave, she shouted.*) HI DEAR!

Friends4Dave: (*Dave logged back in.*) No, definitely not! I told you before why my ex-wife and I separated. I appreciate you saying that you care so much about me. I just want to be sure that you will not do what she did.

Talk2bryan2001: Well I don't know what you think, but I care a lot about you.

Friends4Dave: I appreciate your caring about me. I also care a lot about you. My heart is currently with you. But I just need your assurance that you will not do the same thing she did.

Talk2bryan2001:   Dave!

Friends4Dave: Yes?

Talk2bryan2001:   It's Gracy.

Talk2bryan2001:   Okay? (*Dave did not respond.*)

Talk2bryan2001:   I think I know where all this is coming from. Well, it's okay.

Friends4Dave: I know it is Gracy. You are the only one I am chatting with online right now. I just need to know whether I can depend on you or not.

Talk2bryan2001:   It's well.

Friends4Dave: Why is it difficult for you to give me your assurance that you will not do what she did? Do you have a boyfriend in Nigeria?

Talk2bryan2001:   It's okay dear. Please just know that I care and I will always do.

Friends4Dave: You still did not answer my question. When I love a person, I love with all my heart. I need to know... Do you have a boyfriend or not?

Friends4Dave: (*Gracy did not respond. She stayed online for about fifteen minutes and then logged out. Dave waited for her to log back in but she did not for about thirty minutes.*) Your silence suggests that you do have a boyfriend. But that's okay. If you have a boyfriend, we can still be "just friends"... but nothing more than just friends; because I don't want to have false hopes again like it was with Mitchell who got pregnant by another man as soon as she finished her university. We can continue as ordinary friends and nothing more ... no Honey, no Sweetheart, no Dear, no Baby, or anything like that. Do you understand?

Talk2bryan2001:   (*She logged back in, but still did not answer Dave's question.*) Hey.

Friends4Dave: (*After about another fifteen minutes or so, Dave got upset.*) I truly thought you were different, and I loved you for it. But I was wrong. Please do not put any of my pictures on your phone, and do not use my picture for any reason. I strongly advise you to comply with my humble request that you must not use my pictures for any reason. I also no longer believe that the two pictures you sent me are really you. Goodbye forever.

Talk2bryan2001:   (*She inserted a bawling emoticon indicating that she was crying. Dave ignored her and logged out ... hurt ... really hurt.*)

CHAPTER 22
DAVE FINALLY TALKS TO GRACY

When Dave last chatted with Gracy on July 10, he meant it when he said "Goodbye forever." For the next seventeen days, he did not call nor chat with her. Gracy called Dave on the telephone almost every day, but Dave did not answer when he knew it was Gracy calling. Then she started to call with an undisclosed phone number and, when Dave picked up, she would hand up. This went on for several days. Dave also logged in to his *Yahoo! Messenger* account periodically just to see if Gracy was online. Sure enough, she was always there, apparently waiting for Dave to come online for a chat; or perhaps she was chatting with someone else, he was not sure. Dave did not want to chat with her.

Since Dave was now logging in as "invisible", Gracy did not know that Dave logged in to check on her. Dave was truly hurt and disappointed. He also became very angry because of the fact that all of the people he met online at Flixster.com were not trustworthy. The more he thought about his chats with these Flixster and *Yahoo!* members, the more upset he became and wanted to expose them. That desire to expose the scammers later gave birth to this book. This was the critical moment that Dave decided to compile all of his online chats with the Flixster members, good or bad.

It was true that Dave cared a lot about Gracy. Because of her persistence, Dave gradually began to have compassion for her again; and, finally on July 27th 2009, Dave decided to take Gracy's call. They spoke but got disconnected. Dave called her back but they got disconnected the second ... and third times. Then Gracy suggested that they go online to chat instead and he agreed. Since Dave was using his *Blackberry*, there were no date and time stamps in their conversations below.

Participants: <u>Friends4Dave</u> and <u>Talk2bryan2001</u>:

Friends4Dave: We got disconnected again. I will call you as soon as I am able to log on to the computer.

Friends4Dave: I am still trying to login into Skype so I can call you.

Talk2bryan2001: okay.

Friends4Dave: I tried to call. It says you are busy. I called +234-70-6204-2902.

Talk2bryan2001: Okay try: +2347055799229.

Friends4Dave: Okay.

Talk2bryan2001: Can we just chat since the network is bad?

Friends4Dave: *(Dave tried a few more times to call Gracy on the new number, but he could not get through to her.)* I still can't reach you on that number either.

Friends4Dave: Let me try a few more times again, please. *(Dave dialed both numbers repeatedly a few more times, but the calls still did not go through.)*

Friends4Dave: *(Dave gave up.)* Not successful. Okay, let's chat.

Friends4Dave: *(Gracy did not respond for a few minutes.)* Are you there, Gracy?

Talk2bryan2001: Okay.

Friends4Dave: So, please tell me what happened the other day.

Talk2bryan2001: I'm great as always. *(She probably thought that Dave asked her how she was doing.)*

Talk2bryan2001: Though I missed you a lot.

Friends4Dave: Good. *(Dave sensed that she was evading his question*

	again.) Would you please tell me what happened the last day we chatted?
Talk2bryan2001:	(*After several minutes of silence, she finally responded.*) I slept off while we were chatting because my day was so stressful and before I could reply, you had gone offline.
Talk2bryan2001:	I was short of words when I saw your message because I never expected that from you.
Friends4Dave:	I waited for more than 45 minutes for your response before I logged off. In fact, I actually waited for your response for about one hour before I finally logged out.
Talk2bryan2001:	I am so sorry I fell at sleep.
Friends4Dave:	(*Dave considered her explanation to be a plausible excuse, but he did not want to completely disregard the issue yet.*) How do you really feel about me?
Talk2bryan2001:	I like you.
Talk2bryan2001:	Everything about you.
Friends4Dave:	You said in your voicemail, which you left for me about two weeks ago, that you love me. Is that true?
Talk2bryan2001:	Yeah.
Friends4Dave:	Do you have a boyfriend?
Talk2bryan2001:	Nope.
Talk2bryan2001:	I have got friends anyway.

Friends4Dave: Would you like a long-term relationship with me?

Talk2bryan2001:   I really like you. Okay?

Talk2bryan2001:   (*But she did not seem to want to commit to a long-term relationship right now.*) Let's see how things work out.

Friends4Dave: I know that. But you didn't answer my question, though. (*Dave wanted to know what her real intentions were.*) Would you like to have a long-term relationship with me?

Talk2bryan2001:   Dave!!

Friends4Dave: Please answer my question. (*Dave insisted.*) We will still be friends regardless of your answer. But I just need to know.

Talk2bryan2001:   Are you there?

Talk2bryan2001:   (*Still not willing to commit one way or the other.*) The future will tell. Okay?

Friends4Dave: Okay then, understood. (*Dave concluded that Gracy was cautious but genuine, and he decided to forgive her and resume their friendship; at the same time, Dave was determined not to put all of his hopes on her either. If their relationship were to progress to a long-lasting marriage-type one, fine. But if the relationship did not work out, that was now also fine with Dave.*)

Talk2bryan2001:   How is B? (*Dave did not understand, so he did not respond until it was clarified.*)

Talk2bryan2001:   (*Gracy clarified her last question.*) How is your baby girl?

Friends4Dave:	She is fine.
Friends4Dave:	Thanks for asking. And how is your family?
Talk2bryan2001:	Nice.
Friends4Dave:	How is your family? Your parents, brothers, sisters, etc.?
Talk2bryan2001:	They are doing great.
Friends4Dave:	Wonderful.
Talk2bryan2001:	I am about to take my drugs now. Please give me a second. (*As an American, when Dave first read "drugs", his mind initially went to illicit drugs, and Dave did not want anything to do with a girl who takes illegal drugs. If Gracy were to be a drug-user, Dave would end the relationship right here and right now. But Dave quickly remembered that Nigerians refer to "medications" as "drugs".*)
Friends4Dave:	Okay. Are you ill?
Talk2bryan2001:	Yeah, just thyroid fever.
Friends4Dave:	I'm sorry to hear that. (*Dave was thinking maybe this was the right time to tell her that he was disabled, but then decided not to do so yet.*)
Talk2bryan2001:	Thanks.
Friends4Dave:	What medication are you taking for it?
Talk2bryan2001:	Ciprofloxacin tablets and Paracetamol. Although it's

pretty expensive.

Talk2bryan2001: Are you there?

Talk2bryan2001: (*She buzzed Dave.*) BUZZ!!!

Friends4Dave: Be careful about Ciprofloxacin. I understand that it is a very dangerous prescription medication. When taking it, please take less than the prescribed dosage, if possible.

Talk2bryan2001: Yeah, I know.

Friends4Dave: Are the medications helping?

Talk2bryan2001: Yes, they are.

Friends4Dave: Good. I wish you a speedy recovery, and I will keep you in my prayers. (*Dave was thinking to himself, "That's good. At least, some medications are working for some people. My medications have little or no effects whatsoever. I wish mine would work for me too."*)

Talk2bryan2001: Thanks. Tell me, how did you feel when you got my voice mail. (*Dave did not immediately respond.*)

Talk2bryan2001: Hellooooo.....!

Friends4Dave: I was overwhelmed with affection for you. I had a strong urge to call you back, but I had to resist the urge to call you back. I was struggling every day against that urge to call you. I just didn't want to put myself in the same situation like the one I had with Mitchell.

Talk2bryan2001: Well... that's passed now. Okay? You have to move further and I want to let you know something… that the best is yet to come. I have always known that and it's my belief too.

Friends4Dave: When I love a woman, I love her hard, with all my heart and soul.

Talk2bryan2001:   Hmm...

Friends4Dave: Someone has been calling me almost every day, but when I picked up the phone, the person never spoke and would hang up. Was that you?

Talk2bryan2001:   No, not me. (*But Dave saw her phone number on his caller ID several times. But he did not want to disprove her. There were times, though, that Dave only saw the number "1" on his caller ID.*)[53]

Friends4Dave: Okay. Sorry.

Talk2bryan2001:   And please, if that happens again, you should wait for the person to speak first. Okay?

Friends4Dave: If the person keeps calling, I may have to investigate where the call is coming from; or I may just change my phone number.

Talk2bryan2001:   Please wait for the person to speak first before you say a word.

Friends4Dave: Okay, that's a good idea.

Friends4Dave: Thanks.

---

[53]   Dave later discovered that the unknown and annoying calls were from Hartford Insurance Company, monitoring Dave's disability status.

Talk2bryan2001:   You don't have to change your number just because of one dude.

Talk2bryan2001:   *(She sent a love-struck emoticon to Dave.)*

Friends4Dave: That's true, but the person wakes me up from sleep sometimes.

Talk2bryan2001:   Does the number show on your screen?

Friends4Dave: No. *(Since Gracy already denied calling Dave, he did not want to tell her that he saw her number also show up several times too.)*

Talk2bryan2001:   Hey, is your Skype on?

Friends4Dave: *(Responded to Gracy's question as to whether he saw the number on his phone screen.)* All that I see on my screen is "1". Nothing more.

Friends4Dave: *(Now Dave responded to her question whether his Skype was on.)* No. Let me log back into my Skype account.

******

Dave logged in to his Skype account. But as he logged into Skype, Dave was automatically logged out of his Blackberry *Yahoo! Messenger*. He tried to log back in but could not. He decided to log back into *Yahoo! Messenger* using his laptop instead. Since he was now using his laptop, the date and time stamps were available.

Talk2bryan2001 (July 27 - 3:23:28 PM):   Let me tell you what happened some few months back here. A Nigerian based in South Africa came back home to finish his building. One night he had a call on his cell phone, and as he picked up the call and said "hello" he fell down and that was the end.

Friends4Dave (July 27 - 3:24:59 PM):   *(Dave finally logged back in using his laptop.)* Okay. I'm back. I was logged off and could not sign back in. Sorry about that.

Friends4Dave (July 27 - 3:26:09 PM):   *(Dave noticed what Gracy has written, about the Nigerian who died answering his cell phone, since he was inadvertently logged out.)* What? What do you think happened?

Talk2bryan2001 (July 27 - 3:27:05 PM):   Did you get my story?

Friends4Dave (July 27 - 3:28:01 PM):   Yes. I did. That's why I wanted to know what happened to him. You said that was the end. Do you mean he died?

Talk2bryan2001 (July 27 - 3:28:45 PM):   Yes.

Talk2bryan2001 (July 27 - 3:28:55 PM):   He died.

Friends4Dave (July 27 - 3:29:23 PM):   Wow. *(Dave realized that Gracy was superstitious. But Dave did not believe in any of those superstitious stuff anymore. He used to have such beliefs when he was still living in Nigeria; but not anymore.)*

Friends4Dave (July 27 - 3:29:47 PM):   *(Dave decided to change the subject because he did not want to discuss any superstitious stuff.)* I am on Skype now, too.

Friends4Dave (July 27 - 3:31:52 PM):   Do you have a PC now?

Friends4Dave (July 27 - 3:34:17 PM):   *(Dave realized that Gracy has been communicating with him using two different Yahoo! IDs. He tried to call Gracy's two phone numbers again, but they appear to be busy.*) Are you using two mobile phones now?

Talk2bryan2001 (July 27 - 3:35:27 PM):   I have not gotten a PC yet.

Talk2bryan2001 (July 27 - 3:36:13 PM):   I am using my phone.

Friends4Dave (July 27 - 3:36:57 PM):   Okay. I was trying to call you on Skype, but it says you're "busy".

Talk2bryan2001 (July 27 - 3:39:06 PM):   Well maybe because I am using the phones.

Friends4Dave (July 27 - 3:39:58 PM):   I know, and that's okay.

Friends4Dave (July 27 - 3:40:30 PM):   When are you going to send me your picture?

Talk2bryan2001 (July 27 - 3:42:17 PM):   As soon as I get a PC.

Friends4Dave (July 27 - 3:42:31 PM):   Alright.

Friends4Dave (July 27 - 3:44:03 PM):   Now, please tell me more about the Nigerian guy from South Africa who died when he returned home to finish his building. (*As soon as Dave posted the message, he thought to himself, "Why did I bring that up again?"*)

Talk2bryan2001 (July 27 - 3:45:47 PM):   The police is still investigating the matter.

Friends4Dave (July 27 - 3:46:08 PM):   Did it just happen?

Talk2bryan2001 (July 27 - 3:47:24 PM):   Last month.

Friends4Dave (July 27 - 3:48:18 PM):   That's still very recent in a death investigation. Did the guy have any know enemies?

Talk2bryan2001 (July 27 - 3:52:03 PM):   Well I don't know. Even his wife can't tell. It all happened in her presence.

Friends4Dave (July 27 - 3:52:41 PM):   *(Dave was thinking that either his wife knew what killed the guy or that he might have had a cardiac arrest, if he was out of shape or had some heart disease. Dave did not want to believe in Gracy's superstitious insinuation.)* Was the guy fat and out of shape?

Talk2bryan2001 (July 27 - 3:55:39 PM):   *(Gracy seemed to know exactly what Dave was thinking.)* It's not a heart attack if that's what you think.

Friends4Dave (July 27 - 3:56:01 PM):   That's exactly what I am thinking.

Friends4Dave (July 27 - 3:56:10 PM):   I think he may have died of heart attack.

Talk2bryan2001 (July 27 - 3:56:25 PM):   Well GOD knows it all.

Friends4Dave (July 27 - 3:57:29 PM):   You are absolutely right. He is the only one that knows exactly what happened to the guy. My thinking is only a guess. *(Dave switched over to Skype to join Gracy there, since she has been chatting with Dave on Skype simultaneously, as will be presented in the next chapter.)*

Talk2bryan2001 (July 27 - 3:59:08 PM):   Yeah.

Talk2bryan2001 (July 27 - 4:06:51 PM):   (*Dave was not responding on Yahoo! Messenger because he was responding to Gracy's chat on Skype. But she was trying to get his attention here on Yahoo! Messenger.*)   Helloooow...!

Talk2bryan2001 (July 27 - 4:06:56 PM):   Are you there?

Friends4Dave (July 27 - 4:07:30 PM):   Yes, I am back here. But I was with you on Skype.

Talk2bryan2001 (July 27 - 4:11:20 PM):   Okay. (*Dave and Gracy ended the conversation here on Yahoo! Messenger; and they both continued their conversation on Skype, as presented in the next chapter.*)

CHAPTER 23
DAVE AND GRACY CHAT ON SKYPE

While Dave and Gracy were chatting online via the *Yahoo! Messenger*, they were simultaneously chatting on Skype. After a while of going back and forth between the *Yahoo! Messenger* and Skype, they both abandoned *Yahoo! Messenger* and continued their conversation here on Skype. As mentioned earlier in the previous chapter, Dave placed several telephone calls to Gracy, but none of the calls went through; and the chat presented below indicates some of the phone calls Dave attempted to place to Gracy.

Participants: Friends4Dave (Dave) **and Talk2bryan2001 (Gracy):**

Gracy [July 27 - 3:24:29 PM]:   Hey, good to see you on Skype.

Dave [July 27 - 3:26:36 PM]:   ******* Call to Gracy, no answer. ******* (*Dave tried earlier several times to call Gracy but the calls did not go through. Now, he tried to call her again, but it did not go through either.*)

Dave [July 27 - 3:26:55 PM]:   ******* Call to Gracy, no answer. ******* (*Dave tried to call again, but no success this time either.*)

Dave [July 27 - 3:27:03 PM]:   Hi Gracy, I'm here now. I was logged out of *Yahoo!* and could not sign back in. I am still trying to sign log in to *Yahoo!* now.

Gracy [July 27 - 3:27:37 PM]:   Okay.

Dave [July 27 - 3:30:52 PM]:   I tried to call you several times directly through my phone, but it keeps hanging up. I also tried to call you via Skype without success; and I think Skype has a problem now.

But to be sure, try calling me on Skype, please.

Gracy [July 27 - 3:32:20 PM]:   Sorry, I can't because I am mobile.

Gracy [July 27 - 3:32:27 PM]:   I am not using a PC.

Dave [July 27 - 3:33:32 PM: So, you get Skype on your mobile. That's great.

Dave [July 27 - 3:35:59 PM: *** Call to Gracy, no answer. *** (*Dave tried to call Gracy again, but it did not go through either.*)

Gracy [July 27 - 3:43:07 PM]:   What kind of phone are you using?

Gracy [July 27 - 3:49:18 PM]:   Hope you like the topic?

Dave [July 27 - 3:50:37 PM]:   I'm using my home phone and Skype for calls. But I have a Blackberry cellular.

Dave Washington [July 27 - 3:51:40 PM]:   I am using my computer to chat with you now.

Gracy [July 27 - 3:53:43 PM]:   Nice, you can download Skype onto your Blackberry.

Gracy [July 27 - 3:54:09 PM]:   I will tell you how.

Dave [July 27 - 3:54:51 PM]:   (*Dave tried to download Skype to his Blackberry weeks ago but it was not compatible with Skype.*) I tried to do so already, but my *Blackberry* does not support Skype.

Dave [July 27 - 3:55:33 PM]:   (*Dave decided to give Gracy a chance to show him another way to download the software.*) Well, go ahead, please tell me how I can download Skype.

Gracy [July 27 - 3:58:41 PM]:   (*She shared her expertise.*) I will give you a website address where you will be able to download Skype app. Here: http://www.getjar.com

Dave [July 27 - 3:59:14 PM]:   Thanks.

Gracy [July 27 - 3:59:49 PM]:   Do that now.

Dave [July 27 - 4:00:09 PM]:   Wait a minute, please. (*Dave went to the website through his Blackberry.*)

Gracy [July 27 - 4:00:32 PM]:   Let me direct you on how to go about it.

Dave [July 27 - 4:00:59 PM]:   Okay.

Gracy [July 27 - 4:01:42 PM]:   If the site is open please let me know.

Dave [July 27 - 4:02:04 PM]:   I'm there.

Gracy [July 27 - 4:03:24 PM]:   Scroll down and you will find "Skype Lite."

Gracy [July 27 - 4:04:03 PM]:   If you see it, please let me know.

Dave [July 27 - 4:05:54 PM]:   (*Dave found no option for Skype Lite.*) No "Skype Lite" on my screen.

Gracy [July 27 - 4:08:28 PM]:   Type "Skype Lite" on the search box. And click search. Okay?

Dave [July 27 - 4:08:54 PM]:   Okay (*Dave complied with Gracy's directive, even though he knew what to do. Dave found "IM Plus For Skype" instead.*)

Gracy [July 27 - 4:10:14 PM]:   But do you find other applications?

Dave [July 27 - 4:11:13 PM]:   I found "IM Plus For Skype."

Dave [July 27 - 4:11:55 PM]:   Is that the one you are talking about?

Gracy [July 27 - 4:12:24 PM]:   And Skype Lite?

Gracy [July 27 - 4:12:43 PM]:   And not Skype Lite?

Dave [July 27 - 4:13:04 PM]:   Not Skype Lite.

Gracy [July 27 - 4:14:13 PM]:   What can you find apart from that? IM SKYPE.

Dave [July 27 - 4:16:02 PM]:   Nothing else. (*Dave downloaded and installs IM Plus For Skype.*)

Dave [July 27 - 4:17:15 PM]:   I downloaded IM Plus For Skype.

Gracy [July 27 - 4:18:33 PM]:   Okay, have you tried it now?

Dave [July 27 - 4:21:16 PM]:   I installed it. But it requires me to buy their license first, using a PC. Skype is supposed to be a free software; why are these people asking me to pay for the software? I will check into that later before I decide whether to get it or not.

Gracy [July 27 - 4:23:27 PM]:   Okay.

Gracy [July 27 - 4:24:32 PM]:   With Skype Lite, you don't need to go that far. You don't need to pay for it.

Dave [July 27 - 4:25:43 PM]:   I will search for Skype Lite when I have the time.

Gracy [July 27 - 4:26:01 PM]:   Try this: type Yamee Messenger in the search box.

Dave [July 27 - 4:27:49 PM]:   Hold on a minute, please. (*He obeyed.*)

Gracy [July 27 - 4:28:38 PM]:   If I had a PC, I would have sent the installer right now to you. Because I have it on my flash drive.

Dave [July 27 - 4:30:15 PM]:   Thanks. (*Yamee Messenger did not work for Dave's Blackberry.*) Yamee Messenger is not compatible with my *Blackberry* phone either. I will figure it out later.

Gracy [July 27 - 4:32:46 PM]:   Okay.

Dave [July 27 - 4:34:53 PM]:   I think Skype is probably not compatible with my Blackberry. I tried to install Skype Lite from the Skype website before, my *Blackberry* returned an error message that it was not compatible. I also tried to use the *Blackberry Application Loader* from my PC, and that was not successful either.

Gracy [July 27 - 4:36:18 PM]:   Okay.

Dave [July 27 - 4:39:19 PM]:   I think the Blackberries in the United States are just not designed for Skype yet. I know, however, that Blackberries in some other countries are compatible, because I read about that on Skype website and my friend in London has Skype on his phone. (*Dave continued to explore the website for more information on IM Plus For Skype.*)

Gracy [July 27 - 4:40:33 PM]:   Well, maybe.

Dave [July 27 - 4:43:31 PM]:   I just read more about "IM Plus For SKYPE." It is not free. It required a subscription. It is a Third Party software making money off SKYPE. I am not interested in it and I will delete the program from my phone. (*Dave deleted IM Plus For Skype from his Blackberry phone.*)

Dave [July 27 - 4:44:42 PM]:   I just deleted the program.

Dave [July 27 - 4:45:20 PM]:   What time is it in Nigeria now?

Gracy [July 27 - 4:46:34 PM]:   9:49 p.m.

Dave [July 27 - 4:48:53 PM]:   Okay, thanks. The time on your Skype profile says "8:48 p.m.". That's why I asked what time it was in Nigeria. Here in the United States, our time keeps changing, depending on the season and time zones.

Dave [July 27 - 4:52:41 PM]:   *** Call to Gracy, no answer. *** (*Dave tried to place another call to Gracy again. No success.*)

Dave [July 27 - 4:52:51 PM]:   *** Call to Gracy, no answer. *** (*He tried one more time. Same result.*)

Dave [July 27 - 4:53:21 PM]:   Are you still there?

Gracy [July 27 - 4:53:54 PM]:   Okay.

Dave [July 27 - 4:55:11 PM]:   I need to go now, please. I am very hungry. I have not eaten anything since morning and I need to go and cook, eat and take my medications.

Gracy [July 27 - 4:57:08 PM]:   Okay then.

Gracy [July 27 - 4:57:43 PM]:   Sweet dreams and I miss you.

Dave [July 27 - 4:57:58 PM]:   Thanks a lot for your help on the Skype
Lite, and for calling me today.

Dave [July 27 - 4:58:13 PM]:   You, too.

Dave [July 27 - 4:58:21 PM]:   Good night.

Gracy [July 27 - 4:58:46 PM]:   Thanks.

Gracy [July 27 - 5:07:46 PM]:   Missing you already.

Dave and Gracy both logged out.

CHAPTER 24
DAVE QUESTIONS GRACY'S TRUE IDENTITY

𝕬lthough Dave and Gracy had had pretty good conversations during their last chats on Yahoo! and Skype, Dave now had good reasons to question Gracy's true identity. For the next five days following their last conversations, Dave was not able to communicate with Gracy due to his exacerbated pain levels. He was in so much pain that he could not even sit, stand, or walk in his apartment for more than five to ten minutes at a time. Such levels of pain were not unusual for Dave. He experienced excruciating pains every day, but there were times that he could not even function at all. This was one of those numerous times. On July 29th and August 1st, Gracy left the following short messages for Dave on *Yahoo! Messenger* and Skype.

When Dave logged into his Skype account on August 2nd, he noticed that Gracy has changed her name from "Gracy" to "Lora Terry". He also noticed that Gracy contacted him on *Yahoo! Messenger* with a second and totally different *Yahoo!* ID.[54] Dave was not comfortable with these name changes and he began to question Gracy's true identity in his mind. Incidentally, Dave had come online that day to obtain Gracy's full contact information so that he could send her the money he had promised to send to her in August. Seeing this change of identity by Gracy made Dave very suspicious and he decided not to send her the money because he really did not know who this girl truly was anymore.

Lora.Terry [July 29 - 4:21:59 PM]:   Just thought of you...

Lora.Terry [August 01 - 1:27:34 PM]:   Hi dear.

Dave was not online the two days that Gracy left the two short messages above. However, Dave and Gracy were able to chat on August 2nd below.

---

[54] "Isyluvy2k9" was yet another *Yahoo!* ID that Gracy now used also online. Dave was not pleased with Gracy for using multiple online identities.

Friends4Dave (August 02 - 2:55:44 PM):   Hi Gracy! I'm here waiting for you. (*Gracy was not yet online, and Dave left to do something else around his apartment. He was still in severe pains as usual, but he was a little better than the last five or six days.*)

isyluvy2k9 (August 02 - 3:08:15 PM):   Are you there? (*Gracy inquired of Dave but Dave was not back yet and therefore not available at the moment.*)

Friends4Dave (August 02 - 3:15:09 PM): (*Dave returned.*) Hi. I am back. (*Dave and Gracy left Yahoo! Messenger and continue their conversation on Skype.*)

****

Dave Washington [2:56:33 PM]:   *** Call to Lora.Terry, no answer. *** (*Dave called her on the telephone and on Skype but they did not go through.*)

Dave Washington [2:57:35 PM]:   *** Call to Lora.Terry, duration 00:53. *** (*Dave tried the again and it went through this time but they got disconnected after about 53 seconds. Then Dave's computer started acting up. He had to turn off the computer and turn it back on before he could log in to Skype again. This took about 14 minutes.*)

****

Lora.Terry [3:11:02 PM]:   (*As soon as Dave logged back in, Gracy greeted him.*) Hello.

Dave Washington [3:23:07 PM]: (*Dave greet back.*) Hi.

Dave Washington [3:23:25 PM]:   How was your week?

Lora.Terry [3:27:22 PM]:   Fine.

Dave Washington [3:28:37 PM]:   *(Dave went straight to the point.)* I
                                 noticed you have changed your name to Lora
                                 Terry. Why did you change it, if I may ask?

Gracy [3:30:56 PM]:   *(Rather than answering Dave's question,
                                 Gracy immediately changed her name again
                                 from Lora Terry back to Gracy, and then she
                                 asked Dave what he saw now.)* So, what can
                                 you see now?

Dave [3:31:17 PM]:   Gracy.

Gracy [3:31:31 PM]:   How has your weekend been dear?

Dave [3:31:51 PM]:   *(As usual, Dave did not want to complain
                                 about his pains and suffering.)* Great, Thanks.

Dave [3:32:12 PM]:   How has your day been?

Gracy [3:32:49 PM]:   *(Gracy probably did not see Dave's last
                                 question.)* I Miss You.

Dave [3:33:00 PM]:   I missed you, too.

Dave [3:33:44 PM]:   *(Up till now, Gracy had posted someone else
                                 picture, an Indian girl, as her picture on her
                                 profiles on Flixster, Skype, and Yahoo!
                                 Messenger. If the Indian girl was really
                                 Gracy, Dave would have loved it, because the
                                 Indian lady was very attractive; but Dave no
                                 longer wanted to be looking at someone else's
                                 picture while he was chatting with Gracy. He
                                 wanted her to post her true picture on her
                                 profile so that he could see the real Gracy.)* I
                                 really would like to see your picture on your

profile, instead of this Indian girl.

Gracy [3:34:34 PM]:   *(Gracy ignored Dave's question and changed the subject and Dave did not like that.)* How often do you study your bible?

Dave [3:34:48 PM]:   Every day.[55]

Gracy [3:35:30 PM]:   Good.

Dave [3:35:44 PM]:   Do you read the Bible?

Gracy [3:36:02 PM]:   And how often do you pray?

Dave [3:36:43 PM]:   *(Dave was tempted to say, "It's none of your business how often I pray to my God, but he felts that would be rude and condescending. Then he answered politely but honestly.)* I really don't tell people how often I pray because that...

Gracy [3:36:47 PM]:   *(Gracy now answered Dave's reciprocal question whether she, too, reads the Bible.)* Sure, I read my bible.

Dave [3:37:19 PM]:   I really don't tell people how often I pray because that is something private between God and me.

---

[55] Dave was in fact studying at least three chapters of the Bible everyday; and he had been doing so now for the past eight to nine months. He wanted to ready everyone in the Bible. Although he had pretty much read the entire Bible before, this was the first time that he embarked on a Personal Bible Reading Project to study the entire Bible sequentially on his own from Genesis to Revelation; word by word, and page by page. Furthermore, he had been disfellowshipped as a Jehovah's Witness for the past six years and he was now making earnest efforts to return and be reinstated as Jehovah's Witness. He hoped that he would be reinstated within the next year.

Gracy [3:37:33 PM]:   Why?

Gracy [3:37:51 PM]:   Okay.

Dave [3:38:25 PM]:   (*Dave was offended that she asked him "why" when he just told her that it was something private between God and him.*) Because that is how it should be. It is something confidential between you and your God, and between me and my God.

Gracy [3:38:31 PM]:   (*She changed the subject again.*) How many are you in your family?

Dave [3:38:58 PM]:   (*Dave was glad that Gracy changed the subject, but he found her new question puzzling.*) What do you mean?

Gracy [3:39:22 PM]:   Number of male and female?

Dave [3:40:00 PM]:   Immediate or extended? (*While Dave's immediate family was small, his extended family was too large to number. For example, on his paternal grandfather side alone, Dave had over 200 cousins as of May 1977. Add that number to his maternal family side, plus his extended Royal Family members; the total number was truly too large to count and unknown to Dave.*)

Gracy [3:40:40 PM]:   Immediate.

Dave [3:40:53 PM]:   Six alive.

Dave [3:41:03 PM]:   What about you?

Gracy [3:41:35 PM]:   (*Gracy ignored Dave question again and Dave did not like that at all. He began to think that Gracy was on a fishing expedition. Gracy asked Dave another personal question instead of answering his questions.*) And what number are you in the family?

Dave [3:41:56 PM]: You did not answer my questions. (*Dave insisted sternly.*)

Gracy [3:42:24 PM]: (*Gracy complied.*) We are Four excluding dad and mom.

Dave [3:42:34 PM]: One. (*Dave then answered her question about what number he was in the family.*)

Dave [3:42:46 PM] : And you?

Gracy [3:43:15 PM]: Are you the first?

Gracy [3:43:25 PM]: Four. (*She answered Dave's question about what number she was in her family.*)

Dave [3:43:57 PM]: Yes. (*Dave missed her answer to his question and asked her again.*) What number are you?

Gracy [3:44:39 PM]: Number of male and female?

Dave [3:45:17 PM]: You have not answered my question. (*Dave was no longer in the mood to let his question go unanswered again.*)

Gracy [3:45:45 PM]: Four.

Gracy [3:46:16 PM]: And I am the fourth.

Dave [3:46:27 PM]: Do you mean that you are the fourth?

Dave [3:46:38 PM]:   Thanks.

Gracy [3:46:39 PM]:   I am forth.

Dave [3:46:53 PM]:   We are four boys and two girls.

Dave [3:47:00 PM]:   What about you?

Gracy [3:47:11 PM]:   Thanks for what?

Dave [3:47:27 PM]:   Thanks for answering my question.

Gracy [3:48:12 PM]:   What's the number of male and female in your family?

Dave [3:48:30 PM]:   Four males and two females.

Dave [3:48:38 PM]:   What about you?

Gracy [3:49:08 PM]:   Wow...

Gracy [3:49:29 PM]:   Two males and two females.

Dave [3:49:42 PM]:   Well balanced.

Gracy [3:50:00 PM]:   Two males and two females.

Dave [3:50:29 PM]:   *(Dave resurrected his previous concern about Gracy's posted picture on her profiles.)* I really would like to see your picture on your profile, instead of this Indian female's picture you have posted there.

Gracy [3:51:07 PM]:   *(Again, Gracy ignored Dave's request, and she continued to pry into Dave's personal background.*) So tell me where are your brothers now?

Dave [3:51:39 PM]:   (*Dave was offended that she ignored his request again, which he believed was a deliberate action on her part. Therefore he insisted that she answered his questions before proceeding any further.*) Please respond to my humble request about your picture.

* * * * * * *

Gracy refused to respond. She was silent online for about twenty minutes. Then Gracy logged out without responding to Dave's request. He was very upset about this and he decided to end their relationship. He was very disappointed that every so-called friend he met on Flixster had turned out to be unreliable. He refused to go online for about a week. Later, he decided he must cancel his Flixster account.

Thus, on August 8, 2009, at 02:04 hrs in the wee hours of the morning, Dave canceled his *Flixster* account, as the confirmation indicated below:

Your account has been canceled.

"Your account has been canceled. We have removed your content and details from the site, and others will not be able to access it.

If you would like to reactivate in the future, we'd love to have you back. Just log in with your username and password, and we will automatically reopen your account. You are welcome to cancel again at any time.

Flixster."

* * * * * * *

CHAPTER 25
DAVE INVESTIGATES "ROSE GRAND" FURTHER

Dave decided to return to "Rose Grand" to investigate him/her further; because Dave was now very disappointed with the people he met on Flixster. Dave is using the pronouns "he/she" and "him/her" because "Rose Grand" may or may not be a female as claimed on online. Dave also decided to investigate some of the people he had had encounters with online, whom he now believed were nothing but greedy scammers; possibly including even Gracy herself. One most notorious among these scammers was the person who called himself/herself "Rose Grand." The first sign of fraud that Dave noticed on Flixster was that of Rose Grand's posting on Dave's profile. As indicated in Chapter 2 of this book, Dave's further exploration into Rose Grand's background showed that he/she had written similar fraudulent postings on many of Flixster members' profiles. An example of such fraudulent postings is reprinted here in this chapter.

Below was the message posted on Musah Issifu's profile (as well as Dave's profile and hundreds of other members' profiles) by Rose Grand on Flixster. Rose used about 40 different profiles (accounts) utilizing different pictures on Flixster to defraud people. Dave did not believe that any of the pictures used really belonged to this scammer, nor did he believe that "Rose Grand" was the scammer's real name. Below was one of the messages Rose posted on members' profiles, including those of Dave and Musah Issifu.

"Hotel Omni Mont-Royal
1050 Sherbrooke Street West
Montreal, H3A 2R6 CA.

Welcome To Omni Mont-Royal Hotel Canadian Employment Offer

Good day,

I am Rose from Canada, the manager of Omni canadian hotel, pls i want to inform you about the vacancies in our hotel, The management needs men and women, married and not married, who will work and live in canada .The hotel will pay for his flight ticket and assist him to process his visa in his country, if you are interested contact us via E-mail: omni.montroyalhotels@yahoo.ca. And the Hotel informations will be sent to you immediately.

Thanks.

From the Hotel manager.
TEL...   001-606-259-4052 OR +44-703-187-1148.
Fax: (440)348-7275 .
E-MAIL : omni.montroyalhotels@yahoo.ca
HOTEL WEBSITE. www.omnimontroyalhotels.com"

* * * * * *

When Dave read the above message for the first time, he knew right away that this was a scam. For example, listing a United Kingdom telephone number and an Ohio fax number while claiming to live in Canada did not make any sense to Dave. Besides, Rose Grand's writing skills were definitely deplorable. She did not write as a real manager of a reputable hotel in Canada should write. Rose Grand's writing style was fraught with grammatical, punctuational, and spelling errors. Moreover, Dave believed that there was no way that a reputable Omni Hotel would use a *Yahoo!* email account as its official email address. In Dave's view, the hotel's employment email address was more likely to be similar to one or more of the following:

jobs@omni.ca; jobs@omni.com; info@omni.ca; jobs@omnihotels.ca; jobs@omnihotels.com; info@omni.com; info@omnihotels.ca; or info@omnihotels.com.

Omni Hotel's employment email address should be something along those lines above; but certainly not omni.montrooyalhotels@yahoo.ca nor hotelcanadians@yahoo.com, as Rose Grand claimed. Dave also believed that the hotel may not even have any email address specifically for job applications because jobs seekers may be required to apply for jobs directly online. These obvious inconsistencies made Dave very suspicious of Rose Grand.

Below was another one of Rose Grand's postings on Vinayaamatya's profile on Flixster at: http://www.flixster.com/user/vinayaamatya:

"hotelcanadians …

i am rose from canada, i am the manager of canada hotels, pls hotel need man and woman who can work and live in canadian hotel Canada, hotel will pay for his ticket and his visa in his country, if you are interested contact me back o.k email hotelcanadians@yahoo.com".

Dave did some more digging into Rose Grand's exploitation on Flixster's website, and when Dave found out that Rose Grand had many fraudulent accounts of Flixster, he reported the scammer to Flixster's administration again. Months later, at the time of initiating the writing of this book, Dave went back to query the name again and found that, even though some of Rose Grand's accounts were still open, most of the fraudulent messages had been deleted. It was not clear whether "Rose Grand" deleted those messages or if the Flixster administration did.

Because of the obvious fraud that Rose Grand had been perpetuating on Flixster, Dave posted the following warning for some of the Flixster members on whose profiles Rose Grand had posted fraudulent messages. Below was the warning Dave posted on those members' profiles to alert them to the dangers of Rose Grand's machinations.

Friends4Dave:

"WARNING: I just wanted to post a response to the message by this lady who calls herself "Rose". She claims to be the Manager of a major hotel in Canada and that she is hiring. Well, there is no major hotel in existence in the United States and Canada that uses a *Yahoo!* email address as its official email address. Besides, one of her telephone numbers is a United Kingdom phone number, not Canadian. The second phone number and the fax number are both in the United States. Before you fall for such an obvious fraud, you may want to ask her to post publicly online here the name and address of the hotel, as well as her supervisor's name. Then "Google" (search for) the hotel at www.google.com or go to www.whitepages.com and try to locate the hotel's information. If you are able locate it, then call the number listed on google.com or whitepages.com to see if a person by the name of "Rose Grand" really works there as a manager. Please do not call the phone numbers she listed in her profile. Just be careful... all of you reading her profile. You don't even know if this person is truly a female as claims to be."

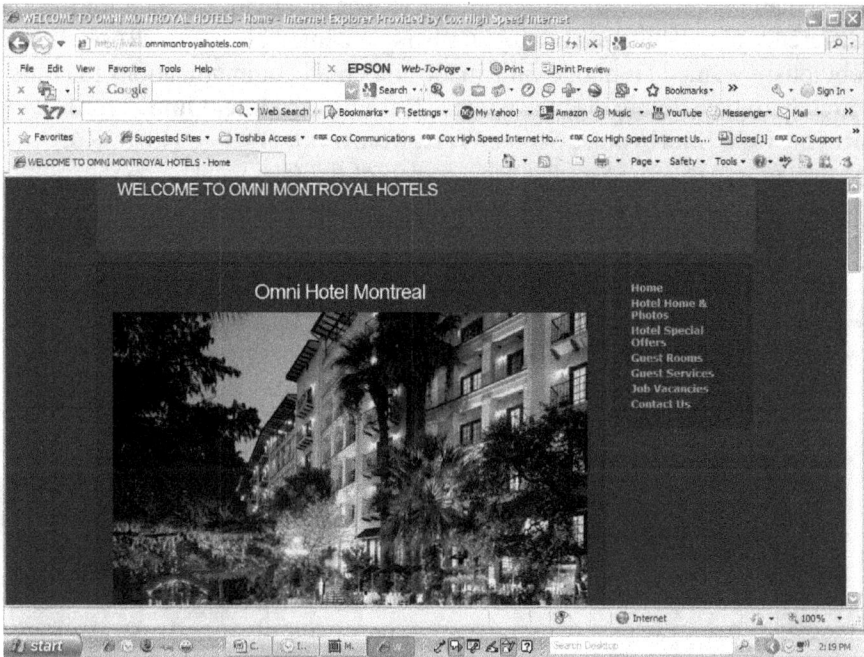

The website's print-screen above, whose fake URL Rose Grand listed on her fraudulent messages, appeared to be genuine on the surface – even to the most cautious individuals. This was the website address that Rose Grand listed, which many gullible people may easily believe to be genuine and legitimate: http://www.omnimontroyalhotels.com.[56] However, clicking

---

[56] When Dave checked this website again seven years later, he noticed that the website was no longer in existence. As indicated in this chapter during Dave's chat with a true representative of the hotel, Dave reported Rose Grand's fraudulent use of the hotel's name to scam innocent people. Therefore, he now believes that Rose Grand's fraudulent website, http://www.omnimontroyalhotels.com, was perhaps shut down as a result of Dave's

on the link would take you to a website that was reprinted in the print-screen above. But don't be fooled. That website was fake. Rose used copy-and-paste photographs from the genuine website; but Rose Grand's fake Omni Hotels website was by far inferior in its design and contents to the genuine Omni Hotels' official website.

Another revelation: the physical address listed on the fake website was the same address on the genuine website, but the telephone and fax numbers and email addresses were different. There was an obvious reason for the differences in telephone and fax numbers and email addresses. Rose obviously wanted all phone calls made and email communications to come directly to her. Below was the address Rose listed: **Hotel Omni Mont-Royal, 1050 Sherbrooke Street West, Montreal, Quebec H3A 2R6.** However, please compare the print-screen of the fake website on the previous page with the print-screen of the genuine website's homepage below (as of 2009):

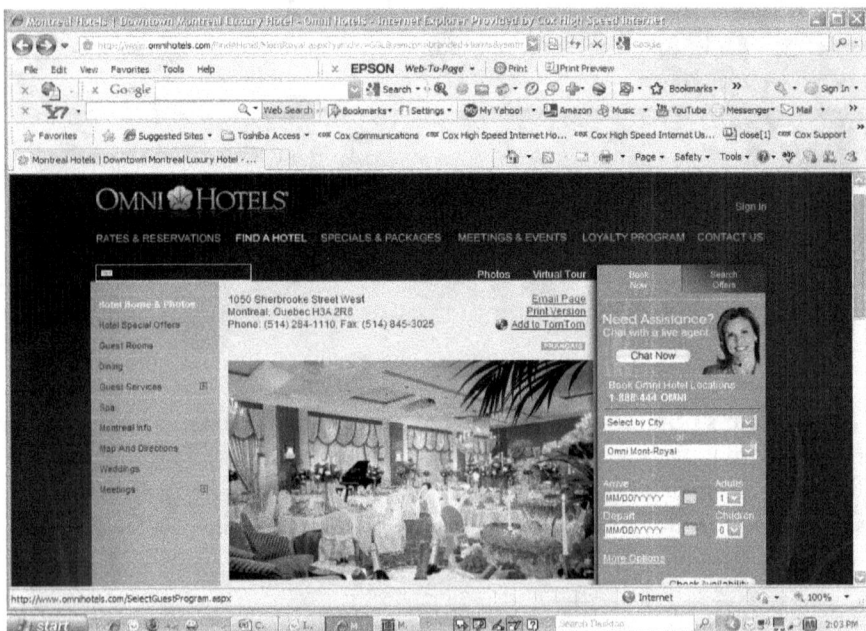

The picture you see on the fake website above was actually one of the

investigation and subsequent reporting to the real Omni Hotels.

pictures on the genuine website in 2009; but this picture was no longer on the homepage as of 2016. The URLs for the genuine website for Omni Hotels that Rose claimed to work for were as indicated below: [57]

> http://www.omnihotels.com/FindAHotel/MontRoyal.aspx?ysmchn=GGL &ysmcpn=branded+terms&ysmtrm=omni+montreal&ysmtac=PPC&ysm grp=Montreal.

AND

> https://www.omnihotels.com/hotels/montreal-mont-royal.

AND

> http://www.omnihotels.com. (Omni Hotels Headquarters in the United States.)

Some of the email addresses of the genuine Omni Royal Hotels that Dave found during his investigation in 2009 were:

NSO.Leads@omnihotels.com AND guestrelations@omnihotels.com.

* * * * * * *

Dave also cross-checked information above with that of Omni Hotels Headquarters' directory and the address and telephone and fax numbers matched those that were listed on the hotel's website in Montreal also. Below is the information as it was written on the Omni Hotel chain's directory:

"Canada:

Hotel Omni Mont-Royal
1050 Sherbrooke Street West
Montreal, Quebec H3A 2R6
Tel: (514) 284-1110
Fax: (514) 845-3025"

Having satisfied himself regarding a probable cause to suspect that Rose

---

[57] It should be noted that seven years later, in 2016 and after the print-screens were printed in 2009, the pictures on the pages of the genuine website have also changed, although the website was still active.

was indeed a fraud, Dave decided to make contact with a representative of Omni Hotels in Montreal, Canada; the same hotel that Rose Grand claimed to be working for as its Manager. Dave returned to the genuine Omni Hotels website and initiated a live chat with one of its online representatives (Miranda). Dave was the "You" in this conversation.

Their conversation was reprinted with the permission of the Omni Hotel representative (Miranda) below:

* * * * * * *

"Please wait for an agent to respond. All agents are currently assisting others. Thanks for your patience. An operator will be with you shortly. (*It took a while for an available representative to come online to chat with Dave. There were no date and time stamps in the chat conversation.*)

You are now chatting with 'Miranda'

Miranda:	Hello. How can I help you today? (*The Omni Hotel representative began a conversation with Dave.*)
You (Dave):	Hi. (*Dave greeted Miranda.*)
You (Dave):	Please, what is your email address to submit an employment application? (*Dave did not want to ask her any leading questions.*)
Miranda:	We do not have an email address. You can submit them on the web site. (*Just as Dave had suspected that the hotel probably did not have any employment-related email address, as opposed to what Rose Grand had posted in her fraudulent schemes.*)
You (Dave):	Thank you for confirming my suspicion.
Miranda:	Is there anything else I can help you with?

You (Dave):   (*Dave decided to tell her why he was contact Miranda's company.*) I am investigating someone who has been using your company's information to defraud other people online.

You (Dave):   Here is an example of the information that this person is posting online: (*Dave copied and pasted Rose Grand's fraudulent message on Flixster.*) "hotelcanadians … i am rose from canada, i am the manager of canada hotels, pls hotel need man and woman who can work and live in canadian hotel Canada, hotel will pay for his ticket and his visa in his country, if you are interested contact me back o.k e mail hotelcanadians@yahoo.com."

Miranda: Yes, we know they are out there. It is a scam. They are not part of the Omni Hotels.

You (Dave):   (*Dave disclosed the fake website.*) And the person has a fake website: http://www.omnimontroyalhotels.com.

Miranda: Yeah, they are not part of us. All our opening for jobs is posted on the web site.

You (Dave):   I have reported this person to the Flixster administration where most of his/her fraudulent practices have been perpetuated and I have warned some of the potential victims.

You (Dave):   If you visit Flixster.com, click on Find User and type in "Rose Grand". It will give you many of the fake names the person has used on that website.

Miranda: Yes, we know that.

You (Dave):   Anyway, I am currently writing a book to expose this person and others like him/her.

You (Dave):   Thank you for confirming my suspicions. I just wanted to make sure and to get the truth from the true source before I complete my book. My name is Dave Washington.[58]

Miranda: Okay, I am glad to be a help.

Miranda: Is there anything else I can help you with?

You (Dave):   If you have any other information that you would like me to include in my book, please email it to investigations@ washingtondivision.com. (*Dave gave the correct email address to Miranda but he changed the email address here in order to prevent spam in his inbox.*)

Miranda: I will do, thank you.

Miranda: Thank you for chatting with us. We value your feedback. Please click the CLOSE button at top right to answer a few questions about your experience with us today.[59]

You (Dave):   You are welcome. Have a blessed day. I intend to copy and paste this conversation to include in my book. Goodbye."

* * * * * *

---

[58] The name was changed to Dave Washington here in this book; however, Dave used his real name and contact information when he chatted with the hotel's representative.

[59] Dave complied as instructed when their conversation ended; and he indicated in the survey that he would reprint his chat with Miranda in this book.

CHAPTER 26
DAVE AND GRACY RECONCILE AGAIN

$ince August 2ⁿᵈ, when Dave and Gracy last chatted online, they had not spoken to each other. Gracy had been trying to call Dave on the phone, but Dave refused to take her calls. Dave was just tired of Gracy logging out whenever she was upset or decided she did not want to answer Dave's questions. This time around, Dave canceled his Flixster account and he was sure that his relationship with Gracy was over for good. However, after repeated and relentless phone calls from Gracy, he decided to answer her last call. Gracy asked Dave why he had been refusing to answer her calls for more than two weeks. Dave replied that he decided that it was best to end their relationship. Gracy then begged Dave to come online to chat with her. Dave was silent for a while, as Gracy waited anxiously for his response. Finally, he agreed to come online, but he was still resolved not to resume the relationship between them. He was fed up. Nevertheless, they ended up reconciling during their online chat.

Friends4Dave (August 18 - 2:51:12 PM):   You just called and asked me to come online. What do you want from me?

Talk2bryan2001 (August 18 - 2:53:38 PM): *(Gracy attempted to pacify Dave.)* Good to see you online honey.

Friends4Dave (August 18 - 2:53:55 PM):   Thanks.

Talk2bryan2001 (August 18 - 2:55:06 PM): Why are you sounding like there is something wrong? Please, I beg of you... tell me.

Friends4Dave (August 18 - 2:55:42 PM):   Because there is something wrong here.

Talk2bryan2001 (August 18 - 2:56:11 PM): What? Please tell me.

Friends4Dave (August 18 - 2:57:44 PM):   I am not sure who or what really you are. I've answered all of your questions, but you hesitate when answering my questions and you do not answer some of my questions at all. Why? (*Dave was still pissed off.*)

Talk2bryan2001 (August 18 - 3:00:06 PM): I am so sorry dear. I can't remember not answering your question. Please what were your questions?

Talk2bryan2001 (August 18 - 3:00:06 PM): (*She impatiently and anxiously buzzed Dave.*) BUZZ!!!

Friends4Dave (August 18 - 3:03:44 PM): I had asked you what "Nwaokoro means", you did not answer but logged out instead. I asked you whether you have a boyfriend, but you did not answer and logged out instead, too. Then, I asked you if you would please post your real picture on your profile that shows on my screen, but you did not answer and logged out instead, also. There are other questions that you did not answer which I cannot remember right now.

Talk2bryan2001 (August 18 - 3:08:10 PM): Oh, I am so sorry, my login off could be as a result to my network or low battery on my phone. Please dear, forgive me.

Friends4Dave (August 18 - 3:09:17 PM): But you remained online for a while each time before you logged out, though. (*Dave has always been willing to forgive anybody who truly apologizes for his or her wrongdoing and is truly remorseful; but right now, he did not want to let Gracy off the hook that easy this time.*)

Talk2bryan2001 (August 18 - 3:12:38 PM): (*Gracy made an earnest effort to answer one of Dave's questions.*) I don't know the meaning of Nwaokoro but maybe I will ask my father.

Friends4Dave (August 18 - 3:12:55 PM):   Ok.

Friends4Dave (August 18 - 3:13:35 PM):   You don't have to know the meaning. I just thought maybe it means something. That's all.

Talk2bryan2001 (August 18 - 3:14:51 PM):   (*Gracy called her dad on the phone to ask him about the meaning of her last name, Nwaokoro.*) I am speaking with my dad now. Please hold.

Talk2bryan2001 (August 18 - 3:14:54 PM): I'll be right back.

Talk2bryan2001 (August 18 - 3:15:21 PM): Let me ask him.

Talk2bryan2001 (August 18 - 3:18:10 PM):   (*Gracy returned with the meaning of her last name.*) NWAOKORO means "child of a strong man".

Friends4Dave (August 18 - 3:18:24 PM):   That is a great name.

Friends4Dave (August 18 - 3:18:33 PM):   Thanks for finding out.

Friends4Dave (August 18 - 3:19:21 PM):   (*Dave's anger subsided and he forgave her.*) The sad thing about our last chat is that, I had called you to come online so that I could get your information to send you the money I promised you. But when you logged out, I used the money for other pressing bills instead. Now, it will have to be another month or so before I can send you anything.

Talk2bryan2001 (August 18 - 3:20:59 PM): Okay.

Friends4Dave (August 18 - 3:21:24 PM):   I am sorry about that.

Talk2bryan2001 (August 18 - 3:22:49 PM): Will.... (*Obviously
                                    disappointed.*)

Talk2bryan2001 (August 18 - 3:23:08 PM): Well....

Friends4Dave (August 18 - 3:23:34 PM):   Well what, please?

Talk2bryan2001 (August 18 - 3:26:57 PM): It's okay.

Friends4Dave (August 18 - 3:27:13 PM):   (*Even though he had forgiven
                                    her, Dave thought that this was the time to find
                                    out more about Gracy. For example, he
                                    wanted to know the "Bryan" in Gracy's
                                    Yahoo! ID and email address.*) Who is Bryan?

Talk2bryan2001 (August 18 - 3:27:58 PM): Me.

Friends4Dave (August 18 - 3:28:32 PM):   (*Dave was surprised by her
                                    response.*) But Bryan is a male's name,
                                    though. Right?

Talk2bryan2001 (August 18 - 3:29:20 PM): Have you heard of Westlife?

Friends4Dave (August 18 - 3:29:36 PM):   (*Dave had never heard of that
                                    name.*) No. What is it?

Talk2bryan2001 (August 18 - 3:31:00 PM): Artist.

Friends4Dave (August 18 - 3:31:26 PM):   Okay. Who is this artist?

Talk2bryan2001 (August 18 - 3:32:47 PM): Westlife.

Talk2bryan2001 (August 18 - 3:33:18 PM): They are group singers.

Friends4Dave (August 18 - 3:33:24 PM):   What does Westlife do, and how is he/she related to Bryan?

Friends4Dave (August 18 - 3:34:10 PM):   Okay. What relationship do they have with Bryan?

Talk2bryan2001 (August 18 - 3:36:02 PM): The name of one of them is Bryan.

Friends4Dave (August 18 - 3:36:17 PM):   Okay. I see. (*Dave began to think that Bryan is perhaps Gracy's boyfriend or that she maybe a member of the singing group.*)

Friends4Dave (August 18 - 3:36:42 PM):   Are you a member of Westlife.

Talk2bryan2001 (August 18 - 3:37:43 PM): No, they used to be by best artist.

Friends4Dave (August 18 - 3:38:11 PM):   Okay. Is Bryan your boyfriend?

Talk2bryan2001 (August 18 - 3:39:04 PM): NO...

Friends4Dave (August 18 - 3:39:24 PM):   Was Bryan ever your boyfriend?

Talk2bryan2001 (August 18 - 3:39:32 PM): I just like the name... that's all.

Friends4Dave (August 18 - 3:41:01 PM):   (*Dave was thinking to himself, "If Gracy is a female, why is she bearing a male's name? Or, could she be a male?"*) You are a female, right?

Talk2bryan2001 (August 18 - 3:42:47 PM): Yes.

Friends4Dave (August 18 - 3:43:38 PM):   I just want to make sure that you are neither a transvestite nor a transsexual. Are you?

Friends4Dave (August 18 - 3:44:13 PM):   (*Dave decided to soften the blow with a smile.*)

Talk2bryan2001 (August 18 - 3:45:21 PM): Hey! (*Gracy did not think that was funny.*)

Friends4Dave (August 18 - 3:45:34 PM):   Yes?

Talk2bryan2001 (August 18 - 3:46:00 PM): I am just a female... GOD'S own creature.

Talk2bryan2001 (August 18 - 3:46:06 PM):   (*Gracy was hot with anger.*)

Friends4Dave (August 18 - 3:46:17 PM):   LOL. (*Dave tried to diffuse the situation, indicating that he was only joking by laughing out loud; but he was serious.*)

Friends4Dave (August 18 - 3:46:54 PM):   (*Dave apologized for offending her with his question.*) I didn't mean to make you angry. I am sorry. I was just trying to establish the truth with a joke.

Friends4Dave (August 18 - 3:47:28 PM):   Please, do not blush ... or get angry.

Friends4Dave (August 18 - 3:48:56 PM):   Now, how was your week?

Talk2bryan2001 (August 18 - 3:50:04 PM): (*Gracy calmed down.*) Great.

Talk2bryan2001 (August 18 - 3:50:30 PM): My week has been great.

Friends4Dave (August 18 - 3:50:48 PM): Good.

Friends4Dave (August 18 - 3:51:48 PM): Someone has been calling me and hanging up since that last time you and I chatted online. Was that you that called?

Talk2bryan2001 (August 18 - 3:52:13 PM): No. (*Dave sensed that her denial was a prevarication because he saw her number on his caller ID a few times.*)

Friends4Dave (August 18 - 3:52:47 PM): Did you ever call me since then … not including today?

Talk2bryan2001 (August 18 - 3:53:03 PM): Though I tried calling but it wasn't going through.

Friends4Dave (August 18 - 3:53:29 PM): It was ringing here.

Talk2bryan2001 (August 18 - 3:53:55 PM): Yes.

Friends4Dave (August 18 - 3:54:36 PM): Where do we go from here now?

Talk2bryan2001 (August 18 - 3:55:03 PM): (*Gracy missed Dave's last question.*) I used a friend's PC to call through Skype.

Friends4Dave (August 18 - 3:55:31 PM): Okay. I see.

Talk2bryan2001 (August 18 - 3:55:33 PM): It wasn't going through.

Talk2bryan2001 (August 18 - 3:57:06 PM): I taught you went outside your state.

Friends4Dave (August 18 - 3:57:40 PM):   What do you mean? Please I
          do not understand.

Talk2bryan2001 (August 18 - 3:58:32 PM): Thought you traveled.

Friends4Dave (August 18 - 3:59:12 PM):   No, I did not travel. I truly
          cannot afford to travel right now.

Talk2bryan2001 (August 18 - 4:00:57 PM): There's nothing impossible for
          GOD to do.

Talk2bryan2001 (August 18 - 4:01:42 PM): I believe so much in prayer.

Friends4Dave (August 18 - 4:01:50 PM):   That is very true, and I agree.

Talk2bryan2001 (August 18 - 4:01:52 PM): Do you?

Friends4Dave (August 18 - 4:02:02 PM):   Yes, I do.

Friends4Dave (August 18 - 4:02:15 PM):   What is your religion?

Talk2bryan2001 (August 18 - 4:04:09 PM): *(She ignored Dave's question
          again.)* From today I will be praying for you
          concerning your present situation.

Friends4Dave (August 18 - 4:04:28 PM):   What situation is that? *(Dave
          was thinking to himself and he hoped that
          Gracy was not indulging in Spiritism, because
          Dave did not want anything to do with
          Spiritism, which is idolatry and in violation of
          God's commandments. The Bible specifically
          condemns any involvement with the practice of
          Divination or Spiritism.[60] And Dave did not
          want to be involved in any way with anyone or
          anything having to do with Spiritism.)*

---

[60] Leviticus 19:26, 31; Deuteronomy 18:10, 11; Galatians 5:19-21; and Revelation 21:8.

Talk2bryan2001 (August 18 - 4:04:44 PM): Get ready for a change.[61]

Talk2bryan2001 (August 18 - 4:05:31 PM): (*Gracy now responded to Dave's question about what situation she was talking about.*) That you can't afford to travel.

Friends4Dave (August 18 - 4:05:43 PM): I appreciate that.

Friends4Dave (August 18 - 4:06:09 PM): I truly appreciate your concern and prayers.

Talk2bryan2001 (August 18 - 4:06:54 PM): Ok.

---

[61] In fact, within a month-and-half of this conversation (on September 24th), a big change did occur. Dave's situation became much worse than it had ever been. Hartford Insurance Company stopped his Disability Payments, claiming that Dave was not disabled, even though he actually was and still is disabled to this very day. Since Dave was already on a five years Supervised Release (Federal Probation for the crime he did not commit and for which he was sent to prison in 2003-2004), Hartford took advantage of that unfortunate situation and then falsely accused Dave of insurance fraud. Hartford insurance did this so that the company would not have to pay Dave's disability insurance benefits, which included substantial monthly income and Life insurance benefits. Based on this false accusation, Dave's Probation Officer at the time said that Dave violated the terms of his Supervised Release, revoked it just two days before he was supposed to be completely free, and then sent him to federal prison the second time for six months; plus an additional five years of Supervised Release, making it a total of 10 years of Supervised Release for a crime he did not commit and for which he was sent to prison twice. Dave completed his 10 years Supervised Release in February 2015. As for the false insurance fraud charge that Hartford Insurance Company falsely accused him of, Dave was prosecuted by the federal government again for the crime he did not commit; but, this time, he was found "Not Guilty" because Dave fought back this time, unlike the first time when he was sent to prison and was not allowed to defend himself. Besides, he did not commit any crime anyway. Unfortunately, Hartford Insurance Company refused to reinstate Dave's benefits, even after the federal court found that Hartford Insurance Company's allegations were false. Furthermore, with no income coming in, and being sent to prison for six months, Dave lost his home and became homeless. Dave searched for attorneys to represent him to sue Hartford Insurance; however, because it was an ERISA case, no attorney wanted to represent Dave against Hartford Insurance Company even though the attorneys believed that Dave had a good case. The reason was that there is no money in ERISA cases. So it was not worth the attorneys' time and efforts. Years later, Dave decided to do it on his own and he sued Hartford Insurance Company in federal court for unlawful termination of his disability benefits and for wrongful and malicious prosecution. Hartford Insurance Company fought back hard with powerful and experienced attorneys on their side, and they came at Dave with everything they've got; but in the end, Hartford settled the case out of Court.

Friends4Dave (August 18 - 4:07:07 PM):   And I will remember you in
                    my prayers, too.

Talk2bryan2001 (August 18 - 4:07:23 PM): Do you fast and pray?

Friends4Dave (August 18 - 4:11:35 PM):   I would love to answer your
                    question, but because of Matthew 8:5-8, 16-18,
                    I am not at liberty to discuss whether I fast and
                    how often I pray. I am trying to obey what the
                    Bible tells me to do. Hope you understand.

Talk2bryan2001 (August 18 - 4:12:52 PM): Okay.

Friends4Dave (August 18 - 4:13:13 PM):   I really appreciate your
                    understanding in this matter.

Friends4Dave (August 18 - 4:14:20 PM):   When you have time, please
                    read Matthew chapter 8, verses 5-8 and verses
                    16-18. You will see why I cannot discuss
                    them.

Talk2bryan2001 (August 18 - 4:15:45 PM): Okay.

Friends4Dave (August 18 - 4:16:16 PM):   I appreciate that.

Talk2bryan2001 (August 18 - 4:17:14 PM): Okay.

Friends4Dave (August 18 - 4:17:22 PM):   By the way, I am ready for a
                    major change in my life, just as you have said.[62]

Friends4Dave (August 18 - 4:17:52 PM):   A major positive change in my
                    life for sure.

---

[62] In hindsight, Dave wished he had never said that, in view of the very bad experiences he
has endured since then.

Friends4Dave (August 18 - 4:19:16 PM):   And I believe that you, too, will benefit somehow from my positive changes in life.

Talk2bryan2001 (August 18 - 4:20:27 PM): GOD is able... more than able to cause a change in your life.

Friends4Dave (August 18 - 4:20:51 PM):   That is definitely true.

Friends4Dave (August 18 - 4:22:30 PM):   *(Dave changed the subject.)* You will be going back to school soon, right?

Talk2bryan2001 (August 18 - 4:23:41 PM): It goes along with faith. If GOD makes it happen in your life, don't be carried away. Ok? *(It was amazing that Gracy said this to Dave, because this has been one of Dave's main philosophies, which is "Humility is a Virtue to be Pursued"; and he has promised himself that when his situation improves in the future, he would still be down to earth as he has always been, including the time when he was well-off in the past.)*

Talk2bryan2001 (August 18 - 4:24:17 PM): I am in school now.

Friends4Dave (August 18 - 4:24:50 PM):   It is amazing that you have just said what I have been telling myself for some time now.

Friends4Dave (August 18 - 4:25:30 PM):   Oh great. When did your school start?

Talk2bryan2001 (August 18 - 4:25:59 PM): Last week.

Friends4Dave (August 18 - 4:27:04 PM):   It is truly surprisingly reassuring how well you have just expressed my philosophy not to be carried away when things begin to improve again for me.

Talk2bryan2001 (August 18 - 4:27:33 PM): Let it be as you believe you
are blessed.

Friends4Dave (August 18 - 4:28:57 PM):   Yes, indeed. But, even if I
remain poor financially, I still believe that I am
blessed. There are so many things for me to be
thankful for besides financial wealth.

Talk2bryan2001 (August 18 - 4:30:46 PM): GOD KNOWS EVERYTHING, I
am not a prophet. But GOD uses me in HIS
own way.

Friends4Dave (August 18 - 4:31:22 PM):   Point well taken.

Talk2bryan2001 (August 18 - 4:31:35 PM): Good.

Friends4Dave (August 18 - 4:31:46 PM):   And may God bless you, too.

Talk2bryan2001 (August 18 - 4:33:52 PM): Okay.

Friends4Dave (August 18 - 4:35:42 PM):   (*Dave changed the subject.*)
Different subject: Has there been fighting in
Northern Nigeria? I read a news headline that
over 400 people have died in the fighting. Is
that true?

Talk2bryan2001 (August 18 - 4:36:16 PM): Yes.

Friends4Dave (August 18 - 4:36:30 PM):   What is the fighting about?

Talk2bryan2001 (August 18 - 4:37:37 PM): Before I forget, if I go offline
it's because of my airtime. Ok?

Friends4Dave (August 18 - 4:37:51 PM):   Ok.

Friends4Dave (August 18 - 4:39:08 PM):   If you need to go, that's fine
with me. We can chat at another time, if you
would like.

Talk2bryan2001 (August 18 - 4:40:41 PM): Ok, when are you going to be
online again?

Friends4Dave (August 18 - 4:41:23 PM):   9:00 p.m. your time.

Talk2bryan2001 (August 18 - 4:41:51 PM): Tomorrow?

Friends4Dave (August 18 - 4:41:52 PM):   Is that good for you, or do you
want a different time?

Friends4Dave (August 18 - 4:42:05 PM):   Yes, tomorrow.

Talk2bryan2001 (August 18 - 4:43:14 PM): Let's make it 7:00 p.m. my
time or what do you think?

Friends4Dave (August 18 - 4:43:41 PM):   That is fine with me. I will see
you then.

Friends4Dave (August 18 - 4:43:59 PM):   Good night.

Talk2bryan2001 (August 18 - 4:44:30 PM): GOODNIGHT DEAR (*They
both logged out.*)

CHAPTER 27
DAVE CONSIDERS FACEBOOK AND
A RETURN TO NIGERIA

The relationship between Dave and Gracy has normalized as they have put the past behind them, even though a telephone call to Dave from someone else almost derailed his conversation with Gracy. They discussed the possibility of Dave joining Facebook.[63] Gracy had been a member of Facebook for a few years now. Dave even began to make some long-term plans with Gracy when he discussed his intention to return to Nigeria in the future. Today, the two lovebirds continued from where they left off in their chat yesterday.

Talk2bryan2001 (August 19 - 2:12:24 PM): Hello.

Friends4Dave (August 19 - 2:14:06 PM):   Hi.

Friends4Dave (August 19 - 2:17:08 PM):   How are you doing?

Talk2bryan2001 (August 19 - 2:17:27 PM): Hello.

Talk2bryan2001 (August 19 - 2:17:58 PM): I'm fine, and you?

Friends4Dave (August 19 - 2:21:18 PM):   *(Dave's telephone rang and he answered the call. The call was from his friend's fiancée in Canada. She had recently lost her baby in a miscarriage. Dave wanted to be available to her and her fiancé for comfort, especially during their period of grief.)* Please hold on. I am on the phone.

Talk2bryan2001 (August 19 - 2:26:26 PM): Ok.

---

[63] Dave did not want to join Facebook largely due to privacy issues with that social medium.

Talk2bryan2001 (August 19 - 2:31:17 PM): Hellooo.... (*Gracy was growing impatient.*)

Friends4Dave (August 19 - 2:34:34 PM): (*Dave decided to interrupt his phone conversation to respond to Gracy.*) How are you doing?

Talk2bryan2001 (August 19 - 2:34:56 PM): I am great and you?

Friends4Dave (August 19 - 2:35:11 PM): I can chat with you, but slowly because I am still on the phone.

Talk2bryan2001 (August 19 - 2:35:38 PM): (*She was impatient.*) Are you through with your call?

Friends4Dave (August 19 - 2:36:41 PM): No, not yet.

Talk2bryan2001 (August 19 - 2:37:01 PM): Okay.

Friends4Dave (August 19 - 2:39:39 PM): How was your day at school?

Talk2bryan2001 (August 19 - 2:40:30 PM): Fine.

Talk2bryan2001 (August 19 - 2:40:31 PM): And how has your day been?

Friends4Dave (August 19 - 2:42:47 PM): Great. Thanks. (*Dave's telephone conversation was going longer than he would have liked it to be.*)

Friends4Dave (August 19 - 2:45:09 PM): (*Apologetically*) I am really sorry.

Talk2bryan2001 (August 19 - 2:46:12 PM): (*Gracy made her umbrage known.*) I am not enjoying this chat. Maybe I will wait till you are through with your call.

Friends4Dave (August 19 - 2:46:43 PM):   (*Dave apologized again.*) I am really sorry about this. I am almost done. (*Dave decided to end the phone conversation prematurely.*)

Friends4Dave (August 19 - 2:46:56 PM):   I am done.

Friends4Dave (August 19 - 2:47:57 PM):   I was trying to resolve an issue with my friend who lost her baby a few weeks ago.

Friends4Dave (August 19 - 2:48:51 PM):   You have my full attention now. And I am very sorry again. I did not expect the phone call. (*Dave was automatically logged out; but he was able to log back in almost immediately.*)

Friends4Dave (August 19 - 2:49:55 PM):   I was automatically logged out.

Friends4Dave (August 19 - 2:50:17 PM):   Are you there?

Talk2bryan2001 (August 19 - 2:51:00 PM): Yeah.

Friends4Dave (August 19 - 2:51:11 PM):   Please forgive me. (*Dave continued to apologize.*)

Friends4Dave (August 19 - 2:52:44 PM):   Are you upset with me?

Talk2bryan2001 (August 19 - 2:53:43 PM): Well not really.

Friends4Dave (August 19 - 2:54:03 PM):   I am truly sorry. Please forgive me.

Talk2bryan2001 (August 19 - 2:55:13 PM): It's okay.

Friends4Dave (August 19 - 2:55:34 PM):   How is the weather in Nigeria? (*Dave was inadvertently logged out again. It took him about three minutes to be able to log back in again.*)

Talk2bryan2001 (August 19 - 2:57:54 PM): It was sunny today.

Friends4Dave (August 19 - 2:58:20 PM):   What did you do today?

Talk2bryan2001 (August 19 - 3:04:55 PM):   (*She sent a love-struck emoticon to Dave.*)

Talk2bryan2001 (August 19 - 3:05:12 PM): Yes I am with you.

Friends4Dave (August 19 - 3:05:26 PM):   I am having some connection problem. It is logging me out and it takes some time to log back in. Sorry.

Friends4Dave (August 19 - 3:05:45 PM):   (*Dave sent her a love-struck emoticon to Gracy too.*)

Friends4Dave (August 19 - 3:06:11 PM):   Did you have a great day?

Talk2bryan2001 (August 19 - 3:07:03 PM): Yes, I did.

Friends4Dave (August 19 - 3:07:12 PM):   Wonderful.

Friends4Dave (August 19 - 3:07:27 PM):   I am been thinking about you all day.

Friends4Dave (August 19 - 3:07:55 PM):   I mean, I have been thinking about you all day.

Talk2bryan2001 (August 19 - 3:09:03 PM): Really, so tell me what have been going through your mind?

Friends4Dave (August 19 - 3:09:34 PM):   Good stuff. I think you are a good person.

Talk2bryan2001 (August 19 - 3:09:56 PM): Thanks.

Friends4Dave (August 19 - 3:10:11 PM):   You have just been on my mind ... just sitting there, watching everything I do.

Talk2bryan2001 (August 19 - 3:10:16 PM): I think of you too.

Friends4Dave (August 19 - 3:10:23 PM):   Thanks.

Friends4Dave (August 19 - 3:11:22 PM):   I wish you were living in the same city as I do.

Talk2bryan2001 (August 19 - 3:12:47 PM): Wow... it would have really been nice.

Friends4Dave (August 19 - 3:13:20 PM):   Yes, indeed.

Friends4Dave (August 19 - 3:14:15 PM):   What classes are you taking this semester?

Talk2bryan2001 (August 19 - 3:14:43 PM): Nine.

Friends4Dave (August 19 - 3:15:16 PM):   You are taking nine classes? That's too many classes! (*Dave was thinking that taking nine university classes was insane.*)

Talk2bryan2001 (August 19 - 3:15:33 PM): Yeah.

Friends4Dave (August 19 - 3:15:48 PM):   What are the classes?

Talk2bryan2001 (August 19 - 3:16:50 PM): It's much and I can't start listing.

Friends4Dave (August 19 - 3:17:35 PM):   I see. (*Dave thought either she was lying about the number of classes she is taking or perhaps she was not even going to the university as she claimed. Or perhaps she meant to say "nine credits"?*)

Friends4Dave (August 19 - 3:18:11 PM):   (*Dave probed further.*) How are you able to handle nine classes?

Talk2bryan2001 (August 19 - 3:19:20 PM): Well, not in a day.

Talk2bryan2001 (August 19 - 3:19:56 PM): Two-three classes a day.

Friends4Dave (August 19 - 3:20:27 PM):   I know that. (*In his mind, he was thinking, "Please tell me what I don't know."*) But nine university classes in a single semester is still too much school work. (*Dave was thinking of when he was in college and graduate school and how people, including some professors, thought that Dave was crazy to be taking five to six classes per semester. Therefore, nine classes per semester was definitely out of the picture and purely insane for any student.*)

Friends4Dave (August 19 - 3:25:42 PM):   (*Gracy did not respond for more than five minutes.*) Are you with me dear?

Talk2bryan2001 (August 19 - 3:26:03 PM): Yes dear.

Friends4Dave (August 19 - 3:26:27 PM):   How many credits for each of the classes you are taking? (*Dave asked this question to see if she was really attending a university.*)

Talk2bryan2001 (August 19 - 3:27:41 PM): (*Gracy misconstrued Dave's question.*) The last semester was 7 credits and 2 passes.

Friends4Dave (August 19 - 3:28:23 PM): That was great! (*Dave said great because when Dave was in Nigeria, "credit" meant "Excellent" which was equivalent to an "A or A-" grade in the United States.*)

Talk2bryan2001 (August 19 - 3:28:39 PM): Really?

Friends4Dave (August 19 - 3:29:44 PM): (*A "Really?" response from Gracy to Dave's accolades signaled to Dave that perhaps a grade of "Credit" was no longer that good anymore. In any case, that was besides the point here; and Gracy's responses so far have not addressed Dave's question about the number of credits each class has; so, he redirected Gracy to answer his question.*) But my question is different: I meant how many credits (credit hours) does each one of your current classes have?

Friends4Dave (August 19 - 3:30:56 PM): For example, in the United States, some classes have 3 credits each, while some have 4 or 4.5 credits each.

Talk2bryan2001 (August 19 - 3:32:02 PM): Yes, same here.

Friends4Dave (August 19 - 3:32:16 PM): I see. (*Dave was now inconclusive as to whether Gracy was really a university student as she claimed.*)

Friends4Dave (August 19 - 3:32:52 PM): When are you graduating?

Talk2bryan2001 (August 19 - 3:33:59 PM): Next year.

Friends4Dave (August 19 - 3:34:11 PM):   Good.

Friends4Dave (August 19 - 3:35:05 PM):   (*Dave changed the subject.*)
                                            How are your parents?

Talk2bryan2001 (August 19 - 3:36:05 PM): Fine. They called me.

Friends4Dave (August 19 - 3:36:17 PM):   Good.

Friends4Dave (August 19 - 3:37:00 PM):   (*Dave envisioned Gracy
                                            laying on her bed while chatting with him now,
                                            and he decided to ask her what she was doing
                                            at the moment.*) What are you doing right
                                            now?

Talk2bryan2001 (August 19 - 3:38:14 PM): Just on my bed.

Friends4Dave (August 19 - 3:38:49 PM):   That was exactly what I
                                            thought!

Talk2bryan2001 (August 19 - 3:39:56 PM): Really.

Friends4Dave (August 19 - 3:40:08 PM):   Yes.

Talk2bryan2001 (August 19 - 3:40:50 PM): You are right.

Friends4Dave (August 19 - 3:40:58 PM):   (*Dave changed the subject
                                            again.*) I saw you on Facebook.

Talk2bryan2001 (August 19 - 3:42:44 PM): Really?

Friends4Dave (August 19 - 3:43:08 PM):   Yes. That was a few days ago.

Talk2bryan2001 (August 19 - 3:43:33 PM): Add me.

Friends4Dave (August 19 - 3:45:36 PM):   I do not have a Facebook account yet. But when I do, I will add you.

Talk2bryan2001 (August 19 - 3:49:01 PM): How come you saw me on Facebook?

Friends4Dave (August 19 - 3:50:39 PM):   I was on Google. And Gracy Isy came up on my search results. I clicked on it and it took me to your Facebook profile.

Talk2bryan2001 (August 19 - 3:51:08 PM): Ok.

Friends4Dave (August 19 - 3:51:25 PM):   There are many Isys on Facebook.

Friends4Dave (August 19 - 3:51:51 PM):   Do you know any of those people also?

Friends4Dave (August 19 - 3:52:43 PM):   One of them is Tilda Isy in Nigeria.

Talk2bryan2001 (August 19 - 3:52:46 PM): No I don't.

Friends4Dave (August 19 - 3:53:01 PM):   Okay. (*Dave sensed some resentment from Gracy.*) Just asking.

Talk2bryan2001 (August 19 - 3:54:21 PM): Okay.

Friends4Dave (August 19 - 3:54:44 PM):   Someone recently invited me through an email to join him on Facebook. I really don't know much about Facebook yet; but I have been thinking maybe I should join Facebook. What do you think?

Talk2bryan2001 (August 19 - 3:55:30 PM): Please do.

Talk2bryan2001 (August 19 - 3:56:36 PM): I have been on Facebook for four years now.

Friends4Dave (August 19 - 3:56:48 PM): I did not like my experience with Flixster. That's why I closed down my account there. And that is one of the reasons why I am hesitant in joining any online social networking sites like Facebook. But my main concern with Facebook is that of privacy.

Friends4Dave (August 19 - 3:57:22 PM): What has been your experience on Facebook for the past four years?

Talk2bryan2001 (August 19 - 3:58:51 PM): It has been okay.

Talk2bryan2001 (August 19 - 3:59:20 PM): You get to meet old friends.

Friends4Dave (August 19 - 3:59:34 PM): I just might join soon. But I will let you know if I do join.

Talk2bryan2001 (August 19 - 3:59:42 PM): It's fun.

Friends4Dave (August 19 - 3:59:57 PM): Okay.

Talk2bryan2001 (August 19 - 4:00:42 PM): Yeah.

Friends4Dave (August 19 - 4:01:39 PM): Are you on Twitter?

Talk2bryan2001 (August 19 - 4:03:54 PM): No.

Friends4Dave (August 19 - 4:04:33 PM): That's another social networking site I thought about maybe joining someday.

Talk2bryan2001 (August 19 - 4:05:37 PM): I am on Facebook, hi5 and

Flixster.

Friends4Dave (August 19 - 4:06:01 PM):   What is hi5?

Talk2bryan2001 (August 19 - 4:06:30 PM): It's like Facebook.

Friends4Dave (August 19 - 4:06:56 PM):   Okay. I never heard of it.

Talk2bryan2001 (August 19 - 4:07:03 PM): Visit www.hi5.com... (*Dave clicked on the link and took off exploring the website.*)

Talk2bryan2001 (August 19 - 4:07:22 PM): And learn more.

Talk2bryan2001 (August 19 - 4:09:50 PM): Hello dear. (*After a few minutes of apparent inactivity from Dave, Gracy tried to get his attention.*)

Talk2bryan2001 (August 19 - 4:10:01 PM):

Friends4Dave (August 19 - 4:10:05 PM):   (*Dave returned to the Yahoo! Messenger chat with Gracy.*) I just checked it out. I don't think I like it. It seems that you have to join before you can know more about the site. And according to the TV program, *In Living Color*, in the 1990s: "Homey don't play that!"

Friends4Dave (August 19 - 4:10:56 PM):   I'm here with you. (*Dave waved his hand back.*)

Talk2bryan2001 (August 19 - 4:11:29 PM): Ok.

Friends4Dave (August 19 - 4:12:46 PM):   (*Again, Dave changed the subject. Dave was getting pretty good at changing the subject now.*) Who is the

President of Nigeria now?

Friends4Dave (August 19 - 4:18:41 PM):   *(Gracy did not respond for six minutes.)* Are you asleep?

Talk2bryan2001 (August 19 - 4:20:03 PM): Musa.

Talk2bryan2001 (August 19 - 4:20:12 PM): No, I am not asleep.

Talk2bryan2001 (August 19 - 4:20:31 PM): Musa Yaraduwa.

Talk2bryan2001 (August 19 - 4:20:59 PM): From the north.

Friends4Dave (August 19 - 4:21:21 PM):   *(Dave was thinking, "They are always from the North and I am sick of it!".)* Was there an election recently? When did Musa become president?

Talk2bryan2001 (August 19 - 4:22:50 PM): 3 years ago.

Friends4Dave (August 19 - 4:23:15 PM):   I really don't know much about Nigeria anymore.

Friends4Dave (August 19 - 4:23:21 PM):   That is sad.

Friends4Dave (August 19 - 4:25:14 PM):   Is Lucky Igbinedion still the Governor of Edo State?

Talk2bryan2001 (August 19 - 4:25:43 PM): Hmm...

Talk2bryan2001 (August 19 - 4:28:17 PM): No.

Talk2bryan2001 (August 19 - 4:29:29 PM): Adams Osurmole.

Friends4Dave (August 19 - 4:29:59 PM):   I am really lost about Nigerian politics!

Talk2bryan2001 (August 19 - 4:30:29 PM): Yeah.

Friends4Dave (August 19 - 4:31:28 PM):   (*Dave sensed that Gracy was thinking that Dave did not know anything about Nigeria at all.*) It's okay for you to laugh at me .... I deserve it.

Talk2bryan2001 (August 19 - 4:34:00 PM): It's funny.

Friends4Dave (August 19 - 4:34:29 PM):   Yeah, I know. And I plead guilty.

Talk2bryan2001 (August 19 - 4:36:14 PM): Yeah, you should.   (*She rubbed it in.*)

Friends4Dave (August 19 - 4:36:50 PM):   Please rub it in. I deserve it.

Talk2bryan2001 (August 19 - 4:37:31 PM): What's the time there?

Friends4Dave (August 19 - 4:38:22 PM):   I was just exploring *Facebook*, and I found someone called David Washington on Facebook. But that is not me! So, there is someone out there with the exact same name as myself; and I am sure we are related also. As you are probably aware, it is only my family that bears my last name.

Friends4Dave (August 19 - 4:38:46 PM):   The time is 16:38 hrs. (*Dave sometimes forget that not everybody knows military time. He often wrote in military time.*)

Friends4Dave (August 19 - 4:38:56 PM):   4.38 p.m. (*He then quickly corrected himself.*)

Talk2bryan2001 (August 19 - 4:39:43 PM): Yes, that's true. Only one family bears that name. Okay.

Friends4Dave (August 19 - 4:40:04 PM):   Do you have to go now?

Talk2bryan2001 (August 19 - 4:40:33 PM):   *(She missed or ignored Dave's question. Dave was not sure which.)* So are you going to join Facebook?

Friends4Dave (August 19 - 4:42:40 PM):   I still have not decided whether to join Facebook yet.

Talk2bryan2001 (August 19 - 4:42:52 PM):   Ok.

Friends4Dave (August 19 - 4:42:54 PM):   But I am thinking about it.

Talk2bryan2001 (August 19 - 4:45:42 PM):   Are you missing someone?

Friends4Dave (August 19 - 4:46:09 PM):   Yes. You.

Talk2bryan2001 (August 19 - 4:46:40 PM):   How much?

Friends4Dave (August 19 - 4:47:02 PM):   As much as wanting you here with me.

Talk2bryan2001 (August 19 - 4:47:33 PM):   Wow... nice. *(Gracy loved that.)*

Talk2bryan2001 (August 19 - 4:47:59 PM):   How is your baby girl?

Friends4Dave (August 19 - 4:48:13 PM):   She is fine, thanks.

Friends4Dave (August 19 - 4:48:28 PM):   I miss her too.

Talk2bryan2001 (August 19 - 4:48:49 PM):   Call her.

Talk2bryan2001 (August 19 - 4:49:00 PM):   How old is she?

Friends4Dave (August 19 - 4:49:08 PM):   I cannot call her right now because she is not at home now.

Friends4Dave (August 19 - 4:49:18 PM):   17.

Talk2bryan2001 (August 19 - 4:50:22 PM): Where is she now?

Friends4Dave (August 19 - 4:50:36 PM):   She is visiting friends. (*The friends that Dave's daughter was currently visiting are Jehovah's Witnesses. Since Dave was disfellowshipped from the organization in 2003, Jehovah's Witnesses did not speak to Dave. Hence, Dave was not allowed to call even his own daughter in the people's home that his daughter was visiting. No resentments, but that's just the way it was; and for very good reasons.*)

Talk2bryan2001 (August 19 - 4:50:50 PM): Ok.

Talk2bryan2001 (August 19 - 4:51:33 PM): Do you speak with her mom?

Friends4Dave (August 19 - 4:52:17 PM):   Yes. We are still friends. We are just not husband and wife anymore.

Talk2bryan2001 (August 19 - 4:52:44 PM): Ok.

Friends4Dave (August 19 - 4:53:23 PM):   What is the time there?

Talk2bryan2001 (August 19 - 4:54:03 PM): 9:54 p.m.

Friends4Dave (August 19 - 4:54:32 PM):   It's late for you, and you have to go to school tomorrow. Right?

Talk2bryan2001 (August 19 - 4:55:14 PM): Yes, but it's okay.

Friends4Dave (August 19 - 4:55:44 PM):   Okay then, if you insist. Please let me know if you need to go.

Friends4Dave (August 19 - 4:56:24 PM):   Please hold on for just a minute. I will be right back. (*Dave's back, neck, and shoulders pains have greatly intensified. He got up from his recliner, stretched himself, and walked around in his apartment for a little while before returning to the recliner to resume his chat with Gracy.*)

Talk2bryan2001 (August 19 - 4:58:54 PM): What's your girl's name?

Friends4Dave (August 19 - 4:59:38 PM):   (*Dave returned.*) Sorry. I am back now.

Friends4Dave (August 19 - 4:59:48 PM):   Her name is Britney. (*The name of Dave's daughter has been changed here to Britney in order protect her identity.*)

Talk2bryan2001 (August 19 - 5:00:48 PM): Hmm... I love that name.

Talk2bryan2001 (August 19 - 5:01:22 PM): Britney, wow... Lovely.

Friends4Dave (August 19 - 5:01:32 PM):   Thanks. She is one of my many blessings. In fact, she is the best thing that has ever happened to me.

Talk2bryan2001 (August 19 - 5:01:49 PM): Yeah.

Talk2bryan2001 (August 19 - 5:01:54 PM): I know.

Talk2bryan2001 (August 19 - 5:02:35 PM): Do you have her picture on PC?

Friends4Dave (August 19 - 5:04:14 PM):   (*Now, Dave was very protective of his daughter. He definitely did not want to send his daughter's picture to someone he truly does not know and as far away as Nigeria. That will never happen.)* She does not like having her pictures sent to people, especially to people she does not know. Even my brother in Italy asked her to send her pictures to him, but she declined to do so. I don't know why, but I respect her wishes.

Talk2bryan2001 (August 19 - 5:04:51 PM): And how is your mom?

Friends4Dave (August 19 - 5:05:04 PM):   My mom is dead.

Talk2bryan2001 (August 19 - 5:05:22 PM): When?

Friends4Dave (August 19 - 5:05:27 PM):   2008.

Talk2bryan2001 (August 19 - 5:05:45 PM): Last year?

Friends4Dave (August 19 - 5:05:55 PM):   Yes.

Talk2bryan2001 (August 19 - 5:06:06 PM): Where you home then?

Friends4Dave (August 19 - 5:06:39 PM):   *(Confused by the question.)* What do you mean?

Talk2bryan2001 (August 19 - 5:07:32 PM): Did you come home then? What about your dad?

Friends4Dave (August 19 - 5:08:37 PM):   No. I did not go to Nigeria when she died. I sent them the money I had for the burial. My father is still alive and lives in Benin City.

Friends4Dave (August 19 - 5:09:07 PM):   The last time I went to Nigeria was in 2001.

Talk2bryan2001 (August 19 - 5:10:12 PM): Ok.

Talk2bryan2001 (August 19 - 5:10:56 PM): How many brothers do you have?

Friends4Dave (August 19 - 5:11:01 PM): *(Dave was thinking, "Here she goes again with her Nigerian Inquisition", substituting the word "Nigerian" for the word "Spanish".)* But my mother lived with me for two years in the United States before she returned to Nigeria.

Friends4Dave (August 19 - 5:11:55 PM): *(Responding to Gracy's question about the number of brothers and sisters Dave has.)* Three brothers and two sisters are alive.

Talk2bryan2001 (August 19 - 5:13:03 PM): That means you guys are six? *(Dave was thinking, "Didn't we go through this before... I thought we discussed this before on the phone? Why is she asking me again? .... Dave was incidentally logged out of the chat, and he was unable to log back in for several minutes.)*

Talk2bryan2001 (August 19 - 5:23:47 PM): I would love to have one. *(Dave did not know what in the world she said she "would love to have one". Dave did not see this comment, however, until long after he logged back in later on his Blackberry because he had been logged out for several minutes now.)*

* * * * * * *

At the same time Gracy posted her question about Dave having six guys in his family, Dave was inadvertently logged out and he could log back in on his computer. Therefore, he took out his Blackberry and logged back into his account through the Blackberry instead, in order to continue his chat with Gracy.

Participants:[64] __Friends4Dave__ and __Talk2bryan2001__:

Talk2bryan2001:   *(Since Dave was logged out, unbeknownst to Gracy, she buzzed him for attention and to respond to her comment.)* BUZZ!!!

Friends4Dave: *(Dave finally logged back in through his Blackberry phone after about more than ten minutes of absence.)* Sorry, my computer screen just froze up. I had to switch to my mobile phone now.

Friends4Dave: Yes, we are now six.

Talk2bryan2001:   Are you chatting with your phone?

Friends4Dave: Yes, I am now. But I was using my computer before. *(In the interregnum, Dave was simultaneously trying to log back in on his laptop.)*

Talk2bryan2001:   What phone is that?

Talk2bryan2001:   The make?

Friends4Dave: Blackberry.

* * * * * * *

Dave finally succeeded in logging back in on his computer; however, the system automatically disconnected his *Blackberry* connection. Therefore, he continued his conversation with Gracy on his computer.

---

[64]   Dave was using his mobile phone, so no date and time stamps.

Friends4Dave (August 19 - 5:24:13 PM):   Okay. I am back on my laptop computer now.

Talk2bryan2001 (August 19 - 5:24:19 PM): I like Blackberry phones.

Friends4Dave (August 19 - 5:25:03 PM):   Yes, they are good phones. But they have limited features (few apps) and are not compatible with SKYPE yet in the United States. However, Blackberry's encryption is very good and that's why I use it.

Friends4Dave (August 19 - 5:25:39 PM):   Skype is compatible with Blackberry in the United Kingdom, but not here in the United States.

Talk2bryan2001 (August 19 - 5:26:20 PM): (*Gracy's Nigerian Inquisition resumed.*) So tell me... where are your brothers now?

Friends4Dave (August 19 - 5:27:04 PM):   Sorry. I thought I told you before. One is in Nigeria and two are in Italy.

Talk2bryan2001 (August 19 - 5:27:23 PM): Ok.

Friends4Dave (August 19 - 5:27:34 PM):   What about you?

Talk2bryan2001 (August 19 - 5:27:56 PM): (*She ignored Dave's question.*) What about your sisters?

Friends4Dave (August 19 - 5:28:14 PM):   In Nigeria. Both married.

Talk2bryan2001 (August 19 - 5:28:33 PM): Good.

Friends4Dave (August 19 - 5:28:49 PM):   (*Dave repeated his question to Gracy.*) What about you?

Talk2bryan2001 (August 19 - 5:29:18 PM): *(She continued to ignore Dave's questions, and Dave was becoming incensed by her blatant disregard for his questions.)* Your brothers is any married yet?

Talk2bryan2001 (August 19 - 5:30:06 PM): I have two brothers and a sister. *(She finally answered Dave's last question.)*

Friends4Dave (August 19 - 5:30:25 PM): Yes.

Friends4Dave (August 19 - 5:30:46 PM): Where are your brothers and sister?

Talk2bryan2001 (August 19 - 5:33:19 PM): One of my brothers is in Finland with his family and my sister is in lag with her family.

Friends4Dave (August 19 - 5:34:04 PM): Good. What is "lag"?

Talk2bryan2001 (August 19 - 5:34:27 PM): My immediate elder brother is in Lagos too.

Friends4Dave (August 19 - 5:34:58 PM): *(Dave realized that, by "lag", she meant Lagos.)* Okay.

Friends4Dave (August 19 - 5:36:00 PM): How much is a very good flat in a nice area in Lagos? *(Dave had been contemplating a return to Nigeria someday.)*

Talk2bryan2001 (August 19 - 5:36:50 PM): To buy or rent.

Friends4Dave (August 19 - 5:37:02 PM): Both.

Talk2bryan2001 (August 19 - 5:39:37 PM): To rent is N250,000 for two years for a very good house.

Talk2bryan2001 (August 19 - 5:42:32 PM): Do you have webcam on your laptop?

Friends4Dave (August 19 - 5:42:52 PM): *(Dave missed her last question about webcam.)* That is very good. I am thinking maybe I should move back to Nigeria for a while; probably in 2010 or 2011.

Friends4Dave (August 19 - 5:43:49 PM): How much is it to buy the same type of house in Lagos?

Talk2bryan2001 (August 19 - 5:43:57 PM): Okay.

Friends4Dave (August 19 - 5:45:13 PM): *(Dave now answered Gracy's question about webcam.)* No, I do not have a built-in webcam on my laptop because it is more than six years old. But I do have a stand-alone webcam that I can connect to it.

Talk2bryan2001 (August 19 - 5:45:26 PM): *(Gracy responded to Dave's last question about how much it is to buy a house in Lagos.)* With N15 million you can get a duplex.

Talk2bryan2001 (August 19 - 5:46:09 PM): Ok.

Friends4Dave (August 19 - 5:46:36 PM): That's too much money for me.

Friends4Dave (August 19 - 5:46:47 PM): At least for now.

Friends4Dave (August 19 - 5:47:13 PM): But that will not be a problem in the future, though.

Talk2bryan2001 (August 19 - 5:47:55 PM): I believe you.

Friends4Dave (August 19 - 5:48:13 PM):   Where in Lagos will such houses be that you have just given me the prices?

Friends4Dave (August 19 - 5:49:37 PM):   (*Dave repeated his question.*) Where in Lagos will such houses be?

Talk2bryan2001 (August 19 - 5:51:24 PM): Ikeja, Surulere, Ketu, even in Lekki, and Ikotu.

Friends4Dave (August 19 - 5:53:06 PM):   What about houses in Ikoyi and Lagos Island where embassies are located? Those are nice and safe places to live in. (*These areas were among the best in Lagos when Dave last lived or visited Lagos.*)

Talk2bryan2001 (August 19 - 5:53:50 PM): Yes they are.

Talk2bryan2001 (August 19 - 5:55:36 PM): With N21 million you can get a good one in these areas.

Friends4Dave (August 19 - 5:56:16 PM):   I don't know anything about Lekki, Ketu, and Ikotu. However, Surulere and Ikeja used to be very nice. But they seem too rough for my liking now. How much are houses in Ikoyi and Lagos Island to rent?

Talk2bryan2001 (August 19 - 6:01:07 PM): N350,000 to N400,000 for 2-3years.

Friends4Dave (August 19 - 6:03:24 PM):   It is expensive but not too bad. I will let you know to help me look for one if and when I decide I want to go back to Nigeria.

Friends4Dave (August 19 - 6:04:09 PM):   I prefer that area, unless there are other areas that are just as good or even better than Ikoyi and Lagos Island.

Friends4Dave (August 19 - 6:09:35 PM):   (*Gracy did not respond.*) Are you tired?

Talk2bryan2001 (August 19 - 6:10:27 PM): Not really.

Friends4Dave (August 19 - 6:10:44 PM):   Are you ready to go to sleep?

Talk2bryan2001 (August 19 - 6:11:07 PM): Yes please.

Friends4Dave (August 19 - 6:11:42 PM):   Okay, Love. Good night.

Talk2bryan2001 (August 19 - 6:11:45 PM): It is 11:12 p.m. here.

Friends4Dave (August 19 - 6:12:39 PM):   I understand. Good night. I will talk to you this weekend.

Friends4Dave (August 19 - 6:12:57 PM):   Saturday or Sunday.

Talk2bryan2001 (August 19 - 6:13:38 PM): Okay then... remain blessed.

Talk2bryan2001 (August 19 - 6:13:49 PM): Bye.

Friends4Dave (August 19 - 6:13:58 PM):   Thanks. Sweet dreams.

CHAPTER 28
GRACY SHOWS INTEREST IN THEOLOGY

As promised a few days ago, Dave went online this weekend to chat with Gracy. She was not online yet at the time that he logged on. He waited patiently for her and then gradually fell asleep on the recliner. As usual, Dave was drowsy because of the medications he was taking for his pains. So he was dosing on and off his short naps. Later, Gracy came online to meet her lovey-dovey. He was evidently glad to see her online and he initiated a conversation with her. During their chat, Gracy showed interest in Theology.

Friends4Dave (August 23 - 2:57:50 PM):   Hi dear?

Talk2bryan2001 (August 23 - 2:57:59 PM): Hello.

Friends4Dave (August 23 - 2:58:10 PM):   How was your day?

Talk2bryan2001 (August 23 - 2:58:12 PM): How are you?

Talk2bryan2001 (August 23 - 2:58:23 PM): Fine, and you?

Talk2bryan2001 (August 23 - 2:58:38 PM): I thought of you today.

Friends4Dave (August 23 - 2:59:04 PM):   I am blessed, thank you. I fell asleep on the recliner waiting online for you.

Friends4Dave (August 23 - 2:59:28 PM):   I have been thinking of you most of the day too.

Talk2bryan2001 (August 23 - 2:59:38 PM): Oh sweetheart!

Friends4Dave (August 23 - 3:00:14 PM):   What did you do today?

Talk2bryan2001 (August 23 - 3:00:22 PM): I am so sorry, but you should have called me.

Friends4Dave (August 23 - 3:00:57 PM):   That is true. I'm sorry I didn't.
                              Not enough credit to make international calls.

Talk2bryan2001 (August 23 - 3:01:58 PM): I made a trip to a close town
                              where I went to visit my aunty.

Friends4Dave (August 23 - 3:02:23 PM):   Oh, great. How is your aunt?

Talk2bryan2001 (August 23 - 3:03:03 PM): She's fine.

Talk2bryan2001 (August 23 - 3:03:24 PM): Thanks.

Friends4Dave (August 23 - 3:03:32 PM):   Good. And how are your
                              parents and siblings?

Talk2bryan2001 (August 23 - 3:03:58 PM): How has your day been?

Friends4Dave (August 23 - 3:05:00 PM):   My day has been great. I went
                              to the Kingdom Hall. Then when I got home, I
                              ate and came online to wait for you so that we
                              can chat.

Talk2bryan2001 (August 23 - 3:05:20 PM): My parents are fine and I don't
                              have siblings.

Friends4Dave (August 23 - 3:05:46 PM):   Your two brothers and sister
                              are your siblings.

Talk2bryan2001 (August 23 - 3:08:16 PM): Oh I thought you were
                              referring to them as my younger ones because
                              I have none.

Talk2bryan2001 (August 23 - 3:08:29 PM):   *(Gracy's emoticon
                              indicated that she was drooling over Dave.)*

Friends4Dave (August 23 - 3:09:00 PM):   No dear. I meant your brothers and sister. And thanks for drooling over me.

Friends4Dave (August 23 - 3:09:52 PM):   How are your classes coming along?

Talk2bryan2001 (August 23 - 3:10:01 PM): *(Responding to Dave's question about how her siblings are doing.)* They are doing great. Thanks.

Talk2bryan2001 (August 23 - 3:10:34 PM): *(Responding to Dave's question about how her classes were coming along.)* It's going well.

Friends4Dave (August 23 - 3:10:47 PM):   I missed you.

Talk2bryan2001 (August 23 - 3:11:24 PM): Thanks.

Talk2bryan2001 (August 23 - 3:11:31 PM): Me too, I missed you.

Friends4Dave (August 23 - 3:11:42 PM):   Thanks.

Talk2bryan2001 (August 23 - 3:14:24 PM): What did you eat?

Friends4Dave (August 23 - 3:15:04 PM):   Rice.

Talk2bryan2001 (August 23 - 3:16:28 PM): Are you there?

Friends4Dave (August 23 - 3:16:40 PM):   Yes. I am here.

Friends4Dave (August 23 - 3:16:53 PM):   Have you had dinner?

Talk2bryan2001 (August 23 - 3:17:21 PM): Yes.

Talk2bryan2001(August 23 - 3:17:26 PM):   Rice also.

Friends4Dave (August 23 - 3:17:56 PM):   That's a coincidence that we
both ate the same thing. Isn't it?

Talk2bryan2001 (August 23 - 3:18:00 PM): hmm... :: (*She smiled.*)

Talk2bryan2001 (August 23 - 3:18:30 PM): Haha! (*She laughed.*)

Friends4Dave (August 23 - 3:18:37 PM):   How long ago did you eat?

Talk2bryan2001 (August 23 - 3:19:08 PM): 30 minutes ago. And you?

Friends4Dave (August 23 - 3:19:37 PM):   About one hour forty-five
minutes ago.

Talk2bryan2001 (August 23 - 3:19:54 PM): Okay.

Friends4Dave (August 23 - 3:20:00 PM):   And I was thinking about you
as I ate.

Talk2bryan2001 (August 23 - 3:21:07 PM): Wow... Really? (*Gracy
was love-struck for Dave.*)

Friends4Dave (August 23 - 3:21:45 PM):   Yes, you were on my mind.
(*Dave reciprocated that he was also love-
struck for Gracy.*)

Talk2bryan2001 (August 23 - 3:22:15 PM): Thanks.

Friends4Dave (August 23 - 3:22:30 PM):   You are welcome.

Talk2bryan2001 (August 23 - 3:24:57 PM): So, how is my Dave doing?

Friends4Dave (August 23 - 3:25:18 PM):   I am blessed, thank you. I'm
really blessed, even though I am in a lot of
pains.

Friends4Dave (August 23 - 3:25:44 PM):   When was the last time you were in Lagos?

Talk2bryan2001 (August 23 - 3:29:11 PM): March 2009.

Friends4Dave (August 23 - 3:29:38 PM):   Okay. A few months ago.

Friends4Dave (August 23 - 3:30:32 PM):   Do you miss it?

Talk2bryan2001 (August 23 - 3:30:51 PM): Kind of.

Friends4Dave (August 23 - 3:32:21 PM):   Are you interested in coming to the United States?

Talk2bryan2001 (August 23 - 3:36:33 PM): Yeah.

Friends4Dave (August 23 - 3:36:55 PM):   Okay.

Friends4Dave (August 23 - 3:37:40 PM):   Have you heard about the green card lottery that the U.S. government sponsors?

Talk2bryan2001 (August 23 - 3:39:50 PM): Yes.

Friends4Dave (August 23 - 3:40:07 PM):   Have you ever entered?

Talk2bryan2001 (August 23 - 3:47:54 PM): No dear.

Friends4Dave (August 23 - 3:50:09 PM):   Perhaps, you should.

Talk2bryan2001 (August 23 - 3:54:34 PM): Ok, I will try it.

Talk2bryan2001 (August 23 - 3:55:12 PM): I really would love to study in the U.S.

Friends4Dave (August 23 - 3:56:41 PM):   Let me know if you are interested, and I will give you the government website for you to enter. (*Dave now responded to her showing interest in studying in the United States.*) Okay. There are many good schools in the U.S., but they are very expensive.

Talk2bryan2001 (August 23 - 3:57:49 PM): Is the green card lottery on now?

Friends4Dave (August 23 - 3:58:24 PM):   The next lottery is not on yet.

Friends4Dave (August 23 - 3:58:47 PM):   I just checked the website a couple of minutes ago.

Talk2bryan2001 (August 23 - 4:00:56 PM): Ok.

Friends4Dave (August 23 - 4:02:11 PM):   Do you know the website to go?

Talk2bryan2001 (August 23 - 4:02:39 PM): Not really.

Friends4Dave (August 23 - 4:03:18 PM):   This is the U.S. government's website: http://www.dvlottery.state.gov.

Friends4Dave (August 23 - 4:05:18 PM):   When entering, you must follow the instructions exactly as the government instructed, otherwise the person is automatically disqualified. For example, you can enter only one time per entry period.

Talk2bryan2001 (August 23 - 4:08:08 PM): Ok.

Talk2bryan2001 (August 23 - 4:08:43 PM): What are the requirements?

Friends4Dave (August 23 - 4:12:47 PM):   I think the requirements are perhaps different and specific to each entry period. I do not know what the requirements for the next entry period will be. But, for last year, they listed all the requirements on the Instructions page. Such requirements included how you should take your passport photograph, the size and pixels of the picture, the dates within which you must enter, and no multiple entries, etc.

Talk2bryan2001 (August 23 - 4:18:52 PM): Ok.

Talk2bryan2001 (August 23 - 4:19:12 PM): Well, until the next entry.

Talk2bryan2001 (August 23 - 4:23:11 PM): Are you there?

Friends4Dave (August 23 - 4:23:20 PM):   Yes.

Friends4Dave (August 23 - 4:23:46 PM):   What would you like to study in the United States?

Talk2bryan2001 (August 23 - 4:25:09 PM): Teology. (*She mistakenly misspelled Theology.*)

Talk2bryan2001 (August 23 - 4:25:09 PM):

Friends4Dave (August 23 - 4:25:31 PM):   I see.

Friends4Dave (August 23 - 4:25:49 PM):   Why Theology?

Talk2bryan2001 (August 23 - 4:26:45 PM): Oh! Sorry dear, I mean theology. (*She laughed at herself for the typographical error.*)

Friends4Dave (August 23 - 4:27:40 PM):   That's alright. I knew what you meant.

Talk2bryan2001 (August 23 - 4:27:45 PM): What do you think?

Friends4Dave (August 23 - 4:28:50 PM):   I think you have the right to study whatever you want to study.

Friends4Dave (August 23 - 4:29:44 PM):   Whatever you decide to study should have a purpose. What is your purpose for studying Theology?

Talk2bryan2001 (August 23 - 4:29:58 PM): I am glad you know that dear.

Friends4Dave (August 23 - 4:35:09 PM):   What is your purpose for wanting to study Theology?

Talk2bryan2001 (August 23 - 4:41:47 PM): To acquire more knowledge and that will build me up, you know.

Talk2bryan2001 (August 23 - 4:41:47 PM):

Friends4Dave (August 23 - 4:44:06 PM):   You don't have to spend over $50,000.00 of your money (which you are likely to borrow as a loan) in order to accomplish that purpose. You can get more and better theological education for free at the Kingdom Halls of Jehovah's Witnesses than the inaccurate Theology education offered by colleges and universities.

Friends4Dave (August 23 - 4:44:33 PM):

Talk2bryan2001 (August 23 - 4:45:00 PM): I like it when you are happy. I want you to be always happy for me.

Friends4Dave (August 23 - 4:46:11 PM):   Sure, I am happy for you. And

I will always try to be happy for you.

Talk2bryan2001 (August 23 - 4:47:19 PM): My dear, when the time comes $50,000.00 would not be a problem. (*This was not what Dave wanted to hear. He knows that the universities really do not accurately teach what is in the Bible. In any case, he respected Gracy wishes and he recognized that the choice was hers to make, not his.*)

Talk2bryan2001 (August 23 - 4:47:54 PM): I like that. Just be ok.

Friends4Dave (August 23 - 4:48:16 PM): That is so true that money would not be a problem. However, I'm just thinking: Why would you want to spend that much money on something like Theology at a university when you can get a much better education for free?

Talk2bryan2001 (August 23 - 4:50:32 PM): Theology exposes one to a lot of things. (*She obviously did not agree with Dave's line of reasoning.*)

Talk2bryan2001 (August 23 - 4:51:00 PM): Well dear, let's leave that for now. Ok?

Friends4Dave (August 23 - 4:51:39 PM): Alright dear.

Friends4Dave (August 23 - 4:53:52 PM): (*Dave did not want to push the issue if she did not want to discuss it further at this time.*) Please let me know when you would like us to discuss the issue again. I will support you in any wholesome endeavor you decide to undertake dear.

Talk2bryan2001 (August 23 - 4:55:13 PM): Hmm... Thanks dear.

Talk2bryan2001 (August 23 - 4:56:00 PM): So how do you wish to spend the remaining part of your day?

Friends4Dave (August 23 - 4:57:17 PM):   Watch a movie at home. Do some reading.

Friends4Dave (August 23 - 4:57:39 PM):   I have not watched a movie for a long time.

Friends4Dave (August 23 - 4:58:09 PM):   Even though I have a big-screen TV and many movies at home.

Talk2bryan2001 (August 23 - 4:59:16 PM): Ok which of the movies?

Friends4Dave (August 23 - 5:00:34 PM):   I haven't decided which one yet. Maybe "Happy Feet", "Goal", "Taxi", "Garfield", etc. I just don't know yet.

Talk2bryan2001 (August 23 - 5:04:34 PM): Ok. Just have some fun. Ok?

Friends4Dave (August 23 - 5:05:41 PM):   Okay. Thanks, dear. What about you? What are you doing now and about to do as soon as we end this conversation?

Talk2bryan2001 (August 23 - 5:07:39 PM): Sleep off. That's what I feel like doing now.

Friends4Dave (August 23 - 5:08:10 PM):   Okay. We will talk at another time dear.

Talk2bryan2001 (August 23 - 5:08:25 PM): When?

Friends4Dave (August 23 - 5:08:54 PM):   Some time during the mid-week?

Talk2bryan2001 (August 23 - 5:09:40 PM): Will you call me?

Friends4Dave (August 23 - 5:10:20 PM):   Okay. I will as soon as I get
                                            more credit to make international calls, but I
                                            don't know if that will be this week, though.

Talk2bryan2001 (August 23 - 5:11:18 PM): Ok.

Friends4Dave (August 23 - 5:11:28 PM):   Good night.

Talk2bryan2001 (August 23 - 5:11:39 PM): Bye.

CHAPTER 29
DAVE CHATS WITH GRACY AT THE AUTO REPAIR SHOP

𝔇ave had been looking forward to chatting with Gracy. He was, therefore, happy to see her online when he logged in with his mobile phone on August 26th 2009.[65] Dave was in Newport News at the time, waiting for his van to be serviced at the Big Al's Auto shop.

Participants:[66] **Friends4Dave** and **Talk2bryan2001.**

Friends4Dave: Hi baby! (*Excited to find her online. Dave was able to bear his excruciating pains more when he was in company of someone he loves or when he was online or on the phone with someone he loves. So, his back and joint pains felt a little more manageable as he now chatted with Gracy while waiting for his van to be fixed.*)

Talk2bryan2001:   Hello sweetheart! (*Gracy greets similarly.*)

Friends4Dave: How are you doing?

Talk2bryan2001:   I am great. And you?

Friends4Dave: I am blessed, as always.

---

[65] Hartford Insurance Company, mentioned earlier had Dave on surveillance on this date. This insurance company claimed that just because Dave was able to drive his van to drop his daughter off at school, and to take his van to the auto shop for repairs, that he was therefore "not disabled" and Hartford Insurance Company subsequently terminated his disability benefits on September 24th. The fact was, and still is, that Dave experiences excruciating pains every day even though he does a very good job of not showing his pains. In most cases, he just does not want people to know that he is in a lot of pains. Hartford Insurance Company doctored the surveillance video tapes by editing and removing scenes that clearly showed that Dave was indeed experiencing excruciating pains. Dave later sued Hartford Insurance Company and the company settled the case out of court.
[66] There are no time stamps because Dave was using his mobile phone to chat.

Friends4Dave: Thanks.

Friends4Dave: *(Since it was early in the day, Dave was not sure if he was disrupting Gracy in class)* Are you at school or you are back home?

Talk2bryan2001:   I've got cold. I was not able to go to school today.

Friends4Dave: I am sorry to hear that! How long have you had the cold?

Talk2bryan2001:   Since yesterday.

Friends4Dave: I am so sorry honey. Are you taking any medication for the cold?

Talk2bryan2001:   Emm... maybe I'll wait till next week; I've spent my money on textbooks last week and this week. I've got nothing on me now.

Friends4Dave: *(Dave felt so terrible to hear that she did not have the money to buy medications. Dave could relate to such a predicament because he was dealing with the same issue every day, as he often had to decide between having a roof over his head and buying some food versus buying the medications prescribed buy his physicians. Even more painful for Dave was the fact that he had no money to send to Gracy to buy her medication.)* That is so terrible, and I am sorry. I wish I could send you some money now.

Talk2bryan2001:   Hmm...

Talk2bryan2001:   You don't come online this early. *(She was right. Dave usually did not go online that early in the day. He was only online now because he was waiting on his van to be fixed at the auto repair shop and he was thinking of Gracy at the same time. So he hoped she might be online so that they could chat, and he was glad that she was online.*)

Talk2bryan2001: BUZZ!!! (*Dave did not respond because he was speaking with Big Al's Manager, Chuck. Big Al's had done a major repair which took almost the entire day on January 23rd; but the same problem had re-surfaced again. Since the repairs were under one year warranty, Dave took it back to Big Al's today to be corrected today and without charge. So, Dave was talking to Chuck about what needed to be done. While Dave spoke with Chuck, Gracy grew impatient and buzzed Dave twice.*)

Talk2bryan2001: BUZZ!!!

Friends4Dave: (*Dave finally responded to Gracy's last comment.*) You are right, I usually do not come online this early in the day. I am on my mobile and at a mechanic workshop right now. The shop fixed my car months ago but it still has the same problem for months now. I called the shop yesterday and they told me to bring the car in today to correct the problem. Since I am just waiting here doing nothing, I decided to check online to see if you were online; and fortunately, you are.

Talk2bryan2001: Oh nice.

Friends4Dave: (*Dave remembered the natural herbal remedy that his parents used to force him to drink when he was young, and what he voluntarily drank as an adult, in Nigeria and then suggested that Gracy should try it. This natural herbal remedy was known to be very effective, unlike the processed medications manufactured by pharmaceutical companies that are mostly ineffective and have many dangerous side effects.*) You may want to try some *Awolowo* plant leaves. I used to squeeze them in water and drink it whenever I was sick in Nigeria. And it worked very well for me and for most people then.

Talk2bryan2001:   BUZZ!!! (*Gracy continued to buzz Dave until he finished writing his response above.*)

Talk2bryan2001:   BUZZ!!!

Talk2bryan2001:   (*Gracy reacted to Dave's suggestion to her to drink Awolowo plant leaves.*)   Really?

Friends4Dave: Yes, really. Awolowo works wonders. No side effects. And, as you know, *Awolowo* is plentiful in Nigeria. I wish we have it here in the United States. It tastes terrible, though.

Talk2bryan2001:   Okay.

Friends4Dave: (*Dave sensed that Gracy did not want to drink the Awolowo natural remedy.*) You don't like *Awolowo*, do you?

Friends4Dave: BUZZ!!! (*Gracy did not reply, so Dave buzzed her.*)

Talk2bryan2001:   I don't know.

Friends4Dave: Okay. (*Chuck told Dave that they were done with his van, and Dave related the message to Gracy online.*) They are done with my car. I will get in touch with you later.

Friends4Dave: BUZZ!!!

Talk2bryan2001:   Okay then…

Friends4Dave: Goodbye. BUZZ!!! (*Dave logged out, picked up his van, and drove back home.*)

CHAPTER 30
DAVE PROMISES TO SEND GRACY MONEY

𝕷ater in the afternoon, a few hours after Dave got home from repairing his van at the shop in Newport News, he went online as promised and found Gracy waiting for him.

Friends4Dave (August 26 - 3:52:29 PM):   Hi Babee!

Talk2bryan2001 (August 26 - 3:53:58 PM): Hello Sweetheart!

Friends4Dave (August 26 - 3:54:12 PM):   How are you feeling, dear?

Friends4Dave (August 26 - 3:57:30 PM):   Are you feeling any better than earlier today when we chatted?

Talk2bryan2001 (August 26 - 3:58:58 PM): I will be fine.

Talk2bryan2001 (August 26 - 3:59:13 PM): I will be fine, really.

Friends4Dave (August 26 - 3:59:39 PM):   I wish I was with you to personally take care of you.

Talk2bryan2001 (August 26 - 3:59:59 PM): How?

Friends4Dave (August 26 - 4:01:10 PM):   Cook for you. Get you the medication you need. Rub you with menthol, put you to bed, and cover you with blankets, and so on...

Talk2bryan2001 (August 26 - 4:04:46 PM): Really? That's a nice thought.

Friends4Dave (August 26 - 4:05:02 PM):   I mean it.

Talk2bryan2001 (August 26 - 4:05:24 PM): I know.

Friends4Dave (August 26 - 4:05:46 PM): I hope you feel better very soon.

Talk2bryan2001 (August 26 - 4:06:53 PM): Yes, and please dear pray for me. Ok?

Friends4Dave (August 26 - 4:07:13 PM): I definitely will.

Friends4Dave (August 26 - 4:07:51 PM): Have you had dinner?

Talk2bryan2001 (August 26 - 4:07:54 PM): Thanks dear.

Talk2bryan2001 (August 26 - 4:08:17 PM): Yes, I have had dinner.

Friends4Dave (August 26 - 4:08:37 PM): Good. What are you doing now?

Talk2bryan2001 (August 26 - 4:09:34 PM): Just on my bed chatting with you.

Friends4Dave (August 26 - 4:10:34 PM): Okay. Good. I just wanted to make sure that you are not doing chores around the house. You need plenty of rest.

Talk2bryan2001 (August 26 - 4:12:01 PM): Yes and that's what I am doing now.

Friends4Dave (August 26 - 4:12:26 PM): I miss you.

Talk2bryan2001 (August 26 - 4:12:48 PM): Thanks dear, I miss you too.

Friends4Dave (August 26 - 4:13:39 PM): Do you have anybody around to help take care of you while you are ill?

Talk2bryan2001 (August 26 - 4:14:17 PM): Not at all.

Friends4Dave (August 26 - 4:14:38 PM):   That's not good. (*Dave was thinking to himself, "She is just as lonely as I am. Another lonely lover .... What a coincidence!"*)

Talk2bryan2001 (August 26 - 4:14:38 PM): There's no one.

Friends4Dave (August 26 - 4:15:01 PM):   Any family members nearby?

Talk2bryan2001 (August 26 - 4:16:11 PM): No.

Friends4Dave (August 26 - 4:16:24 PM):   Now I am really worried.

Talk2bryan2001 (August 26 - 4:17:40 PM): Hmm...

Friends4Dave (August 26 - 4:18:35 PM):   Perhaps you should go to back Lagos until you are well again.

Talk2bryan2001 (August 26 - 4:20:00 PM): Transport fee for now is not available.

Talk2bryan2001 (August 26 - 4:20:36 PM): And I have lectures to attend too.

Friends4Dave (August 26 - 4:20:55 PM):   I will try and borrow some money and send to you by the weekend.

Talk2bryan2001 (August 26 - 4:22:53 PM): Ok, thanks for your concern dear.

Friends4Dave (August 26 - 4:23:27 PM):   It is my obligation to be concerned about you.

Talk2bryan2001 (August 26 - 4:24:58 PM): If I get the money, I will get

some drugs[67] first before going to Lagos.
(When Gracy said "drugs", she meant
"medications". Nigerians often refer to
medications as "drugs".)

Friends4Dave (August 26 - 4:25:15 PM):   Okay. I understand.

Talk2bryan2001 (August 26 - 4:27:00 PM): Do you have my details?

Friends4Dave (August 26 - 4:27:31 PM):   Please give me your details.

Talk2bryan2001 (August 26 - 4:28:21 PM): NWAOKORO GRACE.

Talk2bryan2001 (August 26 - 4:29:08 PM): What are the details you need?

Friends4Dave (August 26 - 4:29:30 PM):   That's all I need.

Friends4Dave (August 26 - 4:30:26 PM):   Once I get the money and
have sent it, I will contact you to give you the
information you need to collect it.

Talk2bryan2001 (August 26 - 4:31:22 PM): Ok dear.

Friends4Dave (August 26 - 4:31:50 PM):   What time is it there?

Talk2bryan2001 (August 26 - 4:32:30 PM): Through Money Gram?

Friends4Dave (August 26 - 4:32:41 PM):   Yes.

Talk2bryan2001 (August 26 - 4:33:18 PM): Like how much should I
expect?

Friends4Dave (August 26 - 4:34:29 PM):   Depends on what I get. But
between $50 to $100.

---

[67] Nigerians call prescription and over-the-counter medications "drugs".

Talk2bryan2001 (August 26 - 4:40:23 PM): Ok.

Talk2bryan2001 (August 26 - 4:40:28 PM): Thanks.

Friends4Dave (August 26 - 4:41:02 PM): What time is it? (*Gracy did not respond.*)

Friends4Dave (August 26 - 4:45:10 PM): Are you sleepy?

Talk2bryan2001 (August 26 - 4:45:24 PM): 9:48 pm (*She finally responded and Dave suspected that she was probably sleepy.*)

Friends4Dave (August 26 - 4:45:50 PM): Do you need to go to sleep?

Friends4Dave (August 26 - 4:59:05 PM): I guess you have fallen asleep. I will chat with you tomorrow. (*After waiting for several minutes without a response from Gracy, Dave concluded that she had fallen asleep and he logged out.*)

CHAPTER 31
HEALTH CARE SYSTEM IN THE UNITED STATES

Still worried about Gracy's health, Dave tried a few times without success to call Gracy on the telephone. He went online several times to see if she was online but she was not. Later in the day, Dave went online and waited for Gracy to come online. When she finally did, they chatted about health issues, including the funeral of Senator Ted Kennedy and the viciousness of the politicians who are against healthcare reform.

Friends4Dave (August 27 - 3:21:06 PM):   Just a reminder that I am waiting for you online ... (*Gracy was not online yet.*)

Friends4Dave (August 27 - 3:40:01 PM):   (*Gracy came online and Dave immediately initiated a conversation with her.*) Hi dear! How are you feeling?

Talk2bryan2001 (August 27 - 3:40:33 PM):   Hello, I just got back from the church.

Friends4Dave (August 27 - 3:40:46 PM):   Okay.

Friends4Dave (August 27 - 3:41:05 PM):   How is your cold?

Talk2bryan2001 (August 27 - 3:41:39 PM):   I am getting better but I still need to get some drugs.

Friends4Dave (August 27 - 3:41:54 PM):   I understand.

Friends4Dave (August 27 - 3:42:30 PM):   I will send you the money tomorrow as soon as I get it.

Talk2bryan2001 (August 27 - 3:42:45 PM):   I was not comfortable at school today because of my cold.

Friends4Dave (August 27 - 3:43:14 PM):   I am sorry to hear that. I wondered if you were able to go to school at all.

Friends4Dave (August 27 - 3:46:58 PM):   I checked on you a few times earlier today to see if you were online. I also tried to call you on the phone many times without success. I left an online message for you once. Did you get my message?

Talk2bryan2001 (August 27 - 3:47:45 PM): Yes, I just did.

Friends4Dave (August 27 - 3:48:07 PM):   I hope you feel better soon.

Talk2bryan2001 (August 27 - 3:49:15 PM): I will.

Friends4Dave (August 27 - 3:50:02 PM):   Did you fall asleep last night when we were chatting?

Talk2bryan2001 (August 27 - 3:51:12 PM): Not really. It was network. (*The telephone and Internet networks in Nigeria seemed to perform very poorly to the point that almost anyone you have a communications problem with in Nigeria will quickly tell you, "It's the network".*)

Friends4Dave (August 27 - 3:52:18 PM):   Okay.

Friends4Dave (August 27 - 3:53:38 PM):   (*Dave changed the subject as he continued to watch the events unfolding on CNN.*) Are you able to watch CNN?

Talk2bryan2001 (August 27 - 3:54:18 PM): No, why?

Friends4Dave (August 27 - 3:54:34 PM):   I wanted you to tune to it.

Talk2bryan2001 (August 27 - 3:55:01 PM): Why?

Talk2bryan2001 (August 27 - 3:56:42 PM): What are they showing on
CNN?

Friends4Dave (August 27 - 3:57:14 PM):   We recently lost a great
American. Perhaps one of the most prominent
individuals who helped to make the United
States a better place for ordinary Americans
like me. It is a very great loss, especially right
now that the country is trying to pass a health
care reform that will benefit all Americans.

Friends4Dave (August 27 - 3:58:01 PM):   The funeral procession of
Senator Ted Kennedy is on CNN now, and it is
live.

Talk2bryan2001 (August 27 - 3:59:08 PM): I know.

Friends4Dave (August 27 - 3:59:23 PM):   How did you know?

Talk2bryan2001 (August 27 - 3:59:59 PM): I saw it on the internet.

Friends4Dave (August 27 - 4:00:08 PM):   Okay, I see.

Talk2bryan2001 (August 27 - 4:00:46 PM): I used my phone.

Talk2bryan2001 (August 27 - 4:00:59 PM): Two days ago.

Friends4Dave (August 27 - 4:03:12 PM):   The big problem is that, now
that Ted Kennedy is dead, Congress may not
be able to pass the health care reform because
the Republicans are against health care reform.
The politicians, especially the Republicans,
have been ripping ordinary Americans off for

decades and they have been working against the interests of the middle and lower classes of Americans and in favor of rich people, big corporations and special interest groups.

Talk2bryan2001 (August 27 - 4:06:34 PM): Really?

Friends4Dave (August 27 - 4:07:14 PM): I want to make it clear that not all Republicans are bad people, and not all Democrats are good people either. And I do not participate in politics. However, history shows that the Republican law makers have never represented the interests of ordinary Americans. They only care for the interests of big corporations, rich people, and special interest groups. Many of these unscrupulous scoundrels are evil and very corrupt. (*Dave was very upset as he reflected on his past negative and painful experiences in the United States, largely as a result of his skin color.*)

Friends4Dave (August 27 - 4:08:17 PM): Many of the Republicans are racists, and they propose and implement racists policies and agendas.

Friends4Dave (August 27 - 4:08:55 PM): Their comments and actions clearly indicate that they hate Blacks, Jews, Hispanics, and other minority groups.

Talk2bryan2001 (August 27 - 4:08:55 PM): Yes, I think so too.

Friends4Dave (August 27 - 4:10:22 PM): And they are against anything that will benefit Blacks, Hispanics, and other minority groups. They only care about their fellow white people. Yet, they claim to be Christians. And this is sad.

Talk2bryan2001 (August 27 - 4:11:35 PM): Then they are racists. Yes, that is just what they are.

Friends4Dave (August 27 - 4:13:47 PM):   I was hoping that, with Senator Ted Kennedy's help, the Congress will pass a good health care reform; and millions of Americans, including myself, will be able to get health insurance again.

Friends4Dave (August 27 - 4:14:35 PM):   I lost my health insurance more than a year ago.

Talk2bryan2001 (August 27 - 4:15:08 PM): How?

Friends4Dave (August 27 - 4:18:11 PM):   (*Dave decided to tell Gracy about his disability, even though he mentioned it briefly previously and there was no reaction from Gracy then.*) I lost my insurance coverage when I was not able to work because of my injuries. The employment insurance company dropped my insurance coverage. Now, like millions of Americans, I can no longer afford the insurance premiums nor get treatment because of pre-existing conditions. And even if I can afford to pay the monthly premiums, they want me to continue paying the premiums but I am not allowed to use the insurance for 12-24 months. That is ridiculous!

Talk2bryan2001 (August 27 - 4:20:08 PM): Really, that's ridiculous.

Friends4Dave (August 27 - 4:20:14 PM):   Millions of Americans have lost their insurance coverage because they lost their jobs. The United States is the only Western country that does not have a Universal Health Care System. And it is a shame.

Friends4Dave (August 27 - 4:21:42 PM):   Medications are too expensive here in the United States. The same types of medications are much cheaper in other countries than here in the United States. To make matters worse, the Laws here prohibit people from buying medications from other countries where they are much cheaper.

Talk2bryan2001 (August 27 - 4:21:52 PM): Really?

Friends4Dave (August 27 - 4:24:03 PM):   One of my medications is $468.00 per month. Another is about $340.00 per month. I just don't buy them ... period. I can't afford them. I just cannot buy them now. At least, not with my current financial status.

Friends4Dave (August 27 - 4:26:26 PM):   And the same type of medications may cost only $25.00 to $60.00 in other countries; perhaps even much less that that. This does not make any sense.

Talk2bryan2001 (August 27 - 4:27:06 PM): Hmm... don't worry things are going to get better soon.[68] Ok?

Friends4Dave (August 27 - 4:27:16 PM):   And Congress has made it illegal for Americans to buy these medications from other countries where they are cheaper.

Friends4Dave (August 27 - 4:28:56 PM):   Yes, I know that my situation will definitely improve again. But I am concerned about the millions of other

---

[68] Little did Dave know that things were about to get much worse for him. As indicated earlier, Hartford Insurance Company terminated Dave's disability benefits on September 24th under the pretext that he was no longer disabled. The termination, and the subsequent false allegation of insurance fraud and unsuccessful prosecution, led to a series of catastrophic events which have lasted for years, including Dave's homelessness. Details of these unfortunate events and circumstances will be discussed in Dave's upcoming Autobiography entitled: "TAKING A WALK IN MY SHOES – VOLUME THREE: The Tyranny of the American Justice System – More Than A Decade of Misery!"

Americans who need help. I want to be in a
position where I can help others; but it is not
possible for me to help everybody that needs
help.

Talk2bryan2001 (August 27 - 4:32:14 PM): Ok.

Friends4Dave (August 27 - 4:34:35 PM):   (*Dave was so upset about the
health care situation that he did not want to
discuss it anymore. So, he changed the subject
again.*) Do you have any close friends in
Agbor?

Talk2bryan2001 (August 27 - 4:35:30 PM): Well, not really.

Friends4Dave (August 27 - 4:35:47 PM):   I wish you did.

Friends4Dave (August 27 - 4:36:21 PM):   So that there will be somebody
close by to look after you in times like this.

Talk2bryan2001 (August 27 - 4:36:27 PM): Why do you ask? (*Gracy
missed Dave's reason for asking above.*)

Talk2bryan2001 (August 27- :36:44 PM):   Ok.   (*She now realized
why Dave asked the question.*)

Friends4Dave (August 27 - 4:37:31 PM):   (*Dave explained why he asked
the question.*) I asked because I am too far
away from you. It would be better if you had at
least one or two people that have your best
interests at heart to take care of you.

Talk2bryan2001 (August 27 - 4:41:21 PM): I see.

Friends4Dave (August 27 - 4:44:21 PM):   (*Dave looked at the clock and
realized that he needed to leave so that he
could get ready for the meeting at the local*

Kingdom Hall. Even though Dave was no longer a Jehovah's Witness because he had been disfellowshipped more than six years ago, he still attended and enjoyed the weekly meetings of Jehovah's Witnesses at the Kingdom Halls.) I need to go. I have to start getting ready to go to a meeting at the Kingdom Hall.

Friends4Dave (August 27 - 4:45:23 PM):   Thursday evenings is one of their meetings.

Talk2bryan2001 (August 27 - 4:48:43 PM): Ok.

Friends4Dave (August 27 - 4:48:56 PM):   I will be in touch tomorrow.

Talk2bryan2001 (August 27 - 4:49:27 PM): Ok dear.

Friends4Dave (August 27 - 4:49:45 PM):   Good night and get well soon.

Talk2bryan2001 (August 27 - 4:49:52 PM): Thanks a lot for your concern.

Friends4Dave (August 27 - 4:50:01 PM):   You are welcome. (*Dave logged out and began to prepare for the Kingdom Hall meeting. Because of his pains, it was now taking Dave unusually long time to get ready; much longer than it used to take him to get ready.*)

Talk2bryan2001 (August 27 - 4:50:02 PM): Bye.

CHAPTER 32
DAVE SENDS GRACY MONEY

On August 28th, just before leaving home in the morning to go get the money to send to Gracy, Dave went online with his *Blackberry* mobile phone[69] to see if she was there and to find out how she was doing. But Gracy was not online. Dave left a brief message for her to let her know that he was thinking about her. Thereafter, Dave left home, got the money and sent it through MoneyGram as promised.

Participants: Friends4Dave and Talk2bryan2001.

Friends4Dave: BUZZ!!!

Friends4Dave: Hi Babee! I just came online early to check on you... to see how you are feeling. I'll talk with you soon.

* * * * * *

When Dave returned home after sending the money to Gracy, he went online again to see if she was online yet. She was not online. Therefore, Dave left the message below for her to claim the money.

Friends4Dave: Hi Gracy! Hope you are feeling a little better. I have sent you the money I promised. Details are below.

Friends4Dave: My name: DAVE WASHINGTON

Friends4Dave: Your Name: GRACE NWAOKORO

Friends4Dave: Amount Sent: $100 (N15,131)

Friends4Dave: Reference #: 94774206

---

[69]   Again, were no time stamps whenever Dave used his mobile phone to chat.

Friends4Dave: Test Question: WHERE DID WE MEET?

Friends4Dave: Test Answer: FLIXSTER

* * * * * * *

Later on that day, Dave and Gracy met online to chat. But when Dave initially went online[70] at about 15:00 hrs, she was still not there yet. Dave had to wait online for her for about two hours before she came online. Dave feared that the cold might have gotten worse and that she may not have even gotten the money he sent to her. He did not have enough credit to making international phone call to her. So he waited some more. At last, Gracy came online.

Friends4Dave (August 28 - 5:11:33 PM):   Hi! How are you feeling?

Talk2bryan2001 (August 28 - 5:11:35 PM): Hi.

Talk2bryan2001 (August 28 - 5:12:21 PM): Getting better.

Talk2bryan2001 (August 28 - 5:12:29 PM): Thanks a lot.

Friends4Dave (August 28 - 5:12:32 PM):   Great! I'm glad you are feeling better!

Friends4Dave (August 28 - 5:12:42 PM):   Thanks a lot for what?

Talk2bryan2001 (August 28 - 5:13:39 PM): I got your offline message about the money. Thanks.

Friends4Dave (August 28 - 5:13:58 PM):   Okay. You are welcome. Were you able to go to school today?

Talk2bryan2001 (August 28 - 5:14:42 PM): No. I was still cold.

---

[70] The third time he went online today to check if she was online.

Friends4Dave (August 28 - 5:15:21 PM):   I really hope you get better soon. Hopefully you will fully recover in the next few days.

Talk2bryan2001 (August 28 - 5:15:42 PM): Amen.

Friends4Dave (August 28 - 5:16:14 PM):   I missed you.

Talk2bryan2001 (August 28 - 5:16:35 PM): Me too.

Friends4Dave (August 28 - 5:17:03 PM):   How is the weather there today?

Talk2bryan2001 (August 28 - 5:18:19 PM): Cold.

Friends4Dave (August 28 - 5:18:30 PM):   I see.

Friends4Dave (August 28 - 5:18:44 PM):   It is hot here.

Talk2bryan2001 (August 28 - 5:20:03 PM): I wish it's so here.

Friends4Dave (August 28 - 5:20:33 PM):   I know. But I wish it is cooler here.

Friends4Dave (August 28 - 5:21:19 PM):   Maybe we should switch our weathers ...

Talk2bryan2001 (August 28 - 5:23:13 PM): Haha... lol.

Friends4Dave (August 28 - 5:23:48 PM):   Have you had dinner?

Talk2bryan2001 (August 28 - 5:24:35 PM): Yes...

Friends4Dave (August 28 - 5:25:12 PM):   Good. Please try and get the medication as soon as you can.

Talk2bryan2001 (August 28 - 5:25:37 PM): Just a hot cup of tea. I wish we
both had it together.

Friends4Dave (August 28 - 5:26:30 PM):   Thanks. You are kind.

Talk2bryan2001 (August 28 - 5:28:25 PM): Hmm...

Friends4Dave (August 28 - 5:29:00 PM):   Hmmmmmnnnnnn.....

Talk2bryan2001 (August 28 - 5:29:15 PM): Lol.

Friends4Dave (August 28 - 5:29:41 PM):   I am glad you are laughing,
despite your cold.

Talk2bryan2001 (August 28 - 5:30:57 PM): You made it so. Thanks.

Friends4Dave (August 28 - 5:31:17 PM):   I am glad to be of service to
you.

Talk2bryan2001 (August 28 - 5:34:02 PM): How long have you been
online?

Friends4Dave (August 28 - 5:34:27 PM):   Since the third time I cam
online, about two hours before you came
online.

Friends4Dave (August 28 - 5:34:36 PM):   I was waiting for you.

Talk2bryan2001 (August 28 - 5:38:29 PM): I am so sorry about that.

Friends4Dave (August 28 - 5:39:15 PM):   Please, don't worry about it. I
am just glad you are feeling a little better than
yesterday.

Talk2bryan2001 (August 28 - 5:41:19 PM): I knew you are going to be online. That's why I did everything possible to be online.

Friends4Dave (August 28 - 5:41:42 PM): I appreciate that.

Talk2bryan2001 (August 28 - 5:42:32 PM): I had to beg for airtime from the next door neighbor, so that I could come online to meet you.

Friends4Dave (August 28 - 5:42:52 PM): *(Dave completely missed Gracy's comment that she had to beg someone else for airtime in order to be able to come online to meet him. Dave missed that completely; an effort which he would have appreciated very much.)* If you need to go and rest, that is fine with me. I want you to be comfortable my dear.

Talk2bryan2001 (August 28 - 5:44:14 PM): We can chat.

Friends4Dave (August 28 - 5:44:41 PM): Okay. But let me know when you need to go. Will you?

Talk2bryan2001 (August 28 - 5:45:03 PM): Yes I will.

Friends4Dave (August 28 - 5:45:34 PM): Good.

Friends4Dave (August 28 - 5:46:47 PM): You may want to eat something more than the cup of tea you've had. I mean, please get some solid food in addition to tea.

Talk2bryan2001 (August 28 - 5:49:59 PM): I am fine.

Friends4Dave (August 28 - 5:50:47 PM): Okay, dear, if you insist.

Friends4Dave (August 28 - 5:52:33 PM):   I understand that when people are sick, they lose their appetite. It happens to me too. But it is advisable to force yourself to eat anyway, even though you don't feel like eating.

Talk2bryan2001 (August 28 - 5:54:13 PM): Okay.

Friends4Dave (August 28 - 5:57:36 PM):   Thanks. It will give you more energy and it will make me happy.

Talk2bryan2001 (August 28 - 5:58:04 PM): Okay then.

Talk2bryan2001 (August 28 - 6:00:44 PM): I think I am beginning to feel sleepy.

Friends4Dave (August 28 - 6:01:03 PM):   Okay. Good night.

Talk2bryan2001 (August 28 - 6:01:49 PM): Thanks dear.

Friends4Dave (August 28 - 6:02:02 PM):   You are welcome. (*Dave logged out.*)

CHAPTER 33
SIMULTANEOUS CONVERSATIONS ON *YAHOO!* AND SKYPE

Gracy and Dave had simultaneous conversations on *Yahoo!* and Skype. On August 30th, two days after their last conversation, Gracy attempted a few times to call Dave on Skype. She was unsuccessful. She did, however, leave a voice message for Dave. Later in the day, Dave logged in to his *Yahoo!* account to see if Gracy was available, but she was not. So, he left a message for her too. About half an hour thereafter, Gracy called Dave again on Skype, and the call was forwarded to his home telephone; but when Dave picked the call up, he could not hear anything. He suspected that it was Gracy trying to call him. So, he logged back into his *Yahoo!* and Skype accounts.

That was when he noticed on Skype that Gracy had attempted to call him a few times. During the course of their simultaneous conversations on *Yahoo!* and Skype between these two love birds, Dave and Gracy attempted several times to connect via video conference on Skype, but their attempts were unsuccessful and frustrating; this was due to the lack of adequate bandwidth in the Nigerian telecommunications network systems.

The record of their conversation on Skype is first presented below, after which the record of their conversation on *Yahoo! Messenger* will be presented next. The reprint of Dave and Gracy's failed attempts to contact each other on the telephone (in the first part of this chapter) is rather boring; but, they are included here to indicate what actually took place.

Gracy [August 30 - 11:57:31 AM]   *** Call from Gracy, duration 02:06. ***

Gracy [August 30 - 11:59:37 AM]   *** Call ended ***

Gracy [August 30 - 11:59:56 AM]   *** Call from Gracy, duration 00:43. ***

Gracy [August 30 - 12:00:40 PM]   *** Call ended ***

* * * * * * *

Friends4Dave (August 30 - 2:57:49 PM):   Hi Gracy. Just checking on
                                          you. Hope you feeling much better.

Gracy [August 30 - 3:29:18 PM]:   *** Call from Gracy, duration 01:25.
                                   ***

Gracy [August 30 - 3:30:43 PM]:   *** Call ended ***

Gracy [August 30 - 3:38:43 PM]:   *** Call from Gracy, duration 03:07.
                                   ***

Gracy [August 30 - 3:41:52 PM]:   *** Call ended ***

Gracy [August 30 - 3:42:26 PM]:   *** Call from Gracy, duration 03:00.
                                   ***

Gracy [August 30 - 3:45:25 PM]:   *** Call ended ***

Gracy [August 30 - 3:47:52 PM]:   *** Call from Gracy, duration 09:30.
                                   ***

Gracy [August 30 - 3:57:21 PM]:   *** Call ended ***

Dave [August 30 - 4:09:09 PM]:   *** Call to Gracy, duration 00:24. ***

Dave [August 30 - 4:10:42 PM]:   *** Call ended ***

Dave [August 30 - 4:12:33 PM]:   *** Call to Gracy, duration 00:18. ***

Dave [August 30 - 4:13:03 PM]:   *** Call ended ***

Gracy [August 30 - 4:13:28 PM]:   *** Call from Gracy, duration 00:04.
                                   ***

Gracy [August 30 - 4:13:32 PM]:   *** Call ended ***

Gracy [August 30 - 4:13:33 PM]:   *** Call from Gracy, duration 00:11. ***

Gracy [August 30 - 4:13:45 PM]:   *** Call ended ***

Gracy [August 30 - 4:13:54 PM]:   *** Call from Gracy, duration 11:44. ***

Dave [August 30 - 4:13:57 PM]:   *** Call to Gracy, no answer. ***

Dave [August 30 - 4:14:27 PM]:   *** Call ended ***

Dave [August 30 - 4:15:07 PM]:   *** Call to Gracy, no answer. ***

Dave [August 30 - 4:15:11 PM]:   *** Call ended ***

Dave [August 30 - 4:15:20 PM]:   *** Call to Gracy, no answer. ***

Dave [August 30 - 4:15:22 PM]:   *** Call ended ***

Dave [August 30 - 4:15:41 PM]:   *** Call to Gracy, no answer. ***

Dave [August 30 - 4:15:43 PM]:   *** Call ended ***

Dave [August 30 - 4:15:49 PM]:   *** Call to Gracy, no answer. ***

Dave [August 30 - 4:15:56 PM]:   *** Call ended ***

Dave [August 30 - 4:16:31 PM]:   *** Call to Gracy, no answer. ***

Dave [August 30 - 4:16:35 PM]:   *** Call ended ***

Dave [August 30 - 4:16:41 PM]:   *** Call to Gracy, duration 08:15. ***

Dave [August 30 - 4:25:11 PM]:   *** Call ended ***

Gracy[August 30 - 4:26:22 PM]:   Let's chat here. (*Frustrated, she suggested that they should chat on Skype.*)

Gracy [August 30 - 4:26:42 PM]:   Are you there?

Dave [August 30 - 4:27:39 PM]:   Hi Dear. I'm here. I lost you on *Yahoo! Messenger*, though.

Dave [August 30 - 4:29:23 PM]:   *** Call to Gracy, no answer. ***

Dave [August 30 - 4:29:25 PM]:   *** Call ended ***

Gracy [August 30 - 4:29:48 PM]:   *** Call from Gracy, duration 01:50. ***

Gracy [August 30 - 4:31:34 PM]:   *** Call ended ***

Dave [August 30 - 4:31:43 PM]:   *** Call to Gracy, no answer. ***

Dave [August 30 - 4:31:55 PM]:   *** Call ended ***

Gracy [August 30 - 4:32:33 PM]:   (*Gracy became frustrated and impatient.*) Are you there????????

Dave [August 30 - 4:33:05 PM]:   *** Call to Gracy, no answer. ***

Dave [August 30 - 4:33:58 PM]:   *** Call ended ***

Dave [August 30 - 4:35:23 PM]:   Yes. I am here.

Gracy [August 30 - 4:36:23 PM]:   *** Call from Gracy, duration 00:45. ***

Gracy [August 30 - 4:37:36 PM]:   *** Call ended ***

Dave [August 30 - 4:37:42 PM]:   I hear you clearly. Do you hear me?

Gracy [August 30 - 4:38:14 PM]:   I wish we can talk on Skype. The network is so, so, so bad that we can't talk on Skype. Well, I just wish we could. (*She tried to call her lovey-dovey again .... He picked up but the call dropped again.*)

Gracy [August 30 - 4:38:39 PM]:   *** Call from Gracy, duration 00:28. ***

Gracy [August 30 - 4:39:06 PM]:   *** Call ended ***

Dave [August 30 - 4:39:16 PM]:   *** Call to Gracy, duration 00:21. *** (*Dave called her again, too, and asked her if she could hear him.*)

Gracy [August 30 - 4:39:19 PM]:   Yes, I can hear you. (*But then, the call dropped again.*)

Gracy [August 30 - 4:40:45 PM]:   *** Call ended ***

Dave [August 30 - 4:41:25 PM]:   I wish we could really talk on Skype. I can hear you, but you are not hearing me.

Dave [August 30 - 4:42:14 PM]:   I love your voice.

Gracy [August 30 - 4:42:17 PM]:   Do you want us to keep trying??????

Dave [August 30 - 4:42:46 PM]:   I love your voice.

Gracy [August 30 - 4:42:53 PM]:   Oh thanks dear.   (*She smiled.*) Thanks.

Dave [August 30 - 4:43:35 PM]:   Let's try a few more times to see if we can hear each other.

Gracy [August 30 - 4:44:40 PM]:   Ok then, according to your wish.
(They both tried a few more times to call each other; but the calls did not go through and the calls kept dropping after connection, and they were never able to see each other on the webcam as Dave had hoped.)

Dave [August 30 - 4:44:51 PM]:   *** Call to Gracy, duration 00:31. ***

Dave [August 30 - 4:45:36 PM]:   *** Call ended ***

Gracy [August 30 - 4:45:37 PM]:   I am really cold here.

Dave [August 30 - 4:46:03 PM]:   Do you have any kind of heating system in the house?

Gracy [August 30 - 4:46:46 PM]:   And it's affecting my voice.

Gracy [August 30 - 4:47:03 PM]:   Hope you don't mind?

Dave [August 30 - 4:47:20 PM]:   Is it weather cold or fever cold?

Gracy [August 30 - 4:47:43 PM]:   Hope you don't mind? *(Gracy was momentarily logged out, but she logged back in again.)*

Gracy [August 30 - 4:58:37 PM]:   I am back.

Dave [August 30 - 4:59:00 PM]:   Okay, try calling me again please.

Gracy [August 30 - 4:59:43 PM]:   Okay. *(Gracy tried to call but it did not go through.)*

Dave [August 30 - 5:01:08 PM]:   Call me now please.

Gracy [August 30 - 5:01:30 PM]:   I tried your mobile but it says I can't call because I don't have Skype credit.

Gracy [August 30 - 5:01:34 PM]:   *** Call from Gracy, duration 00:22. *** (*Gracy tried to call Dave again but the call dropped again few seconds after Dave answered.*)

Gracy [August 30 - 5:01:57 PM]:   *** Call ended ***

Gracy [August 30 - 5:02:01 PM]:   *** Call from Gracy, duration 00:21. ***

Gracy [August 30 - 5:02:23 PM]:   *** Call ended ***

Gracy [August 30 - 5:02:25 PM]:   I just called you now.

Dave [August 30 - 5:02:54 PM]:   I answered but there was no sound. Did you hear me?

Gracy [August 30 - 5:02:59 PM]:   You are not picking up.

Dave [August 30 - 5:03:22 PM]:   I picked up my dear and I spoke both times. But you did not hear me, and I did not hear you either.

Gracy [August 30 - 5:03:31 PM]:   Ok, let me try again.

Gracy [August 30 - 5:03:48 PM]:   Really?

Gracy [August 30 - 5:04:18 PM]:   Are you on webcam.

Dave [August 30 - 5:05:02 PM]:   No. I am not on webcam. But I can take the laptop computer to another room to connect my standalone webcam. Right now, I am reclining on my *recliner*, because I really cannot sit straight for long periods due to my back pains. So, I recline in the living room while I chat with you, with the laptop on my lap. So the webcam is not attached.

Gracy [August 30 - 5:05:25 PM]:   Are you with your headset now?

Dave [August 30 - 5:05:26 PM]:   Do you want me to connect the webcam?

Gracy [August 30 - 5:05:52 PM]:   I want you to.

Dave [August 30 - 5:05:54 PM]:   No, I don't have a headset on. I am actually using the laptop computer's speakers and microphone.

Gracy [August 30 - 5:06:10 PM]:   Ok.

Dave [August 30 - 5:06:19 PM]:   Okay. (*Dave really did not think that a video conferencing would work because the telephone calls that they tried to make could not even sustain a connection. That's because there was evidently a huge lack of adequate bandwidth in the Nigerian telecommunications network systems. Thus, the network systems would definitely not support video conferencing. However, he was willing to try the video conferencing with Gracy.*) Please wait ... this may take a few minutes ...

Gracy [August 30 - 5:06:39 PM]:   Ok.

Dave [August 30 - 5:11:24 PM]:   *** Call to Gracy, duration 00:15. *** (*Dave initiated a video call after connecting his portable webcam to his laptop. But Gracy could not pick up before the call dropped again.*)

Dave [August 30 - 5:12:00 PM]:   *** Call ended ***

Dave [August 30 - 5:13:56 PM]:   I tried to initiate a video call; it rang but you did not pick up.

Dave [August 30 - 5:14:19 PM]:   You try to call me.

Gracy [August 30 - 5:14:23 PM]:   I did.

Dave [August 30 - 5:14:30 PM]:   *** Call to Gracy, duration 00:39. ***
(Dave called Gracy again but the call dropped as soon as they began to talk.)

Dave [August 30 - 5:15:19 PM]:   *** Call ended ***

Gracy [August 30 - 5:15:58 PM]:   Please try again…

Gracy [August 30 - 5:16:34 PM]:   Please try again. Ok?

Dave [August 30 - 5:16:53 PM]:   *** Call to Gracy, no answer. ***
(Dave tried to call Gracy again, but still no success. He left her a voice mail.)

Dave [August 30 - 5:17:46 PM]:   *** Call ended ***

Dave [August 30 - 5:18:10 PM]:   *** Call to Gracy, no answer. ***

Dave [August 30 - 5:19:00 PM]:   *** Call ended ***

Gracy [August 30 - 5:20:44 PM]:   I got your voicemail. It's so clear.

Dave [August 30 - 5:21:53 PM]:   *** Call to Gracy, no answer. ***
(Dave called her again; but still no answer.)

Dave [August 30 - 5:21:56 PM]:   *** Call ended ***

Gracy [August 30 - 5:23:50 PM]:   *** Call from Gracy, duration 00:51.
*** *(Gracy called Dave again too; but the call dropped after speaking for a few seconds.)*

Gracy [August 30 - 5:24:46 PM]:   *** Call ended ***

Gracy [August 30 - 5:24:49 PM]:   *** Call from Gracy, duration 00:48.
*** *(She tried calling again, but the same thing happened again.)*

Dave [August 30 - 5:24:58 PM]:   *** Call to Gracy, no answer. ***
(Dave called her also with the same result.)

Dave [August 30 - 5:25:37 PM]:   *** Call ended ***

Gracy [August 30 - 5:25:53 PM]:   *** Call from Gracy, duration 01:49.
*** *(Gracy called Dave again with little success, but the call dropped after less than two minutes of conversation without video.)*

Dave [August 30 - 5:26:01 PM]:   *** Call to Gracy, no answer. ***

Dave [August 30 - 5:26:26 PM]:   *** Call ended ***

Dave [August 30 - 5:26:42 PM]:   *** Call to Gracy, no answer. ***

Dave [August 30 - 5:27:43 PM]:   *** Call ended ***

Dave [August 30 - 5:28:07 PM]:   It went into your voice mail again. Please try to call me.

Dave [August 30 - 5:32:05 PM]:   *** Call to Gracy, no answer. ***

Dave [August 30 - 5:33:01 PM]:   *** Call ended ***

Dave [August 30 - 5:34:18 PM]:   *** Call to Gracy, no answer. ***

Dave [August 30 - 5:34:29 PM]:   *** Call ended ***

Dave [August 30 - 5:35:13 PM]:   This is obviously not working, and I
am so disappointed.

Gracy [August 30 - 5:38:59 PM]:   *** Call from Gracy, duration 00:36.
***

Gracy [August 30 - 5:39:13 PM]:   *** Call ended ***

Gracy [August 30 - 5:39:17 PM]:   *** Call from Gracy, duration 00:29.
***

Dave [August 30 - 5:39:21 PM]:   *** Call to Gracy, no answer. ***

Dave [August 30 - 5:39:46 PM]:   *** Call ended ***

Gracy [August 30 - 5:40:07 PM]:   *** Call from Gracy, duration 00:47.
***

Gracy [August 30 - 5:40:52 PM]:   *** Call ended ***

Gracy [August 30 - 5:40:55 PM]:   *** Call from Gracy, duration 00:16.
***

Gracy [August 30 - 5:41:10 PM]:   *** Call ended ***

Gracy [August 30 - 5:42:58 PM]:   *** Call from Gracy, duration 00:39.
***

Gracy [August 30 - 5:46:57 PM]:   *** Call ended ***

Dave [August 30 - 5:49:12 PM]:   I am so disappointed about not being able to see you and you not being able to see me.

Dave [August 30 - 5:51:22 PM]:   *** Call to Gracy, no answer. *** (*Dave tried in desperation to call Gracy one more time. It was the same result. So he gave up calling after this last call. Besides, Gracy had just indicated on their simultaneous chat on Yahoo! that she was feeling sleepy and he would did not want to force her to stay awake chatting with him.*)

Dave [August 30 - 5:52:56 PM]:   *** Call ended ***

Dave [August 30 - 5:52:59 PM]:   Okay, that's it! I'm done.

* * * * * * *

Gracy, on the other hand, continued to call Dave and she left two voicemail messages for him before she gave up calling him too. Both Dave and Gracy logged out of their Skype accounts and continued their conversation on *Yahoo!* to conclude their chats[71] for the day.

Talk2bryan2001 (August 30 - 3:58:00 PM): Hi dear!

Friends4Dave (August 30 - 3:58:27 PM):   Hi. How are you feeling today?

Talk2bryan2001 (August 30 - 3:58:36 PM): I tried calling you on Skype.

Friends4Dave (August 30 - 3:58:59 PM):   I picked up but I did not hear anything.

---

[71] Since these were simultaneous chats on Yahoo! and Skype, their conversations on both social media overlapped in time.

Friends4Dave (August 30 - 3:59:40 PM):   Are you on Skype now?

Talk2bryan2001 (August 30 - 4:04:15 PM): Yes.

Friends4Dave (August 30 - 4:05:13 PM):   I don't see you. You are no longer on my contact list.

Friends4Dave (August 30 - 4:05:35 PM):   Please send me your invitation again.

Friends4Dave (August 30 - 4:06:03 PM):   I am on Skype now.

Talk2bryan2001 (August 30 - 4:06:14 PM): It's network.

Talk2bryan2001 (August 30 - 4:06:24 PM): I am on now.

Friends4Dave (August 30 - 4:08:46 PM):   I see you now. (*But Gracy went offline.*)

Friends4Dave (August 30 - 4:09:00 PM):   You went offline again.

Talk2bryan2001 (August 30 - 4:09:07 PM): Ok.

Friends4Dave (August 30 - 4:10:04 PM):   (*Dave tried to call Gracy on Skype and told her to pick up the call.*) I am trying to call you on Skype now. Can you answer?

Talk2bryan2001 (August 30 - 4:10:56 PM): No, I can't. It's the network.

Friends4Dave (August 30 - 4:11:05 PM):   Okay.

Friends4Dave (August 30 - 4:12:12 PM):   How are you feeling today? (*Gracy went offline again and logged back in about 18 minutes later.*)

Friends4Dave (August 30 - 4:30:35 PM):   Welcome back. I lost you for a moment here.

Talk2bryan2001 (August 30 - 4:31:40 PM): I was logged off.

Friends4Dave (August 30 - 4:32:25 PM):   Did you hear me talking when you just called me on Skype and before the call dropped?

Talk2bryan2001 (August 30 - 4:33:27 PM): Yes I did. Did you hear me?

Friends4Dave (August 30 - 4:33:52 PM):   I heard you before you went offline; but I did not hear you since then.

Talk2bryan2001 (August 30 - 4:40:52 PM): I really want us to talk on Skype.

Talk2bryan2001 (August 30 - 4:41:12 PM): It's free you know.

Friends4Dave (August 30 - 4:41:30 PM):   I wish we could really talk on Skype too. I can hear you, but you are not hearing me.

Talk2bryan2001 (August 30 - 4:50:16 PM): Yeah.

Friends4Dave (August 30 - 4:51:14 PM):   You said it is really cold there. Do you mean weather cold or fever cold?

Talk2bryan2001 (August 30 - 4:52:10 PM): I am having running nose.

Friends4Dave (August 30 - 4:52:28 PM):   I am sorry to hear that.

Talk2bryan2001 (August 30 - 4:53:06 PM): Ok, thanks.

Friends4Dave (August 30 - 4:53:42 PM):   Do you have honey and lemon or lime fruit?

Talk2bryan2001(August 30 - 4:55:06 PM): (*Gracy missed Dave's question.*) Tomorrow I shall return this PC to my course mate.

Talk2bryan2001 (August 30 - 4:55:38 PM): She came to check on me today.

Friends4Dave (August 30 - 4:55:46 PM):   I wish we could talk and hear each other before you return it.

Talk2bryan2001 (August 30 - 4:56:25 PM): And I told her to please bring her PC for me.

Friends4Dave (August 30 - 4:57:21 PM):   I am so sorry we are not able to talk. I was hearing you, but you did not hear me.

Talk2bryan2001(August 30 - 4:57:23 PM): Let's keep trying.

Friends4Dave (August 30 - 4:58:16 PM):   Hold on. Let me check my microphone setting first, please.

Talk2bryan2001 (August 30 - 4:59:04 PM): Okay.

Friends4Dave (August 30 - 4:59:50 PM):   My microphone was on mute. Alright, try calling me again please.

Talk2bryan2001 (August 30 - 5:09:36 PM): Ok. (*A few minutes ago, Gracy requested on Skype that Dave should connect his webcam, and he just did as she requested .... He called a couple of times.*)

Friends4Dave (August 30 - 5:17:34 PM):   I have connected my webcam. I tried to initiate video calls to you a couple of times within the past few minutes without success. I am now calling you again on Skype.

Talk2bryan2001 (August 30 - 5:18:37 PM): Ok.

Friends4Dave (August 30 - 5:19:30 PM): I just called but it went into your voicemail both times.

Friends4Dave (August 30 - 5:19:43 PM): Please you try to call me.

Talk2bryan2001 (August 30 - 5:23:20 PM): I got your voicemail. It's so clear.

Friends4Dave (August 30 - 5:25:25 PM): Thanks.

Friends4Dave (August 30 - 5:25:53 PM): I wish your network was better so that we can see each other.

Talk2bryan2001 (August 30 - 5:26:14 PM): Me too.

Friends4Dave (August 30 - 5:26:31 PM): I am still trying to call you now.

Talk2bryan2001 (August 30 - 5:27:08 PM): Ok.

Friends4Dave (August 30 - 5:34:52 PM): This is not working, and I am so disappointed.

Talk2bryan2001 (August 30 - 5:35:16 PM): Me too.

Friends4Dave (August 30 - 5:35:47 PM): What kind of Internet connection do you have?

Talk2bryan2001 (August 30 - 5:35:53 PM): And it's making me feel sleepy too.

Friends4Dave (August 30 - 5:36:12 PM):   I know. I am so sorry honey.

Friends4Dave (August 30 - 5:37:00 PM):   Let's try one more time. You
                                           try it first; then, I will also try to call you.

Talk2bryan2001 (August 30 - 5:38:10 PM):   I am so sorry too.

Friends4Dave (August 30 - 5:41:31 PM):   Just when I thought we got it,
                                           it got disconnected again.

Friends4Dave (August 30 - 5:41:57 PM):   Did you see me on the
                                           webcam?

Talk2bryan2001 (August 30 - 5:42:01 PM):   Oh sorry.

Talk2bryan2001 (August 30 - 5:42:16 PM):   No, I did not see you on the
                                           webcam.

Talk2bryan2001 (August 30 - 5:42:51 PM):   It didn't come up before it
                                           hung up.

Friends4Dave (August 30 - 5:43:09 PM):   I could see myself at the
                                           bottom of my screen. So, I thought maybe you
                                           saw me too since we were able to hear each
                                           other briefly.

Friends4Dave (August 30 - 5:43:44 PM):   Let's try again. It appears to be
                                           getting better.

Friends4Dave (August 30 - 5:51:09 PM):   If you need to go since you
                                           said you are sleepy, I'll understand.

Talk2bryan2001 (August 30 - 5:52:51 PM):   Ok.

Friends4Dave (August 30 - 5:54:07 PM):   I just tried to call you one

> more time, but it went to your voice mail instead. Let's try to get in touch with each other by the middle of the week please.

Talk2bryan2001 (August 30 - 5:59:47 PM): Okay.

Friends4Dave (August 30 - 6:00:08 PM):   I am sorry sweetheart.

Talk2bryan2001 (August 30 - 6:00:25 PM): Me too.

Friends4Dave (August 30 - 6:00:55 PM):   I'll talk with you then. Good night and be well soon.

Talk2bryan2001 (August 30 - 6:01:19 PM): Thanks dear.

Talk2bryan2001 (August 30 - 6:01:32 PM): Bye.

Friends4Dave (August 30 - 6:01:44 PM):   Sweet dreams. (*Dave logged out.*)

The following day, August 31st, Dave left a voicemail message for Gracy to check on how she was doing. Gracy called back several times on Skype and she left eight voicemail messages for Dave. She also told Dave that she loves him.

CHAPTER 34
YEAH, THESE LOVE BIRDS GOT JOKES

$\mathbf{S}$ure, these love birds got jokes! Gracy has two mobile phones and two different *Yahoo! IDs*, which Dave found rather disconcerting. One of her IDs is **Talk2bryan2001** and the other is **isyluvy2k9**. On September 2nd, as soon as Dave went online, Gracy decided to initiate a conversation with Dave using her **isyluvy2k9** ID. At first, Dave assumed that it was Gracy who initiated the chat with him (rightly so), and he chatted with her without much thought; but when he realized that it was a different user ID, that created some doubts in his mind. He was not so sure anymore, and he almost logged out before Gracy quickly admitted that she was indeed the one chatting with Dave. Few minutes later, Dave tried to pull a fast one on Gracy too, but he soon let her know that he was joking too. Dave began the chat using his *Blackberry* phone,[72] but he later switched to his laptop.

Isyluvy2k9:	Hello Sweetheart!
Friends4Dave:	Hi! 😃 How are you doing?
isyluvy2k9:	Fine.
Friends4Dave:	How has your day been?
isyluvy2k9:	Fine and you?
Friends4Dave:	I am blessed as usual, thanks. (*Dave always said that he was blessed when asked how he was doing, even when things were going very badly for him. He really believed that no matter how bad things were for him, he still had a lot of blessings from the Almighty God and he felt that he should be grateful for those blessings every day, rather than complaining about his*

---

[72] As usual, there were no time stamps for their conversation.

---

*misfortunes which, in fact, were considerably
numerous. As far as Dave was concerned, just waking
up in the morning alone was enough blessing for him
because there were some days that he could even get
up from his bed in the morning because of the pains
associated with his disability.*)

isyluvy2k9:   (*Gracy tried to pull a fast one on Dave.*) Guess you know who you are chatting with?

Friends4Dave: Yes, Gracy. You are the only one that I chat with now. If you are not Gracy, I'm sorry and goodbye. (*Dave was about to log out.*)

isyluvy2k9:   It's me! I miss you...!

Friends4Dave: Okay, that's what I thought. But just to be sure, where did you and I meet? (*Dave turned the table on her.*)

isyluvy2k9:   That's funny.

Friends4Dave: I mean it. Where did you and I meet?

isyluvy2k9:   Ok.

isyluvy2k9:   Lol. (*Thinking that Dave was joking, she continued to giggle her heart out; but Dave was dead serious.*)

Friends4Dave: I am signing out if you cannot confirm where you and I met.

isyluvy2k9:   (*Realizing that Dave was very serious, Gracy quickly answered his question.*) Flixster.

isyluvy2k9:   Hi dear, it's me Gracy.

Friends4Dave: Okay. It is really you, Gracy, then. I am sorry. I missed you too.

Friends4Dave: Lol.

isyluvy2k9:   Just trying to have some fun.

isyluvy2k9:   I'm so sorry about that.

Friends4Dave: Okay. I was about to log out. Lol.

isyluvy2k9:   *(Gracy continued to laugh.)*

Friends4Dave: That alright. I am sorry dear.   *(Dave joined in the chorus of hearty giggles.)*

isyluvy2k9:   It's okay.

Friends4Dave: How are you feeling? Is your cold gone?

isyluvy2k9:   Yes but...

Friends4Dave: But what dear? Is there a problem?

isyluvy2k9:   No... I will be fine. Ok?

Friends4Dave: Please tell me if there is a problem.

isyluvy2k9:   Ok.

Friends4Dave: Did you go to school today?

isyluvy2k9:   Yes.

Friends4Dave: How was it?

isyluvy2k9:   You really relieved me from my debt.

Friends4Dave: What do mean?

isyluvy2k9:   I will always appreciate you. Thanks for being there for me.

Friends4Dave: I really haven't done anything for you; at least, not as much as I would like to do for you.

isyluvy2k9:   I had borrowed some money at school to enable me sort some things out. As soon as I got the money you sent, I had to go and pay the debt off. (*Dave was not so pleased to hear that she used the money for something else other than what the money was meant for; but he understood that sometimes, priorities can change.*)

isyluvy2k9:   So you see why I have to be thankful.

Friends4Dave: I see. No problems. I have used up what I got on September 1st. As soon as I receive my October 1st disability payment,[73] I will try and send you about the same amount I previously sent you.

isyluvy2k9:   Okay.

Friends4Dave: I am sorry to hear that you are in that situation. I understand how hard that must be for you.

isyluvy2k9:   I have a lot of projects this semester.

---

[73] Dave never received his October 2009 disability payment he was expecting because Hartford Insurance unlawfully terminated his disability benefits, claiming that he was not disabled. Consequently, Dave could not fulfill his promise to send money to Gracy. He also lost his home a couple of months later and became homeless. Dave took Hartford Insurance to court years later and the case was settled out of court.

Friends4Dave: I can imagine. Taking nine classes is a lot of work.

isyluvy2k9: Yes, and I need to get my own PC. I am tired of borrowing PCs from people to do my assignment or research works.

Friends4Dave: That is so true.

isyluvy2k9: I had save some money before but spent some part.

(Gracy logged out. Perhaps accidentally.)

* * * * * *

Friends4Dave: *(Dave did not realized that Gracy had been logged out.)* With time, you will get your PC. It's just a matter of time. I need a new one myself. Mine is old and too slow; but I cannot afford another one right now.

* * * * * *

Gracy was inadvertently logged out. But she was soon able to log in again with her other *Yahoo!* ID (Talk2bryan2001). And she resumed her chat with Dave.

Talk2bryan2001: BUZZ!!! *(Gracy buzzed Dave upon her logging back in.)*

Talk2bryan2001: I was logged out.

Talk2bryan2001: I'm so sorry about that.

Friends4Dave: *(Dave decided to pay her back with the same joke she played on him earlier ...)* Who is this? Hey, do I know you? *(... but he immediately signaled to her that it was a joke by laughing.)*

Talk2bryan2001:   Lol.

Friends4Dave: I thought it was your network.

Talk2bryan2001:   Yes, it was network.

Friends4Dave: I am about to switch from my mobile phone to my computer... *(Dave switched from his mobile phone to his laptop computer and they continued their conversation ....)*

* * * * * *

Talk2bryan2001 (September 02 - 5:43:10 PM):   What was the last thing you said before the network interrupted?

Talk2bryan2001 (September 02 - 5:46:33 PM):   Are you there?

* * * * * *

Friends4Dave (September 02 - 5:47:25 PM):   Sorry about that. Even though I had logged back in, I could not write anything because my computer is extremely slow.

Talk2bryan2001 (September 02 - 5:47:57 PM):   Oh.

Talk2bryan2001 (September 02 - 5:49:10 PM):   I am sorry about that.

Friends4Dave (September 02 - 5:49:14 PM):   I don't remember exactly the last thing I said before the network problem, but I think it was ... that with time you will get your computer; and that I need a new computer myself because my laptop is very old (almost seven years old) but I cannot afford another one right now.[74]

Talk2bryan2001 (September 02 - 5:50:12 PM):   Ok.

Friends4Dave (September 02 - 5:50:55 PM):   Have you returned the PC you got from your class mate?

Talk2bryan2001 (September 02 - 5:51:11 PM):   Yes.

Friends4Dave (September 02 - 5:53:14 PM):   I thought maybe you still had it. You left eight messages for me at about 04:00 hrs early this morning. My phones were turned off at the time because I was asleep; that's why your calls could not be forwarded to my home phone. Thanks by the way for your expressions of affection for me.

Talk2bryan2001 (September 02 - 5:53:53 PM): You are welcome. I saved some money then, to buy a PC, but it's not complete and I keep it very far away from me, so that I do not use the money for something else.

Friends4Dave (September 02 - 5:54:03 PM):   I was hoping that if you still had the computer, maybe we should try again to call each other on Skype.

---

[74] Little did Dave know that things were going to turn much worse in less than a month from today.

Friends4Dave (September 02 - 5:55:02 PM):   I understand. You are wise to keep the money far away from you. If you have the money with you, it is more likely to be spent on something else.

Talk2bryan2001 (September 02 - 5:55:22 PM):   She came to pick her computer up today.

Friends4Dave (September 02 - 5:55:30 PM):   I see.

Friends4Dave (September 02 - 5:56:08 PM):   I really would like to see you on the webcam; and I would like you to see me too.

Talk2bryan2001 (September 02 - 5:56:49 PM):   You are so understanding.

Talk2bryan2001 (September 02 - 5:57:02 PM):   And I like that a lot.

Friends4Dave (September 02 - 5:57:30 PM):   Thanks. I believe you are an understanding person too.

Talk2bryan2001 (September 02 - 5:57:49 PM):   Thanks.

Friends4Dave (September 02 - 5:58:39 PM):   I do not have that typical "Nigerian man mentality" anymore. Coming to America has opened my eyes to many things.

Talk2bryan2001(September 02 - 5:59:10 PM):   Really?

Talk2bryan2001 (September 02 - 5:59:35 PM):   That's good.

Friends4Dave (September 02 - 6:00:49 PM):   However, I am not perfect. I have some shortcomings too, like everyone else.

Friends4Dave (September 02 - 6:01:05 PM):   In some areas, I am just like everyone else.

Talk2bryan2001 (September 02 - 6:01:22 PM): Okay.

Friends4Dave (September 02 - 6:02:15 PM):   That is why I find myself saying, "I am sorry" often times.

Friends4Dave (September 02 - 6:02:22 PM):

Talk2bryan2001 (September 02 - 6:02:49 PM):   *(She laughs and, after a moment of silence, she said)*: I am beginning to feel sleepy now.

Friends4Dave (September 02 - 6:03:13 PM):   Alright dear. We will talk at another time.

Talk2bryan2001 (September 02 - 6:03:47 PM): Okay.

Friends4Dave (September 02 - 6:03:58 PM):   Good night.

Talk2bryan2001 (September 02 - 6:05:02 PM): Goodnight dear.

CHAPTER 35
AN ABRUPT END TO AN UNDEFINED LOVE

𝕬 couple of days later, on September 4th 2009, Dave was really missing Gracy. He went online many times to see if she was online, but she was not. Dave left a couple of messages for her, letting her know that he was thinking of her and that he really missed her.

The following day, September 5th, Dave went online again several times early in the morning but Gracy was not online either. He also left another message telling her how much he missed her, and that he would keep checking online to see if she was there so that they could chat.

Later that day, Dave went online again and found Gracy online. He was very pleased to find her there. But she was chatting with someone else. Nevertheless, he greeted her, but she did not respond. Dave waited online for about 30 minutes waiting for Gracy to respond. But she did not. Instead, she logged out.

The next day, September 6th, Dave went online again, giving Gracy the benefit of the doubt that maybe "it was the network" again, as usual. Gracy was online, again chatting with someone else. Dave remained online with Gracy for about 45 minutes but, this time, he did not want to initiate a conversation. He thought to himself, "If she is serious about our relationship, let her initiate the conversation today." But Gracy ignored Dave and did not initiate a conversation with him.

After waiting for a while thereafter, Dave felt hurt at heart and he logged out. And after pondering on the issue for several hours, he also decided to terminate their relationship.

Sadly for both of them henceforth, there would be no more , and no more .

Since that eventfully day of September 6th, Gracy sent Dave numerous electronic messages, and she left numerous voicemail messages, and she called Dave countless times. Gracy even invited Dave to join her at other dating websites, using other fictitious names such as "Isy Bryan" on http://www.Jhoos.com and "Bryan Kim" on http://www.netlogmail.com.[75] But it was too late. Dave was no longer interested in Gracy. Besides, Dave was no longer interested in dating anyone else online, nor was he interested in joining any dating websites. Period.

---

[75] As of February 2014, it appeared that both www.Jhoos.com and www.netlogmail.com were no longer operating as dating sites. The information previously available on these sites in 2009 were no longer available in 2014.

𝔄bout 𝔗he 𝔄uthor

𝔓rince Joe Eweka, PMP®., (also known as "**African Joe**" in the Music Industry) is a member of the extended Royal Family of the Edo Kingdom (the ancient Benin Empire). He is a Nigerian-American currently living in Northern Virginia, United States. Joe was born in Benin City, Nigeria. He was a writer and actor on the "Youth Rendezvous" and "The Assizes" on NTA; and a weekly commentator on "Current Affairs" for Nigeria's national TV network called the Nigerian Television Authority (NTA) for most of the 1980s. He also acted on state-owned Bendel Television (BTV). He immigrated to the United States in late 1980s. He lived in New York City until 1996 when he relocated to Virginia.

Joe Eweka is often referred to, by people who know him very well, as an intelligent results-oriented thinker, legal professional, law-enforcement professional, Security Management Specialist, Real Estate professional, and a Project Management Professional (PMP®); with proven initiatives, trustworthiness, great integrity, resourcefulness, as well as analytical and decision making abilities. Joe is an expert at negotiating contracts to his clients' satisfaction, an expert in organizing and coordinating efforts and multiple projects toward the achievement of desired objectives and deliverables. Some people characterize him as a highly energetic and goals-oriented professional with excellent human relations skills. Most people know him to be a person unsurpassed abilities to identify and analyze complex issues, to reach appropriate resolutions, able to implement complex strategies, and to produce timely solutions and deliverables.

Joe's past and current memberships in professional organizations include: Project Management Institute (PMI®); National Authors Registry; American Society of Composers, Authors and Publishers (ASCAP®); American Criminal Justice Association; Professional Investigators & Security Association; Association of Certified Fraud Examiners; International Society of Poets; National Association of Investigative Specialists; and many others.

Joe was amongst the top 1% of all students in the American Universities and Colleges. He obtained his Bachelor of Science & Master of Arts degrees in *Criminal Justice* and *Law* simultaneously (both with *Summa Cum Laude*) from John Jay College of Criminal Justice, City University of New York (CUNY); and his *Specialization* was in *Criminal Law and Procedure*. Furthermore, he attended Walden University for his Ph.D. program. Moreover, he has other Diplomas in *Legal Studies*. He attended another Master's Degree program in *Management Information Systems* at Strayer University. He possesses other diplomas, certifications, and licenses in the Real Estate, Project Management, Investigations, Security, Behavior Management, Legal Compliance, Healthcare, and many more.

Joe's scholastic, leadership, and professional awards and honors include, but not limited to, the following: Student of the Year Scholarship Award; AFRICADEMICS Highest Award; Thematic Studies Honors Program Award; National Dean's List Awards every year; John Jay College of Criminal Justice Dean's List Awards every year; Who's Who Amongst Students In American Universities & Colleges; Belle Zeller Scholarship Honorable Mention; Business of the Week Award by the Williamsburg Chamber of Commerce; International Poet of Merit and Poet of Merit Medallion Awards by the International Society of Poets; City University of New York (CUNY) Outstanding Leadership Award (within the entire CUNY system); Most Disciplined, Most Punctual, & Most Regular Actor of the Year by the Nigerian Television Authority (1985) Award; Distinguished Service Award by John Jay College of Criminal Justice; Outstanding Service Award by John Jay College of Criminal Justice; Leadership Excellence Award by the Judicial Board of John Jay College of Criminal Justice; etc. In fact, Joe received eight graduation awards at John Jay College of Criminal Justice in 1996.

Areas of Joe's expertise encompass Strategic Business Development, Human Services, Criminal Justice and Law, Law Enforcement, Civil Litigation, in courts, Social Policy Analysis, Research, Leadership Styles, Investigations, Security, Corrections Management, Real Estate, and Project Management.

Joe is also a Song-Writer, Singer/Performer, Music Producer, and Sound Engineer. His songs are mostly poetic and sociological in nature. He has also written about love, religion, life, humor, and the hope for the future; as well as other subject matters. His songs and poems are based on his real life experiences and observations.

Joe's songs are also based on his strong sense of justice. For example, despite his numerous outstanding qualifications, he was repeatedly rejected for employment within his professions, apparently because of his color and/or nationality, or strong accent. He detests corruption, violence, terrorism in any form, hypocrisy, oppression of the poor and defenseless, any kind of injustice, and police brutality (although he himself was once a law enforcement officer). However, as a former law enforcement officer, he knows that many police officers are good and highly skilled professionals; and, unfortunately, the news media usually ignore such good law enforcement officers because such stories do not result in the news media's high ratings. But he also knows that some police offers are corrupt and many are racists. And these bad qualities influence their discretionary decisions including: pulling motorists over, issuing traffic tickets, as well as disproportionately arresting and criminally charging people who are Blacks and other people of color.

Although Joe attained a level of academic excellence and distinguished service only imagined and dreamed of by most people, he has repeatedly been victimized by several misfortunes since his arrival in the United States (mostly because of his race and/or nationality and strong African accent). Frankly, the "American Dream" turned out to be an "American Nightmare" for him. Books will be written about his experiences soon.

Nevertheless, determined not to be a burden on society, he established a limousine business in 1991 (after he had an on-the-job accident) in New York City, while he was still studying Criminal Justice and Law. The limousine business later became "the best" in a tightly competitive environment in Virginia. Based in the Your County, Virginia (the capital of the racists enclave) Joe's limousine business had vehicles which no other company in Virginia had at the time. In fact, he revolutionized the Limousine Industry in Virginia. That fact, also resulted in his downfall because his closest White competitor, who could not compete on the merits, conspired with the racist York County Government to unlawfully shut his business down in 2001. And they got away with it.

Unfortunately, Joe has repeatedly been victimized by America's racist super-structure, and the institutionalized racism within the American society. And, as already mentioned above, Joe was illegally forced out of business in 2001 by racist York County local government, who conspired with his White competitor that could not compete on the merits.

To mention just a few more, Joe was also assaulted by a New York City police officer in 1995 when he went to the police precinct for help because of the white clients who refused to pay and then damaged his super-stretch limousine after service. Besides, he was also a victim of the notorious racial profiling and other unlawful conducts by the New Jersey State Police on the New Jersey Turnpike in 1998, and the New Jersey State Police was protected by the Courts from the subsequent lawsuit that ensued, on a claim of *Sovereign Immunity*; claiming that since the New Jersey State Trooper was on duty when he violated Joe's constitutional rights, he could not be prosecuted nor sued in Court. Even after the Court dismissed Joe's unlawful arrest and ordered the New Jersey State Police to return Joe' handgun to him (because he should not have been arrested because he was a law-enforcement officer legally in passion of his firearm), which the State Troopers confiscated during his arrest after racially profiling him; the New Jersey State Police defied the Court Order and refused to return Joe's handgun. These all happened while Joe himself was a law-enforcement officer and a Criminal Justice Expert. None of his outstanding credentials and service to society could shield him from such governmental abuses.

Moreover, as if the above were not bad enough, Joe was unjustly and unfairly prosecuted by the Federal Government without being read his *Miranda Rights* in 2003-2004 and sent to prison for a crime he did not commit. And while he was in Federal Prison, he was forced to perform unsuitable and horrendous work duties that later caused him to be totally and permanently disabled. Later, he was also maliciously accused of Insurance Fraud in 2010 by Hartford Insurance Company (who just wanted an excuse not to pay his disability benefits", and he was prosecuted by the Federal Government for this crime that he did not commit; but, this time, he was rightly found "not guilty."

These unfortunate and nightmarish events have had negative effects not only on Joe himself, but also on his daughter who later decided not to become a medical doctor because of having witnessed the fruitless results of her Dad's incessant labors to attain the highest academic achievements. She also decided not to got college at all, even though she was a straight A student like her Dad, Joe. Her decision not to go to college devastated Joe. He respects her decision, since she is an adult.

Prince Joe Eweka's music industry trade name is "African Joe". His genre is *Reggae*. At a tender age, Joe's daughter contributed to his first released music CD album in 2001 entitled "Mighty Babylon". Another album was produced in 2009 but never released. Nevertheless, six more reggae music albums were produced in 2016-19 and released in 2019. All African Joe's Albums are sociological, pensive, educational, and historical real-life stories presented in entertainment form.

Despite the seemingly satirical nature of some of African Joe's songs, they are all intended to promote human rights, equality, justice, racial unity and harmony, and the seemingly utopian concept of World Citizenship and Peace; which, paradoxically, the Bible promises will soon be fulfilled. And it will!

Although Joe has been repeatedly victimized by the United States' racist super-structure and the institutionalized racism within the American society and culture, Joe is very forgiving and strongly believes that many white people and law-enforcement officers are good-natured, just as there are in other races too. Examples include the many law enforcement officers whom he has either worked with in the past, or are formerly or currently his friends; and as evidenced by his white spiritual brothers and sisters, friends, acquaintances, colleagues, fellow scholars, and clients. However, he also knows that America is deeply rooted in racism and other forms of prejudice, and he strongly believes that until the arrival of God's Kingdom (according to Daniel 2:44; Matthew 6:9-11; and Revelation 21:3-5), there will be no "True Peace" and "Real Justice" in America and the rest of the World.

Some of Joe's songs and poems dating back to the early 1980s, which specifically address such issues include: Mighty Babylon; Africanism; Blacks & Whites Unite; Divine Embezzlement; Why? Is It The Color Of My Skin?; Apartheid; All We Need Is Liberty; Stealing In The Name Of The Lord; Lament; Jealous; Victim of Circumstance; I'm Feeling Ghetto Fabulous; War In No Man's Land; Religious Robbery; Love; Midday

Darkness; Beauty In Diversity; My Heart Is In Inferno; Utopia; This World Is Not Mine; Rock My World; Now You Know…What I Know; World Peace; Love To Have My Blackness Back; Sun Rays; When Will You Come To My Rescue?; Posthumous Fame; New York; Kindness; We Are Inmates; African Identity; Unforgiving Society; and many others that he has written since the early 1980s.

Many of Prince Joe Eweka's songs were first written as poems. For more information and details of his poems, songs, and plays, please read one of his books entitled, *"This Star Is An African: A Collection of Poems, Songs, and Plays Based on Real-Life Experiences and Observations.* (Available soon online, in bookstores, and in libraries near you.)

BOOKS BY PRINCE JOE EWEKA, PMP.®

1. CONFESSIONS OF A LONELY LOVER: *An Exploration Of Online Dating Scams.*

2. THIS STAR IS AN AFRICAN: *Oberservations From the Land of Alkebulan. (A Collection of Poems, Songs, and Plays Based on Real-Life Experiences and Observations.)*

UPCOMING BOOKS BY PRINCE JOE EWEKA, PMP.®

3. READINGS – VOLUME ONE: *An Interdisciplinary Collection of Essays, Articles, Research Studies, Discussions, and White Papers.*

4. READINGS – VOLUME TWO: *A Scholarly Collection of Essays, Articles, Research Studies, Discussions, and White Papers.*

5. PLEADINGS: *Hearings, Transcripts, Pleadings, and Legal Briefs.*

6. TAKING A WALK IN MY SHOES – VOLUME ONE: *A Victim of Circumstance.* (Autobiography)

7. TAKING A WALK IN MY SHOES – VOLUME TWO: *Pursuit of "The American Dream."* (Autobiography)

8. TAKING A WALK IN MY SHOES – VOLUME THREE: *The Tyranny of the American Justice System – More Than A Decade of Misery!* (Autobiography)

9. TAKING A WALK IN MY SHOES – VOLUME FOUR: *Another Half-a-Decade of Misery – Just Because They Can!* (Autobiography)

10. HOW AMERICA BETRAYED ITS CITIZENS.

11. DISASTERS: *Act of God or Man-Made?*

REGGAE MUSIC CD ALBUMS BY AFRICAN JOE

1. AFRICANISM
2. BEAUTY IN DIVERSITY
3. CHILD ABUSE
4. MIGHTY BABYLON
5. MY HOOPTY HAS GOT AC
6. UNFORGIVING SOCIETY
7. WAR IN NO MAN'S LAND

WEBSITES

https://www.Joe-Eweka.com
https://www.African-Joe.com
https://www.Joe-Eweka.org

THIS PAGE WAS INTENTIONALLY LEFT BLANK

ISBN 978-1-944429-90-4

US$29.95

ISBN: 978-1-944429-90-4

www.ingramcontent.com/pod-product-compliance
Lightning Source LLC
Chambersburg PA
CBHW070542270326
41926CB00013B/2175